Native Acts

Native Acts

Law, Recognition, and Cultural Authenticity

JOANNE BARKER

DUKE UNIVERSITY PRESS
Durham & London 2011

© 2011 Duke University Press. All rights reserved. Printed in the United States of America on acid-free paper ∞. Designed by Jennifer Hill. Typeset in Arno Pro by Tseng Information Systems, Inc. Library of Congress Cataloging-in-Publication Data appear on the last printed page of this book.

Contents

....

Acknowledgments

....

I thank my Mom — Sally Mae Anslyn — for her loving support in a process that I know she finds confusing for its endless supplies of acronyms and mysterious demands on my time and attentions. I simply could not have made it through the labored process of writing a book without her.

I also had the bearings of friendship along the way. Dont Rhine has loved me always and generously. Dianne Cantor listened to near daily rants on my ever-shifting levels of motivation in working on a manuscript for what seemed like a decade. J. Kēhaulani Kauanui took invaluable time at crucial moments to encourage and support me and my work. Clay Dumont offered many hours of critical insight on difficult issues. Alice Sunshine is the best roommate and kitty co-staffer ever. Melissa Nelson has been a good friend over many necessary hours of excursion from work.

I am deeply grateful to colleagues and friends who provided me with comradeship and many necessary hours of conversation and support over the years, especially Tomás Almaguer, Falu Bakrania, Luz Calvo, Robert Keith Collins, Jon Daehnke, Catriona Rueba Esquibel, Colin Farish, Jack D. Forbes, Velia Garcia, Andrew Jolivétte, Phil Klasky, Amy Lonetree, Bob McAndrews, Keta Miranda, Alfreda Mitre, Betty Parent, John Carlos Perea, Roberto Rivera, Gabriela Segovia-McGahan, Amy Sueyoshi, and Kathy Wallace.

I am indebted to advisors who spent invaluable time and energy with me, guiding me through the difficult theoretical and methodological aspects of this book. In its dissertation form, Donna Haraway, Louis Owens, and Angela Davis provided countless hours of counsel and direction. As dissertation advisor, Donna earned sainthood (if you believe in that sort of thing) for her skillful and steady negotiation of my stubbornness, density, and panic. Louis became a good friend when we were both at Davis, and he is now sorely missed. Angela posed provocative questions and challenges along with gentle guidance and direction.

I am indebted to Ken Wissoker, editorial director, Duke University Press, for his leadership and encouragement, and to the readers who provided me with invaluable editorial and bibliographic suggestions. Thank you also to Anitra Grisales for copyediting assistance at an especially crucial moment and to Timothy Elfenbein, assistant managing editor at Duke University Press, and copy editor Christine Dahlin, for their careful guidance through the final stages of production.

I was invited to present material from this study in various forums, where discussions provided me with provocative and interesting perspectives on the issues I have taken up in this book. Thanks to J. Kēhaulani Kauanui for inviting me to participate in a same-sex marriage debate with David Cornsilk and Craig Womack at the Native American and Indigenous Studies Conference at the University of Oklahoma, Norman, in May 2007. Thanks to Jean O'Brien for inviting me to participate in a round-table discussion about recognition with J. Kēhaulani Kauanui, Amy Den Ouden, and Malinda Maynor Lowery at the Native American and Indigenous Studies Conference at the University of Georgia, Athens, in April 2008. Thanks to David Shorter, Jessica Cattelino, Mishuana Goeman, Maylei Blackwell, and other members of the Indigenous Sovereignty Research Group for reading with me the introduction and chapter six and for hosting a public presentation on disenrollment at the University of California, Los Angeles, in June 2010. Thanks to Jennifer Denetdale and Alyosha Goldstein for hosting a brown bag discussion and presentation on chapter four at the University of New Mexico in October 2010.

Several individuals gave invaluable counsel on specific chapters. All faults in the resulting arguments are my own, but I am particularly indebted to the generosities of John A. Gomez Jr., David Cornsilk, and Rusty Creed Brown for providing keen insights and sharing resources.

Postdoctoral fellowships were provided by the Ford Foundation (2005–6), San Francisco State University President's Sabbatical (Spring 2010), and the American Indian Studies Center at the University of California, Los Angeles (2010–11).

As a note of acknowledgment, while our works are very different, the title of this book was inspired by Lisa Lowe's *Immigrant Acts: On Asian American Cultural Politics* (1996), for its multiple plays with the idea of legal acts as cultural acts of identity formation.

Introductions

....

W hen I was born in Southern California in 1962, my paternal grandparents, then living in Los Angeles, initiated the process for my enrollment with the Lenape nation (the Delaware Tribe of Indians). At the time, the tribe possessed federal recognition status, reflecting its historic relations with the colonies dating back to the early 1600s, and with the United States dating back to 1778. But in 1979, ten years after my grandparents returned to live in Oklahoma and a decade after President Nixon suspended tribal termination as a policy goal, the Delaware Tribe was terminated by the Bureau of Indian Affairs (BIA) at the political behest of the Cherokee Nation of Oklahoma. In 1996, the Delaware successfully appealed the decision and were reinstated. Within two years, the tribe built a basic infrastructure through federal grants for an elder-care program, child care, language revitalization, and housing. When the Delaware began to explore the possibility of land restoration and gaming operations in Oklahoma, the Cherokee filed a lawsuit to challenge the Delaware's legal status as a tribe. In 2004, the U.S. Tenth Circuit Court of Appeals ruled in favor of the Cherokee, resulting in the second termination of the Delaware. In 2009, after a controversial memorandum of understanding with the Cherokee Nation regarding Delaware rights to lands and economic development in Oklahoma, the BIA reinstated the tribe.[1]

Like many other Native people in the United States, I was socialized from an early age into the arbitrariness and absolutes of federal categories of Native legal status and rights and into the difficult work the categories do in mediating the social terms and conditions of Native political and interpersonal relations.[2] And yet most of the challenges about my identity have not been on the point of the law. While legal discourses about recognition and enrollment provide one means of articulating these challenges, I have never been asked for my tribal card or proof of enrollment (though I know others who have been). I have, however, been questioned repeatedly on authenticity grounds.[3]

I have often been challenged on blood quantum. Sometimes at annual holiday parties, a member of the Norwegian/Irish maternal side of my family has asked "how much Indian" my father or grandparents *really* were. These types of questions have also been posed from advisors and colleagues. As one of my graduate school advisors suggested to me the week before my qualifying exams, "Maybe you are only doing mixed-blood studies to legitimate your own identity as an Indian?" Or the professor of Egyptology in the College of Ethnic Studies at San Francisco State University (SFSU), who, one morning in the copy room, asked me very loudly about my "exact" blood quantum. When I explained briefly and somewhat awkwardly as others entered the room why I did not answer that question, he replied indignantly, "Well, do you even have an Indian name?" As if my reasons for not answering him were because I did not have any Indian blood and not for those I explained.

All of these questions and remarks are intricately tied to racialized perceptions about physical appearance and biological difference, where degrees of blood are assumed to be equated with degrees of cultural identity. There was the hairdresser who insisted to me that I "did not look like an Indian." As proof, she pulled a photo inserted into the frame of the mirror in front of us. It was a picture of her standing with a group of Native people with whom her daughter had done missionary work the previous summer.

"See how dark they are? Their facial features? Their hair is so thick." She continued to stare at the photo and my reflection in the mirror, returning the photo to its place and giving me a look that I could only infer was one of deep confusion.

In these exchanges, people are looking to resolve preconceptions about Native peoples that my physical appearance and presumed blood degree contradicts. Often these efforts just make me tired, particularly of the disrespect to me and my family that I experience in these kinds of interactions. So much so that on occasions when I have gone out after work for drinks with colleagues, when I just want to relax and unwind, I have disguised the work that I do so that I do not have to deal with the questions about my identity that its disclosure too often solicits. One evening a couple of colleagues (both of them from the sociology department, one Native and one Brazilian) and I went out for a beer in San Francisco's West Portal district. In an unguarded moment I told the bartender that I was a faculty member in American Indian Studies. He quickly dropped what he was doing and asked in due sincerity—and urgency—whether or not I was an Indian. I said yes. He put his hands on the bar and leaned forward, "So, how much Indian are you?" He was so excited to know. I said one-third. He stood back. "Wow. One-third. That's a lot." "I know," I said. He was impressed, happy, and relieved. He returned to his work, obviously resisting the urge to ask me the slew of questions that seemed to flood his mind. Meanwhile, my colleagues had turned their heads to muffle their confused laughter. "Is that even possible?" my fellow Native asked. I took another sip of my beer and began, "I was the product of a ménage à trois. . . ."

Unfortunately for Native peoples throughout the United States, my experiences are not unusual and rarely amusing. Our families, histories, and personal ethics are constantly called into question as everyone else seems to know exactly what a Native person is and looks like and just how far any one of us deviates from it (Barker and Teaiwa 1994; Vizenor 1994; Owens 1998; P. Deloria 2004; Kauanui 2008). But the questions and remarks about blood and appearance are not merely breaches in decorum—a faux pas of social etiquette or arrogance. They are interpersonal instances of deeply entrenched social ideologies and identificatory practices of race within the United States. What is more, these ideologies and practices have been employed to legally and popularly contest the authenticity of Native genealogical ties in order to contest the legitimacy of Native legal status and rights. If you are not *really* Native, after all, then you do not deserve what are often perceived as the "special benefits" reserved for Native peoples under the law (Barker 2005/2006).

It all begins with federal recognition policies and the historically central role of race and racialization in constructing the "Indian tribe" (Drinnon 1980; Dippie 1982; R. Williams 1990). These policies were necessary for purposes of allocating federal dollars, services, and programs that provisions of treaties and congressional statutes mandated to recognized tribes. Ideologies of race and racial difference demanded tribal cultural authenticity which was assumed to be measurable by their blood-as-cultural degrees of isolation from other societies (Barker 2004; Whitt 2009). In other words, the more isolated a tribe was socially, the more authentic it was presumed to be as a tribe. Language fluency and blood quantum were used as special tools for measuring isolation and, hence, authenticity against the presumed historical forces of assimilation that resulted in language loss and compromised blood degrees.

In fact, congressional records are full of discussions by House and Senate representatives obsessed with the number of original speakers and the prevalence of blood quanta among Native groups (Kauanui 2008). Linguistic and biological differences were assumed to provide scientifically "objective" and "reasonable" indications of cultural authenticity and were the only valid reason for establishing or maintaining the recognition of Native peoples' legal statuses and rights.

These presumptions resulted in federal policies for tribal enrollment, instituted during the administration of the General Allotment Act of 1887 which unevenly deployed language and blood to measure "competency" and land entitlement. Similarly, blood degree was perpetuated for Native Hawaiians by a 50 percent criteria within the Hawaiian Homes Commission Act of 1920 (Kauanui 2008) and for Alaska Natives by a 25 percent criteria within the Alaska Native Claims Settlement Act of 1971.

While originating in federal policy, blood degree criteria were folded into tribal governance and enrollment policies. These policies were instituted within allotment agreements with those tribes in Indian Territory who were originally exempt from the statute (Bledsoe 1909). They were then carried into tribal constitutions established under the terms of the Indian Reorganization Act of 1934 (F. Cohen 1940) in which "Indian" was defined as including "all persons of Indian descent who are members of any recognized" tribe, "all persons who are descendents of such members . . . residing within the present boundaries" of tribal reservations, and "all other persons of one-half or more Indian blood" (Section 19).

The constitutive role of racist ideologies and identificatory practices in federal recognition, and their impact on tribal governance and enrollment policies, contribute to the always-present futures and social agencies of U.S. national narrations—the grand meta-stories of national progress, civilization, democracy, freedom, liberty, and equality. Therein, the story goes, those whose current positions of power were historically defined within U.S. colonial and imperial formations have evolved past their roles in Native genocide, dispossession, and exploitation to embody an ever-present multicultural humanism that recognizes and celebrates the intrinsic value of Native cultures and identities (Povinelli 2002).[4] These discursive maneuvers enable U.S. nationalism and citizenship to be reinvented as relevant and meaningful. Those who have historically benefited from histories of Native oppression—especially including genocidal violence and land dispossession—can now perceive their positions of power and legal entitlements as somehow inevitable by recognizing and celebrating Native cultures and identities (even more so in claims of ancestral ties to Native royalty! [R. Green 1990]). This recognition and celebration works to perpetuate the *progressive* historical trajectories of national narrations—beginning with tales of Native savagery and ending with those in power finding resolution and affirmation—but only if the Native recognized and celebrated is authentic.

Within the narrative practices of nation formation, laws that regulate Native status and rights are central in defining the conditions of power for those classified as "white." These laws have worked so concertedly over time to normalize the legal, social, and economic positions of privilege for "whites" over Native lands, resources, and bodies that those classified as white have come not only to feel entitled to their privileges and benefits under the law—in fact, expecting the law to continue protecting those privileges and benefits—but also to enjoy the right to exclude them from nonwhites (Harris 1993). The power of exclusion deeply informs the social status and reputation of whites that comes from being legally invested with power and finding the law to protect those investments over time (Frankenberg 1993; López 1996; Lipsitz 1998; Kauanui 2008). Native legal status and rights to sovereignty and self-determination confront the presumed normalcy and righteousness of this system of entitlements and exclusions. Keeping the threats posed by Native governance and territorial rights at bay demands a reinforcement of racist ideologies and identificatory practices of Native authenticity. Natives are never quite Native enough to deserve the distinction and rights granted to them under the law, which extends "special" rights and privileges to Natives out of the benevolence of those in power. This discursive posturing is fortified further by the "scientific proof" of biological-as-cultural difference that deploys such tools as blood quantum and physical appearance as objective and rational measures of Native authenticity as well as a counter to culturally biased and politically motivated Native genealogical claims and cultural practices that establish affiliation and belonging in other ways (such as by making families through love, adoption, or naturalization).

The rub, as it were, for Native peoples is that they are only recognized as Native within the legal terms and social conditions of racialized discourses that serve the national interests of the United States in maintaining colonial and imperial relations with Native peoples. Natives must be able to demonstrably look and act like the Natives of national narrations in order to secure their legal rights and standing as Natives within the United States.[5] How Native peoples choose to navigate these demands and the implications of their choices within Native social formations is the focus of this book.

In this book I interrogate the configurations and workings of U.S. national narrations and their coproductions by ideologies of race, gender, sexuality, and severe religious conservatism in mediating the social terms and conditions of Native legal status and rights in the United States. But while federal laws and legal discourses are central to these configurations and operations, I examine them specifically from within the historical contexts in which they have mediated Native political and interpersonal relations. In other words, my critical focus is on the political and ethical implications of how Native peoples choose to navigate the legal and cultural demands for their authenticity with one another. The core, indeed sacred, concepts of Native culture and identity that inform these choices are not merely articulated by national narrations about Native peoples; they are articulated by Native peoples within their intellectual, political, and creative work. Therein, the concepts and assumptions of cultural authenticity within Native communities potentially reproduce the very social inequalities and injustices of racism, ethnocentrism, sexism, homophobia, and religious conservatism that define U.S. nationalism and Native oppression. Until the hold of these ideologies is genuinely disrupted *by Native peoples*, the important projects for Native decolonization and self-determination that define Native movements and cultural revitalization efforts today are impossible. These projects fail precisely in the ways that they reinscribe notions of authenticity that are not only defined in nationalisms to uphold relations of domination between the United States and Native nations, but within Native political and interpersonal relations. Native peoples must take on the challenge of decolonizing their concepts and projects for self-determination that retain the politics of authenticity within them.

Some Methodological Musings on "the Law"

> It is more proper that law should govern than any one of the citizens.
>
> — ARISTOTLE, *Politics*

> We must eschew the model of Leviathan in the study of power. We must escape from the limited field of juridical sovereignty and state institutions, and instead base our analysis of power on the study of the techniques and tactics of domination.
>
> — MICHEL FOUCAULT, "Two Lectures"

This book does not offer a case study or other disciplinary exegesis of the laws that have concerned Native legal status and rights, even as those laws are a critical focus of it.[6] Instead, following the methodological approaches of such poststructuralists as Michel Foucault (1975, 1977) and Stuart Hall (Morley and Chen 1996), I analyze how federal and tribal laws arbitrating the terms and conditions of Native status and rights work in the ongoing processes of social formation. This does not mean that I consider the law to be ahistoric. But contrary to Aristotelian philosophy, I do not treat the law as canonic or as an integral, isolated whole. The law cannot govern from on high or in the abstract, and it is not politically disinterested. The law is a discourse that operates in historically contingent and meaningful ways, articulated to other discourses ideologically, strategically, and irrationally. It informs the constitution and character of the relations of power and knowledge between Native peoples and the United States, and within Native communities.

Ineluctably, the law enables the state to subject groups and individuals to its authority (Foucault 1979; Hunt and Wickam 1994). This occurs in multiple ways. It occurs through the knowledge the state claims about its subjects, engulfing them under its jurisdiction as police, judges, criminals, terrorists, victims, inmates, guards, ex-cons, and parole officers (Althusser 1971). It occurs through the institutionalization of that knowledge in mechanisms of regulation like surveillance, fines, and incarceration (Ross 1998; Davis 2003). And it occurs through the privatization and diffusion of the state's control throughout multiple service sectors and routine administrative procedures (Ong 1995). These processes normalize the state's domination, even or especially in the context of criticisms of its failures to meet the demands of public safety and national security, requiring still further controls to improve its operations.

Even more important are the complexities of how power is constituted through the actions of those subjected through legal discourse (Althusser 1971; Lacan 1977): the inmate who disciplines himself to avoid punishment (or not) and so makes himself governed as an inmate under the guard's watchful authority, and therefore the state's control (or not); the inmate who represents herself as obedient because she understands the significance of the panopticon, which in turn represents the attendance of surveillance and punishment even in the absence of the guard from the tower (Foucault 1979).

Historical genealogies of how legal discourses are defined and deployed by the state, and how those subjected invite, deflect, ignore, and resist the subjectivities and social conditions they are articulated into, provide a necessary literacy in how power is constituted (Foucault 1977; Ong 1995). They also provide a means for thinking through strategies for opposition that will produce other social formations and other futures (Davis 1983, 2005; Tadiar 2009).[7] Such genealogies reject the conventional, popular treatment of the law as the self-evident arbiter of objectivity, justice, and reason whose developments can be chronicled by case study (Carrillo 2002). By perceiving the law as a discourse, the law is understood within the context of how it is articulated to other discourses and to what (un)intended ends. In this sense, the law has no "necessary, intrinsic, transhistorical belongingness" (Hall, in Grossberg 1996, 142). Its significance comes from how it is articulated to other discourses, as Stuart Hall says of religion: "Its meaning—political and ideological—comes precisely from its position within a formation. It comes with what else it is articulated to. Since those articulations are not inevitable, necessary, they can potentially be transformed, so that religion can be articulated in more than one way" (ibid.).

For instance, given the difficulties of convincing powerful nation-states in North America, the Pacific, and Africa to ratify the Declaration on the Rights of Indigenous Peoples (2007), the United Nations Secretariat of the Permanent Forum on Indigenous Peoples produced a working definition of "indigenous peoples" in 2004. This definition was a response to concerns about the scope of those included as indigenous and their associated legal rights. The definition that resulted characterized "indigenous communities, peoples and nations" as those "having a historical continuity with pre-invasion and pre-colonial societies that developed on their territories, [and] consider themselves distinct from other sectors of the societies now prevailing on those territories, or parts of them" (Secretariat of the Permanent Forum on Indigenous Issues 2004). It also provided that "on an individual basis, an indigenous person is one who belongs to these indigenous populations through self-identification as indigenous (group consciousness) and is recognized and accepted by these populations as one of its members (acceptance by the group). This preserves for these communities the sovereign right and power to decide who belongs to them, without external interference" (ibid.).

This definition is important not as a capture of the essence or truth of what it means to be indigenous, or as an indication of the evolution of international law or legal precepts that have finally recognized the human rights of indigenous peoples. It is important because in the over forty years of labored efforts by indigenous peoples from around the world on the Declaration, it instances the political agendas of those aligned through the United Nations to *rearticulate themselves* as "indigenous communities, peoples and nations" with human rights to self-determination (Wilmer 1993; Anaya 1996; Venne 1998; Niezen 2003). These efforts are embedded within the way that international law has historically subjected indigenous peoples to the absolutes of federal plenary power and programs aimed at their genocide, dispossession, and assimilation (Anaya 1996). Not merely in provision but in process, the Declaration represents indigenous peoples' perceptions of the possibilities of *rearticulation*: the potentially revolutionary shift (never complete) from hegemonic and essentialist formations to those characterized by the antagonisms of a radical democratic politics (Laclau and Mouffe 1985; Grossberg 1996).

This is not to suggest that the rearticulation of the terms of legal status and rights suddenly produces liberation and revolution or that the terms lose their etymological histories and meanings. This would imply that *self-determination* is significant outside the historical contexts of the colonialisms and imperialisms in which it was made meaningful. Rather, it is about the potential of rearticulation to produce political antagonisms that can lead to other social formations (Laclau and Mouffe 1985; Grossberg 1996). This potential is evident not merely in the text of the Declaration but in the conflicts surrounding its ratification in 2007. These conflicts were marked by four votes against it from Australia, Canada, New Zealand, and the United States (all have since reversed their 2007 votes and endorsed the Declaration).

In other words, the Declaration represents indigenous peoples' efforts to rearticulate themselves to other discourses than those of oppression (as the oppressed), to shift the "intelligibility of their historical situation" (Hall, in Grossberg 1996, 142) from the legal constraints of federal plenary power to the internationally recognized legal status and rights of *peoples* to sovereignty and self-determination. The initial vote against and subsequent reversals make it clear that articulatory practices are not about legal provisions or categories *per se*. They are about the radical politics of antagonist reformation (Laclau and Mouffe 1985). The Declaration is important not because its definitions are "right" or because it has fully produced the transformations sought, but because it posits the possibilities for producing other social formations than those characterized by colonialism and imperialism. Simultaneously, it marks the avid refusal of the United States and its variously dominant classes (not merely economic) against having existing power structures in relation to Native peoples disturbed or viably challenged. The Declaration, then, marks both the potential for reform and the vigilant efforts of many powerful nation-states to keep indigenous peoples subjugated to their respective but related regimes of power.

Given histories of genocide, dispossession, assimilation, and discrimination are enacted and rationalized through the law, it is perhaps ironic or simply confusing that the law would continue to be regarded by indigenous peoples or other disenfranchised people as a tactic of resistance or reform.

But the truth is that indigenous peoples, immigrants, minorities, women, queers, the sick, the poor, and ex-cons (not necessarily mutually exclusive categories) look to the law to be a mediator for a more just life. This is evident in the ways that these diverse communities have mobilized human and civil rights to contend social inequality (Young 1990; Markell 2003), and they do so not because they are delusional or confused. Their mobilization of the law is because the law represents a possibility for reform and even revolution, particularly of the state that administers it (Biolsi 2001). This possibility stands up against the concrete ways that the law has benefited some groups and individuals over others (Harris 1993; Kauanui 2002; Moreton-Robinson 2005; Tsosie 2005). Despite this, the promise of the law to bring about justice and equity in a fair and objective, even rational, way compels many different kinds of political constituencies to look to the law as the thing that will compel the state and those in power to conform to a more just standard of action. And in modest ways, this has been true in some legislative and common law decisions: African Americans and women (not necessarily distinct) have been enfranchised; lesbian and gay couples have secured some domestic partnership or same-sex marriage rights in some states; and some Native groups have reacquired aspects of their traditional governance and territories.

The question that lingers is not *why* Native peoples would use the law as a means of reformation (Biolsi 2001, 181) but *how*, in those uses, they seek to rearticulate their relations to one another, the United States, and the international community. How does the law work? When is it promise, arbiter of justice and fairness, rational and truthful, even in the most glaring of historical contexts when it has not been any of those things? How and when do Native peoples reinterpret the law to define and achieve their political objectives? In the remaining chapters of this book, I focus on the complexities of these and related questions. I consider how within discourses of Native legal status and rights, the law holds out its promise for objectivity, equality, and social change. I examine the place of culture and identity in Native articulations of their legal status and rights. I show that federal law demands a particular kind of Native culture and identity in order for Natives to be recognized as legitimately, legally Native. I argue that Native peoples must choose strategically and ethically how they will negotiate these demands as they articulate their cultures and identities as Natives in claims of their legal status and rights.

Some Theoretical Musings on "the Authentic"

Within Native studies in the United States there is an assumed righteousness and rightness in Native peoples' legal status and rights to sovereignty
and self-determination. This owes in part to understandings of the colonial
and racist impact of federal law on Native peoples (Berkhofer 1979; Drinnon 1980; Dippie 1982; R. Williams 1990). The law is read as a tool of oppression and interracial conflict rationalizing Native oppression (V. Deloria 1974; Deloria and Lytle 1984; Rawls 1984; Harris 1993; Vizenor 1994;
Wilkins 1997; Berger 1997; Harring 1994; Ross 1998; Biolsi 2001; R. Miller
2006). It is understood to emerge from dominant ideologies of race that
provide images of an Indian who is always lacking the qualities that would
prove she or he possesses the same status and rights, or even just humanity,
as the white heterosexual Christian civilized norm (Berkhofer 1979). The
law's Indian-who-lacks has been shown to be a complete fabrication or
"simulation" (Vizenor 1994) of dominant ideologies of race that rationalize the still-colonial and imperial relations between the United States and
Native peoples (R. Green 1990; R. Williams 2005).

The paradigmatic focus within Native studies on federal law and dominant ideology leaves unaddressed a myriad of critical questions about the
law and legal discourses (Harring 1994; Lomawaima 1994; Biolsi 2001). This
lack of address could be read as contributing to a romantic stabilization or
essentialism of the righteousness and rightness of Native legal rights, societies, and/or cultures against the social forces of U.S. oppression. Robert
Allen Warrior, in *Tribal Secrets: Recovering American Indian Intellectual Traditions* (1994), and Eva Marie Garroutte, in *Real Indians: Identity and Survival of Native America* (2003), challenge their readers not to be so presum-
ing or dismissive. They argue that such critical work be treated with respect
for the historical and cultural contexts in which the authors are writing and
the intellectual genealogies from which they write. They argue that the stabilization of Native legal status and rights, and its contrast with federal law
and dominant ideology, might be more political strategy than simplistic
essentialist formula.

For instance, in *The Nations Within: The Past and Future of American Indian Sovereignty* (1984), Vine Deloria Jr. and Clifford M. Lytle argue that federal law has undermined the means and abilities of tribes to
exercise their rights to sovereignty. In their introduction "A Status Higher

Than States," they argue that the United States refuses to fully recognize the unique status of tribes as sovereign nations under the precepts of international and constitutional law. Instead, they maintain, the government asserts plenary power over tribes as domestic dependent "nations within" and then exercises that power in legislation that erodes the viability of tribal rights. With the righteousness of tribal status and rights against the United States so demonstrated, Deloria and Lytle then deliver a scathing critique of the Indian Reorganization Act (IRA) of 1934. They focus on the failure of the "nations within" model, perpetuated by the IRA and related statutes like the Indian Civil Rights Act (ICRA) of 1968, to provide the promised framework for the revitalization of tribal self-government and economic self-sufficiency (see Alfred 1999, 2005). They locate this failure in part within the IRA's negation of the diversity of traditional forms of tribal government in its centralization and corporatization of tribal councils in order to facilitate the administration of federal policies.[8]

Deloria's and Lytle's work raises important questions about the viability of tribal governments and the relevance of customary laws and practices. Writing during President Ronald Reagan's administration and its particular assault on tribal sovereignty (backing legislation that greatly restricted land rights claims and enacting severe budget cuts to the BIA), Deloria's and Lytle's assumption of the viability and relevance of tribal law and governance combats dismissals of its backwardness and insignificance. Subsequent authors, like Taiaiake Alfred (1999) and Wallace Coffey and Rebecca Tsosie (2001), have pushed this critique further to argue that the very cultural beliefs and practices of Native peoples define their sovereignty and not the precepts of international or constitutional law.

These arguments must now be pushed to address the important differences in the ways Native cultures, traditions, sovereignty, and self-determination are perceived and represented by Native peoples. In understanding and working toward Native decolonization, these arguments must take on the consequential differences—in contradiction, in disagreement, and in complexity—of Native perspectives about what their unique cultures and traditions are and how those cultures and traditions matter to them in the governance, territorial integrity, and cultural autonomy that they seek.

For instance, discourses of Native legal status and rights often presume a value distinction between the status and rights of the group and those of the individual (Barker 2006, 2008). In this view, group status and rights draw from traditional values that place the needs of the community first; individual status and rights reference "Western ideologies" that advance a more self-centered individualism that puts personal liberty and freedom before the needs of the group. Collective status and rights are affirmed by international law, while civil rights are protected constitutionally. Collective rights address "hard" political issues like self-government and territorial integrity, while individual rights address "soft" political matters like personal freedom and equality. The kind of Native culture and identity through which these various distinctions are articulated assumes two things. First, it assumes a coherent and stable set of traditions about the group and the individual, not so much or merely of the past as bounded and protected from "Western influence" today. Second, it assumes an agreement among all Native traditions that the group is more important than the individual, in the sense that those entities are distinguished in "Western" philosophies, ignoring other intellectual genealogies about the group and the individual that might be defined within Native epistemologies. Indeed, ignored is the discursive role of the "group" and "individual" in the different epistemologies and metaphysical assumptions about Natives and Europeans.

In fact, many Natives have dismissed Native women and their allies for asserting the principles of civil rights and gender equity in tribal government as mere Western ideologues. Positioning feminism and gender equality as "outside" and therefore dangerous to traditional values, Native women have been made complicit and even co-conspirators of the colonization of Native communities by "bringing in" and "forcing" feminist principles on tribal governments and communities. This discursive move pretends that Native women's activism has not been focused on matters of Native sovereignty and self-determination. It reflects a deeper erasure within Native political discourses of the very core constitutive role of gender in Native women's concepts, politics, and efforts for Native sovereignty and self-determination (Barker 2006, 2008). In doing so, it reflects the difficulties facing Native conceptualizations of sovereignty and self-determination. As discussed throughout this book, Native people who have expressed frustration, anger, and disagreement with tribal governments for advancing racist, sexist, homophobic, or extremely conservative religious perspectives have been dismissed as anti-Indian and anti-sovereignty. They have been accused of imposing "outside," "Western" ideologies and values like equality and feminism or homosexuality on tribal governments and communities and so of being complicit with assimilationist efforts aimed at eroding the integrity of tribal cultures. These dismissals and silences have not only chilled public debate and political critique about racist, sexist, and homophobic discrimination and violence within Native communities. They have rearticulated a Native sovereignty and self-determination that perpetuates racism, sexism, homophobia, and severe religious conservatism from within.

In this book, I examine these thick and difficult negotiations. I argue that discourses of Native culture and identity are articulated to discourses of Native legal status and rights in ways that are contextual and conditional. Their particular attachments result from specific struggles over and against "the techniques and tactics of domination" (Foucault 1972, 102) as well as intellectual, political, and cultural histories within Native communities. In other words, Native peoples are not merely the product of the dominant—thinking the "necessary and inevitable thoughts" that belong to their "socio-economic or class location or social position" (Hall, in Grossberg 1996, 142). Their histories matter in consequential ways to the cultures and identities that they claim for themselves as Native, tribal people and that they claim in relation to one another as Natives or tribes. In the agency of social formation, Native peoples participate fully in the configuration of their relationships to the United States and to one another. In that participation, there is great possibility for revolution as well as a deep ethical responsibility for its consequences.

On "the Native" and "Tradition": A Prelude to the Conclusions in Origins

I do not believe that there is a metaphysical Native who possesses essential rights to anything. I do not believe that there is an authentic tradition to be revitalized from a past that transcends "Western ideology." I do not offer this work as a "Native intellectual," authorized by the truths of a Lenape culture and identity.

"The Native" and "tradition" are constructs that function within and are anchored to specific contestations for power between Native peoples and the United States and within Native communities. These constructs result from the political objectives that deploy them. They can no more be extrapolated from their historical situation than they can be from the intentions, passions, devotions, hatreds, and competitions of the groups and individuals that put them to work.

So exactly what am I saying? That Natives do not exist except as mere constructs or inventions? That Native identities are fabrications or simulations, generally of "Western" derivation? That there is no meaning in identifying as Native? That Natives have no traditions of their own? That in the absence of Native authenticity, Native rights to sovereignty and self-determination are flimsy, whimsical, and undeserved? No. And I would like to try to get at the disquiet of these questions by offering a brief etymology of "the Native" and "tradition." However, this etymology leads me to confront a fundamental theoretical conundrum that percolates throughout the book: namely, the paradigmatic authority of theories of assimilation and social evolution in theories of Native culture and identity. These theories assume a historical trajectory for understanding the value and consequence of social change over time along a whole host of progressive lines: from primitive to civilized; from integral and whole to contaminated and fractured; from lived to lost; et cetera. Depending on the perspective, these changes are read as the natural and good result of social development; the inevitable result of contact between a less and a more civil society; a tragic reminder of racially fueled colonial projects aimed at the eradication of all things Native; as indications of compromise, capitulation, or even selling out by Native people to dominant social values and norms. Whatever the conclusion, it seems that cultural authenticity for Native peoples exists only in a pre-colonial — indeed pre-historical — moment that has been forever lost to the natural, inevitable, compromised, or tragic ends of colonialism and imperialism.

Reified by national narrations, these characterizations take for granted the "centrism" of the societies of western Europe and the United States. It presumes that social change for these societies is always about progress, while social change for Native peoples is always about either progress, assimilation, compromise, or loss. It is a narration that celebrates the inevitable and venerated evolution of "the West" against the tragic but unavoidable consequences of that evolution for everyone else. In the end, it seriously distorts the aggressive and violent histories of colonization and imperialism for cultural nostalgia and political apologia (Taussig 1987; Povinelli 2002).

These troubled notions of Native culture and identity attach to Native legal status and rights in ways that force Native peoples to claim the authenticity of a culture and identity that has been defined *for* them. Furthermore, these definitions derive from the very narratives of colonization and imperialism that perpetuate Native domination.

But what if assimilation and evolution are not the best ways to understand histories of social change? What if culture and identity are negotiated within a complex matrix of social interactions and relationships, never whole and integral, always incomplete and unsure, but deeply meaningful and significant?

The Native

"The Native" has multiple genealogies related to but not the same as "the Indian."[9] It originates from the Latin word *nativus* in English use in 1374, meaning innate, produced by birth, to be born, to be related to, to beget, to produce. By 1450, it was used to mean "a person born in bondage." By 1535, it meant "a person who has always lived in a place," and by 1652, it was used to refer to the original inhabitants of European colonies. From 1800, particularly in North America, it was used to mean "the locals."[10] Then, in 1845, "Nativism" took on a particularly anti-immigrant significance, no doubt owing to its etymological links with the "nation" and therefore its use in nationalist ideologies and practices (Onions 1996, 603).

The ideological work of "the Native" is about its political utility. It works to distinguish the descendants of colonials from those who are more recent immigrants (Berkhofer 1979; Vizenor 1994; P. Deloria 1998). For instance, the Daughters of the Lone Star Republic of Texas, formed in 1891, referred to themselves as "Native Texans." This was meant to distinguish their status and rights as descendants of the "pioneering families and soldiers of the Republic of Texas" who "rendered loyal service to Texas prior to its annexation in 1846 by the United States" from those immigrants who arrived after 1846 (Daughters of the Republic of Texas Library n.d.). It thereby displaced—indeed erased—Natives from Texas by suggesting those who descended from the "pioneering families and soldiers of the Republic of Texas" possessed the legal rights of citizenship and land of Natives. This followed from ongoing national narrations. As would happen more and more frequently in the 1800s, "Native," particularly when coupled with

"American," took on the task of differentiating those of English descent from those immigrants of German, Irish, Italian, and other European origins in constructions of the rights and privileges of American citizenship. This citizenship was first and foremost for and by free white men and inextricably linked with property rights (Saxton 1990; Almaguer 1994; López 1996; Lipsitz 1998).

In other words, "Native Americans" worked to preserve and protect a set of legal status and rights to U.S. citizenship and property for those classified as "white." It did so by claiming a Native identity that embodied the rights of possessive descent over the rights of immigrants. Time and again, the legal status and rights of "whites" as "Native Americans" would be affirmed and protected by federal law while that same law stripped Native peoples and recent immigrants of their rights to self-governance, property, and other means to economic self-sufficiency and access to education (Harris 1993).

Beginning in the 1960s, Native peoples reappropriated "the Native" to distinguish themselves as the original inhabitants of the Americas against all other racialized or ethnicized immigrants and minorities. Unlike claims to American citizenship and constitutional rights implied in the terms "African American" and "Asian American," "Native American" intended to distinguish the collective rights of Natives to sovereignty and self-determination under international law from the constitutional or civil protections of immigrants and ethnic minorities (Barker 2002; Kauanui 2002; Wilkins 2002; Champagne 2005).

Today some understand "Native American" to include American Indians, Alaskan Natives, and Native Hawaiians, that is, all of the descendants of the original inhabitants of what are now the fifty states. However, many Native Hawaiians reject this inclusion because they do not want to be placed under the administration of the BIA as "nations within." They prefer to be recognized under the United Nations' classification of Hawai'i as a nation illegally occupied by the United States that qualifies for decolonization (Trask 1993; Silva 2004; Kauanui 2008; Tengan 2008).

Others use "Native" to indicate the indigenous peoples of North, South, and Central America (i.e., of the Western Hemisphere). Many Natives resist this because they perceive it to subsume them under an identification that erases their historical presence in the United States. For example, many Native California Indians have criticized the "hemispheric" perspective as contributing to an erasure of their unique histories and cultures as distinct from Latin, Aztec, and Mayan contexts.[11]

"The Native," then, is put to work in many ways to represent specific political concerns and agendas. As a consequence, who is and is not included as Native is contingent on the social contexts of its use. To assert that there is a stable, *real* group of people, or an essential, organic individual being referred to as Native, is to assert an essentialist definition of what it means to be Native, when essentialism is about claiming a preexistent, metaphysical truth or essence that is *the* Native against which all others are opposed.

The challenge, then, is not how to capture the truth or the essence of the Native in the category of the Native; it is not about which discourse "gets it right." Rather it is to think through the kinds of historical circumstances that have been created to produce coherence in what "the Native" means and how it functions in any given historical moment or articulatory act. That coherence of meaning is historically contingent and not guaranteed for all time and places (see Morley and Chen 1996). What the Native means will change over time and place as various political constituencies lay claim on determining its significance.

So, of course, Native cultures and identities are not "constructs" if what is meant by "construct" is a falsity or falseness. Native cultures and identities are meaningful to the groups and individuals who give them meaning. But these meanings are not static in time or fixed for all time; they do not refer to realities or essences that exist beyond historical and social context and use.

Tradition

Conventionally, "tradition" is understood as that which is "handed down as belief or practice in a community" (Onions 1996, 935). In the introduction to *The Invention of Tradition* (1983), however, Eric Hobsbawm and Terence Ranger argue that traditions ("governed by overtly or tacitly accepted rules and of a ritual or symbolic nature") are actually more recent constructions ("inventions") toward nationalist ends (1-2). In this, they identify three types: "those establishing or symbolizing social cohesion or the membership of groups, real or artificial communities," "those establishing or legitimating institutions, status or relations of authority," and "those whose main purpose was socialization, the inculcation of beliefs, value systems and conventions of behavior" (9). They found that the study of traditions had often presupposed the nation's claim to historical cohesiveness and continuity against the reality that traditions are continually being innovated often toward upholding the nation's claims of being cohesive and continuous (12–14). This has certainly characterized histories within the United States of Native traditions. Inflected through racialized notions of biological-as-cultural authenticity, theories of assimilation and social evolution have been used by federal and military officials to rationalize Native oppression on the grounds of Native heathenism and savagery.

In other words, Native traditions have most decidedly not been considered to be valued or even legitimate cultural teachings and ways of life handed down between the generations. This would mean that by the very character of cultural history and identity formation, traditions would change and be changed over time (Owens 1998). Instead, Native traditions have been fixed in an authentic past and then used as the measure of a cultural-as-racial authenticity in the present.

These perspectives have impacted Native peoples in a number of ways. In the mad rush to preserve and catalogue Native cultural artifacts and human remains in the late nineteenth and early twentieth centuries, some archaeologists and anthropologists seemed to care less about how Natives were living than what they remembered or were willing to recount of their ancestors' traditions (Bieder 1986; P. Deloria 1998). Those Natives considered especially worthy of study were those considered to be less assimilated (the infamous "last of" narratives dominating the popular media and sciences of every kind). These theories were authorized in popular, scientific, and legal representations which seemed to validate racist ideologies that produced everything from images of the Vanishing Noble Savage to policy developments like allotment and boarding schools. Throughout, some archaeologists and anthropologists were assumed to be *the* authorities on Native cultures and identities (Rose 1992), so much so that they were made "expert witnesses" in congressional hearings and court cases in which they evaluated the authenticity of Native groups in ways that undercut those groups' legal claims (Clifford 1988; Carrillo 1998).

Anthropology was central to the production of "colonial cosmologies" of Native cultural authenticities and inauthenticities that furthered colonial aims on racist grounds (Raibmon 2006). These representational practices were wholly political and anticipated nationalist agendas (Hobsbawm and Ranger 1983). They belonged to the moment in which they were produced, informed by the social relations in which they were made meaningful. They reflect, then, the political objectives and social ethics of representing Native traditions and not the truth about Native traditions. Treating Native peoples unethically—robbing their graves; stealing their cultural artifacts; lying about intent, profit, and circulation of work; asserting knowledge or authority over them; betraying them in court—taints anthropologists' methods and conclusions with the stench of political self-interest and self-importance (Dumont 2003, 2008).

Of course, still further, Native articulations of Native traditions make explicit the problematic and complex aspects of Native social politics through which they work. Some Natives have asserted a sovereignty that embraces Western notions of tradition and "nation-ness" (Anderson 1991, 1–2). Others have articulated traditions in discriminatory and hurtful ways with the explicit goal of claiming some and expelling others (Denetdale 2006). But simultaneously, traditions have served as significant sites of political empowerment, coalition, and social work. In the Declaration on the Rights of Indigenous Peoples, traditions stand in for a host of legal rights that are a radical departure from those ascribed to Natives by nation-states. Native groups have likewise used traditions to define cultural revitalization efforts in everything from language retention, agricultural and medicinal practices, and substance abuse programs to K–12 curriculum (Nelson 2008). And, as Owens writes (1998), Natives have insisted that the reality of cultural change and transformation in tradition is not wholly tragic or horrific. In fact, some people, like the Fort Peck Assiniboine woman who described the tribal practice of mutilating the faces of suspected adulterers, or the Pueblo woman who told me about the practice of exiling those who had committed certain types of crimes, think that certain traditions ought to be left in the past. In these multiple articulations, Native peoples shun the notion that the relevance of their cultures and identities is merely collectable, anecdotal, or decorative. They assert traditions as the cultural beliefs and practices that they understand as uniquely their own, not as a yardstick of conformity to an authentic past but as what binds them together in relationship and responsibility to one another in the present and future.

So, it is not about suggesting that Native cultures and identities are "invented" or "false" because they are historically contextual and socially constructed. It is about suggesting that "the Native" and "traditions" are conditional, that they are made meaningful and relevant again and again in the specific contexts in which they are articulated. Both "the Native" and "traditions" are representational strategies of domination at the same time that they are mechanisms and tactics of antagonism and reformation — sometimes at the same time.

An Overview of the Book

Each chapter that follows puts an act of articulation into historical context and examines the social and legal conflicts within Native communities through which it functions. I focus on how articulatory practices provide a historically conditional perspective on the kinds of social relations and conditions that the United States seeks with or for Native peoples and that Natives seek with one another. I show that the practices are mediated by the terms of national narrations and the agencies those narrations ascribe — to the United States and to Native peoples. The book closes in chapter 7, "Origins," by thinking through the ethical implications of how Natives are (un)made by (their own) status and rights talk.

Until "Origins," the book is divided into three parts. In part I, "Recognition," I argue that U.S. agendas have over-determined the status and rights of Native peoples as "Indian tribes." This has occurred through federal efforts to reproduce Native peoples under the absolutes of federal authority. Within these efforts, the recognition of Native status and rights is really about the coercion of Native peoples to *recognize themselves* to be under federal power within federal terms. The importance of these discursive maneuvers is not merely in the subjugation of Native peoples to federal authority but in the kinds of "Indian tribes" that Native peoples see themselves as and then assert in their relationships with one another. Chapter 1, "Of the 'Indian Tribe,'" unpacks these politics through a brief genealogy of "Indian tribes" in federal law. Chapter 2, "In *Cherokee v. Delaware*," examines these politics in the conflicts between the Cherokee Nation of Oklahoma and the Delaware Tribe of Indians over the terms of Delaware legal status and rights in "Cherokee territory."

In part II, "Membership," I argue that tribal membership criteria are a politic of relationship (un)making, as Native peoples negotiate the terms of their legal status and rights in relation to one another as "Indian members." These processes of identification involve multiple mirrorings of what it means to be Native. In one set of reflections, tribes include and expel members as they include and expel themselves as tribes within the parameters of federal law. In another set of reflections, members construct and present themselves as members based not only on their concepts of tribal cultures and identities, but also in relation to their perceptions of other tribal cultures and identities. These various mirrorings of group and individual status and rights, federal and tribal policy and criteria, and notions of Native culture and identity are impossible to untangle. Their significance relates to the kind of self-determination Native peoples claim for themselves and in relationship to the international community, as well as the kind of social relations they seek with one another. Chapter 3, "Of the 'Indian Member,'" provides a brief genealogy of the racialization and gendering of membership policies in federal and tribal law. Chapter 4, "In *Martinez v. Santa Clara* (and Vice Versa)," examines the articulatory practices of tribal membership through the gendered politics of tradition and sovereignty. Chapter 5, "In Disenrollment," unravels membership within the racialized and economic contexts of disenrollment practices in California spawned by the Indian Gaming Regulatory Act of 1988.

In part III, "Tradition," I examine the discursive work of traditions in relation to Native definitions of Native governance. Chapter 6, "Of Marriage and Sexuality," focuses on national and tribal debates that exploded in 2004 over marriage and sexuality. At that time, the elected officials and legal counsel for the Cherokee Nation of Oklahoma and the Navajo Nation passed legislation that imitated the U.S. Defense of Marriage Act (DOMA) of 1996 and the rash of state ballot initiatives banning same-sex marriage rights. What is compelling about these laws is that they were rationalized on the grounds that they reflected the traditions of the tribes as decidedly Christian and American conservative. This chapter examines the contestations within the Nations that followed over their respective traditions regarding marriage and sexuality and the kinds of tribes, and rights, those traditions defined.

The difficult stories within this book are not told to indulge tribal secrets or air dirty laundry. The focus on a very modest part of some of the people in U.S.-Native relations and within Native communities who have been disenfranchised and disempowered by articulations of Native culture and identity to Native legal status and rights is intentional and strategic. The unrecognized and the terminated, the *un-* and *dis-* enrolled, and those treated as undesirable for purposes of defining and asserting Native nationhood and citizenship have paid the highest price for how Native legal status and rights are defined and asserted by Native peoples. Only from a consideration of the discursive work of status and rights in disciplining Native social and interpersonal relationships can the operations and relations of power within Native communities be better understood. Rather, it is a power that regulates a complex social matrix in which *everyone* is awarded his or her agency and, subsequently, ethical responsibilities as the kinds of nations and citizens each seeks to be.

Part I RECOGNITION

recognition [L *recognoscere*, to recall to mind [*re*, again + *cognoscere*, to know: see COGNITION] **1** *a*) a recognizing or being recognized; acknowledgment; admission, as of a fact *b*) acknowledgment and approval, gratitude, etc. . . . . **2** formal acknowledgment by a government of the independence and sovereignty of a state newly created, as by session, or of a government newly set up, as by revolution **3** identification of some person or thing as having been known before or as being of a certain kind **4** notice, as in passing; greeting; salutation.

Webster's New World Dictionary, Third College Edition

1 Of the "Indian Tribe"

The "Indian tribe" is probably one of the most analyzed—and so perhaps one of the most familiar—categories within Native studies. This is because, technically, it indicates that Native groups possess federal recognition status and all commensurate rights under the law, including the right to self-government, sovereign immunity, and tax exemption. But, ideologically, it is a category that works in far more obscure ways to provide for the continued rearticulation of federal authority over Native peoples. It is, in other words, most certainly not about who is and is not recognized so much as it is about the ongoing processes of social formation that work to keep Native peoples subjugated to U.S. power.

For instance, congressional and court authority over who is and who is not recognized is absolute. As of this writing, those with recognition include 565 "American Indian tribes" and "Alaska Native villages" (the villages having been extended the status and rights of "Indian tribes" by the Alaska Native Claims Settlement Act of 1971). Those excluded—as those perceived to fail recognition criteria and so classified as the "unrecognized"—have been estimated to involve between one-third and one-half of all Native peoples in the United States (S. O'Brien 1989). Also excluded from recognition are Natives within U.S.-occupied territories in the Pacific and Caribbean, including the Kanaka Maoli of Hawai'i, the Chamorro of Guam, and the Taíno of Puerto Rico (Barker 2005b).

Through the discourses of recognition, U.S. national narrations represent recognition as an expected outcome of Native cultural authenticity. This is coupled with the deployment of recognition as evidence that the United States has realized itself as a fully democratic, humanist, and civil society, rendering historical violence and fraud against Native peoples an unfortunate aberration that the U.S. has evolved progressively past and that Natives just need to "get over" (Povinelli 2002).

The seamless articulation of Native legal legitimacy to cultural authenticity by recognition, however, marks the racist ideologies and identificatory practices that undergird its function in reinforcing Native subjugation. For even as "Indian tribes" are represented as historically continuous and culturally cohesive legal entities within recognition, their members are characterized simultaneously as inferior, heathen savages living in a permanent state of nature outside the tribunals of the world's civilized nations. The consequences of these representational divides go to the kinds of "Indian tribes" that Native groups are made to *represent* to federal authorities in order to establish and maintain their legal status and rights. In other words, by the terms of recognition, "Indian tribes" are (made) *recognizable* and so *investable* with a unique set of rights under constitutional and common law. In order to be recognized as a legitimate "Indian tribe," Native groups must be recognizable as tribes in federal terms. These conditions are about the effectiveness of U.S. national narrations at maintaining Native dominance on the grounds of U.S. superiority and a Native inferiority that simultaneously codifies Native authenticity as a particular kind of cultural continuity, cohesiveness, and distinction.

As addressed in the next chapter within the context of Cherokee and Delaware conflicts over the terms of Delaware rights in "Cherokee territory," how Native peoples choose to navigate the incongruous and contradictory demands for their cultural authenticity within their struggles for legal standing represent both the conflicts of Native peoples in the United States for sovereignty and self-determination and the kinds of social relations and conditions that Natives seek (to make) with one another as (un)recognized "Indian tribes." For here, the constitutional, congressional, and common law configurations of the "Indian tribe" are unthreaded through the Marshall Trilogy and the BIA's Office of Federal Acknowledgment (OFA) criteria in relation to how they rearticulate the racisms of U.S. national narrations.

The Reconstituted Tribe

Recognition policies derive from the interpretations of the Constitution's "Indian tribe" by the Supreme Court in the decisions known as the Marshall Trilogy: *Johnson v. McIntosh* (1823); *Cherokee v. Georgia* (1831); and *Worcester v. Georgia* (1832).[1] The "Indian tribe" emerged therein from powerful ideologies of nation formation and racism that objectified and rationalized Native domination on the grounds of Native inferiority (Drinnon 1980; Dippie 1982; Rawls 1984; R. Williams 1990, 2005; Newcomb 2008). The ideologies made for some incredibly incoherent legal actions that at once affirmed and undermined tribal rights to self-government and territorial integrity. In both contexts, "Indian tribes" were represented as savage, barbarian, violent, heathen, immoral, backward, and unevolved; they represented every social and moral characteristic considered opposite and opposed to U.S. society and values. At the same time, they were represented as timeless, noble, and proud. So much so, in fact, that many colonial settlers took great pains to learn and emulate Native cultures and identities as their own (P. Deloria 1998).

Robert F. Berkhofer Jr. (1979), Rayna Green (1990), and Gerald Vizenor (1994) aptly explain the reasons for these representational contradictions by showing their ideological consistencies within the racisms of nationalism. They argue that the point of the "Indian" was and is not her or his *accuracy* but her or his *utility* in constituting and perpetuating the national narrations that uphold Native subjugation. This "Indian" was never meant to represent the complexities and diversities of Native peoples' cultural perspectives and experiences. It was meant to fit within the preexisting archetypes of national narrations—having been defined there to *simulate* both the legitimacy of those narratives and the supremacy of U.S. society:

Pocahontas forever falling in love with and choosing the civil and Christian society of John Smith over her own people (R. Green 1990; Barker 2002); Ishi forever embodying the "last of" his tribe in some tragically romantic tale of U.S. progress across the West (Vizenor 1994).

These politics of representation deeply informed the interpretations of the Constitution's "Indian tribe" by the Supreme Court's Marshall Trilogy. These three decisions are an important example of the contradictory work of the racialization of Native legal status and rights through racist ideologies of what is considered authentically Native.[2]

Referred to as "the commerce clause," the Constitution's Article 1, Section 8, provides that Congress has exclusive jurisdiction over the national economy, including the authority to impose taxes, borrow money, and "regulate commerce with foreign nations, and among the several states, and with the Indian tribes."[3] The distinction between foreign nations, states, and Indian tribes has been interpreted by Congress and the Supreme Court to mean that Congress possesses the exclusive power to regulate all aspects of national commerce and trade relations with these different kinds of sovereign entities. By implication, Congress possesses the authority over related matters of jurisdiction, military alliance and passage, and transportation. It so limits the scope of state relations with tribes and tribal relations with foreign nations.

Referred to as "the taxation clause," the Constitution's Article 1, Section 2, stipulates that in determining how congressional representatives and taxes would be apportioned among the states, representation would be decided by "adding to the whole number of free persons, including those bound to service for a term of years, and excluding Indians not taxed, three fifths of all other Persons." Amendment XIV of 1868 modified the clause to read as "Representatives shall be apportioned among the several states according to their respective numbers, counting the whole number of persons in each state, excluding Indians not taxed." In terms of tribal affairs, the taxation clause has been interpreted by Congress and the Supreme Court to mean that because Indians living under the jurisdiction of their tribal governments on treatied lands were without representation in Congress, they were exempt from taxation by Congress.[4] The connotation is that Indian tribes possess a unique legal standing as separate sovereigns within the United States: They are not represented in Congress and so are exempt from being taxed by Congress. The commerce clause thus limits the scope of federal and state taxation of tribes.

Referred to as the "supremacy clause," the Constitution's Article 6, Paragraph 2, provides that treaties are to be regarded as equal with the Constitution and congressional statute as the "supreme Law of the Land" whose provisions demand respect by the "Judges in every State." Through the ratification of 371 treaties with Native nations from 1778 to 1871,[5] Congress affirmed the sovereign status of tribes and obligated juridical and state authorities to adhere to the provisions of ratified treaties (F. Cohen 1940; V. Deloria 1974; Prucha 1994; Anaya 1996).[6]

Read together, the U.S. Constitution's commerce, taxation, and supremacy clauses defined "Indian tribes" as possessing a unique legal status that inferred a government-to-government relationship with the United States, noninterference by foreign nations and states in their governance and territories, exemption from federal and state taxation, and empowerment to treat with the United States over matters such as lands, jurisdiction, trade, and alliance. Significantly, however, as Congress asserted authority in its relations with tribes, it systematically extended by law its authority over tribes, thus limiting the tribal status and rights.

This authority would be seized upon by the Supreme Court in the decisions known as the Marshall Trilogy. These decisions betrayed racist ideologies as tools of nation building. All three decisions forcefully reinterpreted "Indian tribes" as uncivil, un-Christian savages living in a "state of pupilage" that warranted the unilateral subsuming of all of their legal rights and freedoms under the plenary power, care, and protection of the United States (Wilkins and Lomawaima 2001, 64–97). While the United States would be restricted in exercising those powers by the terms of its ratified treaties with tribes and by congressional law (usually because of the absence of laws specifically extending federal authority), the Marshall Trilogy would provide Congress and the courts with the precedent needed to re-situate tribes as quasi-sovereign "nations within" that were dependent on the United States for the recognition and protection of their rights to self-government and territorial integrity.

Delivering the opinions of the court, Chief Justice John Marshall defined tribes as "domestic dependent nations" who had "passed under" the authority of the United States by virtue of their having repeatedly signed treaties proving their dependence on the United States for aid and protection. The reconceptualization of tribes as "domestic dependent nations" assumed a radical repositioning of Native peoples within a colonial order. Outside the purview of foreign or international relations as sovereign nations who could treat, Indian tribes were said to be positioned within the domestic boundaries of a dominant nation-state as dependents. This was rationalized on the basis of the alleged character of Indian tribes. Marshall asserted that tribes were weaker—uncivilized races living as barbarians in a permanent state of nature. Consequently, he concluded,

> Their relation to the United States resembles that of a ward to his guardian. They look to our government for protection; rely upon its kindness and its power; appeal to it for relief to their wants; and address the president as their great father. They and their country are considered by foreign nations, as well as by ourselves, as being so completely under the sovereignty and dominion of the United States, that any attempt to acquire their lands, or to form a political connection with them, would be considered by all as an invasion of our territory, and an act of hostility. (*Cherokee v. Georgia* 1832)

This description of the character of tribes and the authority of the United States over them was explained further by their *usufruct* relationship to the lands on which they "roamed over" to satisfy their immediate needs. This relationship established their "aboriginal title" to use and occupy the lands in contradistinction from the preeminent title or ownership of the lands by the United States (R. Miller 2006).

> The uniform understanding and practice of European nations, and the settled law, as laid down by the tribunals of civilized states, denied the right of the Indians to be considered as independent communities, having a permanent property in the soil, capable of alienation to private individuals. They remain in a state of nature, and have never been admitted into the general society of nations. . . . Even if it should be admitted that the Indians were originally an independent people, they have ceased to be so. A nation that has passed under the dominion of another, is no longer a sovereign state. The same treaties and negotiations, before referred to, show their dependent condition. (*Johnson v. McIntosh* 1823)

Without having achieved proper civilization, Indian tribes were denied a place as equal members in the "tribunals of civilized states," stripped of their full standing and rights as sovereigns to self-government and territorial integrity as possessed by "civilized states." In other words, the indelible links between nationhood and territorial integrity within constitutional and international law were completely severed for tribes. Tribes were found not to possess the full qualities of sovereign nations—and so not to have entered into the "general society of nations" as equals—because they had not evolved into civilization, into an agricultural society in which people owned and cultivated the land for God and country. Instead, Indians wandered over the lands in search of materials to satisfy their immediate needs for clothing, shelter, and sustenance. Such a "race," in encountering a more civilized one, would naturally have "passed under" its authority. No civilized person, and by implication no civilized nation, would expect a civilized people to give up the lands and by implication their collective sovereignty or personal freedoms and liberties to "Indians."

The recognition of "Indian tribes," then, was not about recognizing the character of tribes—as metaphysical beings or through extra-political truths there to be seen and described as Marshall claimed to be doing. Obviously, tribes were not uncivilized infidels wandering over an untouched wilderness, taking brief respites in their otherwise busy days of hunting and gathering to sign treaties for aid and protection with their newly adopted great white father. The recognition of "Indian tribes" was instead about the United States establishing its absolute authority to recognize tribes as dependent and uncivilized and then subjugating them as such to its power.

This disciplining was enforced by the U.S. Supreme Court and Congress, which rationalized their decisions on the grounds of racialized notions of tribal culture and identity—illustrated by Marshall's ridiculous characterizations of Indians but furthered repeatedly in subsequent decisions and congressional hearings that cited Marshall practically verbatim (R. Williams 2005; Newcomb 2008). The racialization of Natives, then, facilitated their subjugation to domination not merely "within" the United States but internationally where European nations cooperated and even aligned their own actions accordingly (Anaya 1996; Ivison, Patton, and Sanders 2000).

Of course, no one wants to be seen as a dictator. Congress and the courts worked very hard to represent their plenary power over "Indian tribes"—

while owing to tribal savagery and weakness — as inherently benevolent and trustworthy. In fact, Marshall's decisions became the foundation of the trust doctrine, which claimed that the United States had a fundamental responsibility to care for and protect Indians based on their dependent, political vulnerabilities (Wilkins and Lomawaima 2001). This doctrine was exemplified in the Supreme Court's decision in *Lone Wolf v. Hitchcock* (1903). The court was asked to consider whether or not Congress had the right to change the terms of ratified treaties without tribal consultation. It found that such a right existed and that it was based on plenary authority over tribes and tribal affairs.

> Plenary authority over the tribal relations of the Indians has been exercised by Congress from the beginning, and the power has always been deemed a political one, not subject to be controlled by the judicial department of the government. . . . When, therefore, treaties were entered into between the United States and a tribe of Indians it was never doubted that the power to abrogate existed in Congress, and that in a contingency such power might be availed of from considerations of governmental policy, particularly if consistent with perfect good faith towards the Indians. (*Lone Wolf v. Hitchcock* 1903)

Remarkably dismissive of the actions of the United States in violating the provisions of virtually every single ratified treaty with tribes, sometimes even within hours of their signing, the court invented a trust that had slid into its benevolent trustworthiness. The court argued that the United States had fulfilled its trust responsibility to act in the best interest of the tribes when modifying treaties without consultation not because it had acted in the tribes' best interest but because it had the power to do so.[7]

This would all be folded into national narrations in the furtherance and absolution of its colonial and imperial objectives. The narrations would claim that *always* the United States had acknowledged the special legal character and rights of tribes, had risen to fulfill its grave responsibilities to care for and protect tribes from adverse political interests and criminal activities, and had acted in trustworthy fashion toward tribes even when its actions were misunderstood by the tribes as doing otherwise.

Of course not just any "Indian tribe" will do. The narrations that reinvent trustworthiness — via the values of multicultural humanism — out of histories of genocide and dispossession rely deeply on its recognition (knowledge) of an authentic "Indian tribe" (Povinelli 2002; Markell 2003). This tribe is made to occupy a decidedly pre-colonial, pre-history of cultural authenticity that allows the United States not only to locate its colonialism and imperialism in the past but to make it a kind of ideological precursor to being recognized in the present. The United States escapes the consequences of its own historical sins by having real Indians situated in a far distant past before colonialism and imperialism mattered and embodying those cultures and identities today as though colonialism and imperialism have had no substantive or significant long-term consequences. Native peoples are confronted with the impossible task of representing *that* authenticity in order to secure their recognition and rights as sovereigns.[8]

The Rearticulated Tribe

The seventies and eighties have been defined as the period of tribal self-government and self-determination (Deloria and Lytle 1984). This is attributed in part to the fact that the Congress passed a number of bills and amendments that transferred the administration of several federal programs like education to tribal governments and extended previously restricted programs and grants by the Indian Reorganization Act (IRA) of 1934 to non-IRA tribes as with housing.

During this period, the BIA established the Office of Federal Acknowledgment (OFA), later known as the Branch of Acknowledgment and Research (BAR), to revise and streamline what had become a murky and criticized process for tribes who had never been terminated to gain recognition status.[9] The BAR is charged with receiving applications from tribes for recognition, researching and reviewing the merits of those applications with BIA legal counsel, sending out initial reviews usually requesting additional information, accepting public comments, and writing a report to the Department of the Interior's (DOI) Assistant Secretary of the BIA. The Assistant Secretary then makes a formal recommendation to the Secretary of the DOI who makes the final determination on recognition (M. Miller 2004).

Requiring extensive evidence including letters of support from neighboring tribes, eligibility for federal recognition by the BAR is determined on the basis of a petitioning tribe's ability to meet seven criteria.[10] The first is that the tribe has been identified "externally" as "an American Indian entity" for a "substantially continuous basis since 1900." Second, the membership of the tribe "comprises a distinct community" that "has existed as a community from historical times until the present." Third, the tribe "has maintained political influence or authority over its members as an autonomous entity from historical times until the present." Fourth, the tribe has documentation of its government structure and membership policies. Fifth, its membership includes "individuals who descend from a historical Indian tribe or tribes, which combined and functioned as a single autonomous political entity." Sixth, the membership is unique and does not include individuals who are members of other recognized tribes. Seventh, the tribe was never terminated or "forbidden" recognition by Congress (summarized in GAO 2001a, 10–11).

Whether or not a tribe meets these criteria is determined by BAR staff members who have degrees and expertise in one or more disciplines — including history, anthropology, sociology, and genealogy. They work closely with BIA attorneys to make their recommendations. But although the criteria have been blasted as being inconsistently evaluated (GAO 2001a) and for shoring up anthropologically centric notions of Native culture and identity (Beinart 2002; M. Miller 2004), some already recognized tribes have found the criteria to be necessarily discriminating (M. Miller 2004).[11]

The BAR's categories were reified by the Federally Recognized Indian Tribe List Act of 1994. The act identifies only three means to recognition status and so inclusion on the required BIA list of federally recognized tribes: "Indian tribes presently may be recognized by Act of Congress; by the administrative procedures set forth in part 83 of the Code of Federal Regulations denominated 'Procedures for Establishing that an American Indian Group Exists as an Indian Tribe' [BAR]; or by a decision of a United States court." Assuming the accuracy of the resulting list of recognized tribes, the act quietly affirms the exclusion of unrecognized groups from federal services and the consultation procedures now required of federal and state governments on the development and implementation of policies and programs that affect all tribes.

Again, what is important about the criteria is not their *accuracy* but their *utility*. Obviously they defy complex histories of tribal conflicts over matters of legal status, treaty rights, and territorial boundaries as well as the historical conditions of colonization and imperialism enacted through federal programs of relocation, dispossession, and termination. In light of these complexities, the question follows: What political purpose do the

BAR's criteria serve?[12] Simply, they serve the interests of the United States. They pull tribes into the mundane administrative processes of the federal government, disciplining them to the terms of federal power as (un)recognized (Foucault 1979; Ong 1995). Against uneven but harsh criticisms of the constitution and exercise of that power, the criteria assert the dispassionate "objectivity" of historical documentation and scientific evaluation required of tribes and enacted through the evaluation process (Beinart 2002; M. Miller 2004).

Meanwhile, in order to secure the recognition of their legal status and rights, Native groups are made to reflect their cultural consistency "from historical times to the present" even as their authenticity is characterized as extra-colonial and ahistorical. These discursive maneuverings facilitate national narrations of the always regretful yet inconsequential effect of colonization and imperialism—Native cultures and identities did not merely survive the histories, but they have remained intact to embody and emulate cultural continuity, cohesiveness, and distinction as tribes authentic.

Some Conclusions on Tribes Undone

Inherent within the legal promise of recognized inclusion are the implications of the exclusions for those deemed unrecognized (unrecognizable). Cheryl I. Harris (1993) has studied the politics of these types of classification schemes in respect to the ways that those classified as "white" have had their rights to property established and protected within the law— including the "property" rights of political participation, wealth, inheritance, and disposition. These rights are inflected not merely through their exercise but through the power of those entitled by them to exclude them from others. According to Harris, these exclusionary rights are fundamentally racialized by the property of whiteness to the domination of all "others" so classified (see Omi and Winant 1986; Almaguer 1994; López 1996; Lowe 1996; Lipsitz 1998; Tsosie 2005).

The property rights of "Indian tribes" are similarly represented in how the United States has mobilized the category to strategically include or exclude Native groups to serve its political and economic interests. The strategic practice of inclusion or exclusion of Native peoples is about the utility of the "Indian tribe" in rearticulating federal and national power over Native peoples.

These politics are examined by J. Kēhaulani Kauanui in *Hawaiian Blood* (2008). Kauanui analyzes the legal category of "native Hawaiians" as defined by a 50 percent blood criterion in the U.S. Hawaiian Homes Commission Act (HHCA) of 1920. The HHCA set aside public lands and revenues from their leasing for the benefit of state citizens and "native Hawaiians." When Hawai'i was admitted as a state in 1959, the administration of the HHCA's obligations was transferred to the state. In 1978, the state created the Office of Hawaiian Affairs (OHA) to fulfill its obligations to "native Hawaiians" as outlined in the HHCA (Kauanui 1999).

Those Native Hawaiians who qualified to lease the lands and share in the revenue under the HHCA had to prove that they satisfied the 50 percent criterion. This criterion was established in the name of "rehabilitating" "native Hawaiians" from their poverty and unemployment owing to land dispossession to a self-sufficiency both symbolically and legally related to land use. Kauanui shows how this criterion served to racialize Native Hawaiians as "beneficiaries" of state programs against the recognition of their collective claims to sovereign status and land entitlement under international law. Concurrently, the racialization of Native Hawaiian status undermined Native Hawaiian epistemologies of belonging and affiliation reckoned through genealogy.

But of course, federal law has been inconsistent in its interpretations of "native Hawaiian" legal status and rights. Congress ratified five treaties with the kingdom before it backed the illegal overthrow of the kingdom by a "provisional government" in 1893. Within its treaties with Hawai'i, the kingdom never ceded its lands to the United States, which were illegally seized and ceded to the United States by a "provisional government" that was backed by congressional vote (Trask 1993). Still, in over 160 federal statutes dating to at least 1903 (Kauanui 2005), Native Hawaiian legal status and rights have been recognized as analogous to that of "Indian tribes" for the purposes of fulfilling U.S. obligations to Native Hawaiians (Kauanui 2002). In *Rice v. Cayetano* (2000), however, the Supreme Court ruled that even though U.S. obligations to Hawaiians are administered by the Office of Hawaiian Affairs (OHA), and even though the right to vote for OHA's Board of Trustees is based on the unique legal status of Native Hawaiian people in light of these obligations, it found that the state's electoral restrictions enacted race-based voting qualifications and therefore violated the Constitution's Fifteenth Amendment (Kauanui 2002, 2005)."

The contradictory decisions regarding the inclusion or exclusion of "native Hawaiians" and Native Hawaiians from the legal status and rights of "Indian tribes" is entrenched within the consistently colonial and imperial aims of the United States toward Hawai'i. This is represented by the continued racialization of Native Hawaiians by blood quantum in order to reinforce the articulation of a particular kind of Hawaiian cultural authenticity for a federal recognition of Hawaiian legal legitimacy, always "in the service of settler colonialism" (Kauanui 2008, 25).

The inclusion or exclusion of the "Indian tribe" and its specific work in racializing the blood of Native cultural authenticity and so legal legitimacy is evident likewise in the Alaskan Native Claims Settlement Act of 1971. The act extended the legal status and rights of "Indian tribes" to Alaskan Native "villages" incorporated under the act's provisions. It reserved 44 million acres of public lands and $962 million as compensation for the additional or other lost lands composing Alaska. Those who qualified to reside in the villages and share in the funds were those who met the following criteria:

> "Native" means a citizen of the United States who is a person of one-fourth degree or more Alaska Indian (including Tsimshian Indians not enrolled in the Metlaktla Indian Community) Eskimo, or Aleut blood, or combination thereof. The term includes any Native as so defined either or both of whose adoptive parents are not Natives. It also includes, in the absence of proof of a minimum blood quantum, any citizen of the United States who is regarded as an Alaska Native by the Native village or Native group of which he claims to be a member and whose father or mother is (or, if deceased, was) regarded as Native by any village or group. Any decision of the Secretary regarding eligibility for enrollment shall be final.[13] (Alaska Native Claims Settlement Act 1971)

For those who qualified, the act established 211 villages and 13 regional corporations (one outside of Alaska) to manage the reserved lands and funds on their behalf. Those who met the requirements could enroll in either or both of the villages and regional corporations of their traditional territories and receive one hundred shares of stock in land revenue. Concurrently, federal rights, programs, funds, and services reserved for "Indian tribes" and administered under the BIA were extended to Alaskan Natives (thereafter defined in the federal statute as "American Indians/Alaskan

Natives"). Fueled by oil interests in Alaska, the 1971 act was meant to settle any future claims by Native peoples of Alaska to state lands or oil shares. Alaskan Natives were thus made to fit within and under the legal categories and administration of the "Indian tribe" in the interests of colonial and imperial projects in and for the state (Dombrowski 2001). As for American Indians and Native Hawaiians, this was facilitated through the racialization of Native legal status by blood—a process that allows the state to *individualize* Native legal rights and so defer attention from the *collective* rights Native peoples possess to sovereignty and self-determination under international and constitutional law.

The "Indian tribe" is fundamentally a racialized construct of national narrations that continually rearticulate Native cultures and territorial rights in the service of U.S. colonial and imperial efforts at maintaining federal power over the terms of Native governance and territories. In doing so, it is a legal category that participates fully in the reinvention of U.S. democracy and humanism out of histories of colonization and imperialism, specifically through the recognition and provision of Native legal status and rights on the grounds of Native authenticity (Povinelli 2002). The consequences of this multidimensional disciplinary work (Foucault 1979; Ong 1995) is to how Native peoples choose to navigate the demands for their cultural authenticity in order to secure some measure of stability in their rights to sovereignty and self-determination.

2 In *Cherokee v. Delaware*

O n November 16, 2004, the U.S. Court of Appeals for the Tenth Circuit issued its ruling in *Cherokee Nation of Oklahoma v. Delaware Tribe of Indians et al.*[1] The Cherokee Nation challenged a BIA decision in 1996 to reinstate the recognition status of the Delaware Tribe, which had been terminated by the BIA in 1979. The Court of Appeals found that the BIA had overstepped its authority in reinstating the Delaware, ignoring the significance of U.S. Supreme Court decisions in 1894 and 1904 that ruled that the Delaware had been "incorporated" as "native Cherokee" into the Cherokee Nation under the terms of a Cherokee-U.S. treaty in 1866 and a Cherokee-Delaware agreement in 1867. Dismissing the relevance of a Delaware-U.S. treaty in 1866 and a 1977 Supreme Court ruling that reversed the 1894 and 1904 decisions, the court concluded that the Delaware had not been an "independent" tribe since 1867. Following the ruling, the BIA removed the Delaware from its list of recognized tribes in March 2005. In 2006 the Delaware appealed to the Supreme Court, which declined to hear the case.

Following the 2004 decision, the BIA instructed the Delaware Tribe that in order to be reinstated it would have to reach an agreement with the Cherokee Nation. The resulting agreement has been much criticized by Delaware people as relinquishing too many rights of governance and territorial integrity to the Cherokee, including submitting the tribe to pay revenue shares to the Cherokee on certain kinds of businesses and agreeing not to apply for certain federal services otherwise available to recognized tribes.

Moderated by the BIA's office in eastern Oklahoma, an election was held in May 2009 to approve the Constitution and By-Laws and accept the agreement with the Cherokee Nation. While the membership was supplied with a copy of the Constitution and By-Laws last amended in December 2008 (and equally contested), the agreement with the Cherokee Nation was not included in the voting information packet. Even then, with the promise of recognition before them, the tribe's membership approved the Constitution and By-Laws and the Cherokee agreement (1,138 voted to approve, 19 voted against it, and thus only 1,157 of the roughly 10,800 members voted); the vote was then ratified by the DOI. In August 2009, the Delaware Tribe was relisted by the BIA as federally recognized.

It is not so easy to summarize the intertribal and social conflicts between the Cherokee and Delaware. They do not merely bear out the political burdens of the "Indian tribe"—the suggested course of analysis given my arguments in the previous chapter. It is also not about offering up these conflicts as a self-contained, representative example of an Althusserian "interpolation" (Althusser 1971) or a Laclauen and Mouffean "radical antagonism" of the tribes against U.S. authority (Laclau and Mouffe 1985)—the reductive conclusion to the arguments of the previous chapter. Rather, it is about suggesting that the "Indian tribe" provides a complex discursive and ideological field in which the legal status and rights of Native peoples are contested between those (un)identified as "Indian tribes." The Cherokee and Delaware legal conflicts over the terms and rights of Delaware status in "Cherokee territory" is one such example.

The Historical Conditions of an Intertribal Conflict:
The Tribes in Treaty

By the 1860s, the Cherokee and Delaware had each ratified about twenty treaties with the United States that brought about their relocations into "Indian Territory."[2] The unique histories that informed the treaty negotiations and relocations are far too complicated for this chapter. They include the repeated failure of the United States to honor the treaties (such as allowing immigration into tribal territories and state interference in tribal government), armed conflict between the United States and the tribes (particularly over territorial rights), and intertribal and civil conflicts within and between the tribes (F. Cohen 1940; V. Deloria 1974; Weslager 1978; Prucha 1994; Perdue and Green 2004). Repeatedly, it was made clear to both the Cherokee and Delaware that the political and economic interests of the United States would overpower their own. In contextualizing the 2004 legal conflict and court decision about Delaware status and rights in relation to the Cherokee, therefore, I begin with the tribes' discrete treaties with the United States in 1866. These treaties subjugated the Cherokee and Delaware to the needs of nontribal agendas and were crucial to the legal conflicts between them that followed.

While the official position of the Cherokee Nation during the Civil War was neutrality, many outside of the elected council entered into treaty relations with the Confederate states, with some Cherokee even serving in the Confederate Army. As a result, after the war, the Congress expected the Cherokee Nation to go through a "reconstruction" process much like the southern states. The result for the Cherokee was a "reconstruction treaty" that was signed similarly with other tribes who had aligned themselves with the Confederacy during the war (Wardell 1938; Perdue and Green 2004).

Within the Cherokee Nation, various political parties fought hard for control during treaty negotiations, with several attempts by some to unseat Principal Chief John Ross and to withdraw as a separate tribe with a separate reservation and modified rights to slavery. But the National Council was able to control the process largely because it was backed by the United States (Wardell 1938, see 177–208). The "reconstruction treaty" that resulted was signed by the Cherokee National Council in July 1866 and ratified by Congress in August.

The treaty nullified the 1861 treaty between the Confederate states and the "Southern Cherokee." It granted general amnesty but required that those residing in the Nation who had or would commit crimes in the United States must be turned over to officials of the United States. It repealed Cherokee confiscation laws (by which the Council had seized the property of those serving in the Confederate Army). It granted rights to settle and occupy certain lands within the Nation to "freed persons who were formerly slaves to any Cherokee, and all free negroes not having been such slaves" and granted those persons rights to be represented on the National Council.[3] It declared that "all laws of the Cherokee Nation shall be uniform throughout said nation," granted the president of the United States the right to intervene if the laws were not uniformly applied, and established "a fair and equitable application and expenditure of the national funds as between the people of this and of every other district in said nation." It established courts within Indian Territory but recognized Cherokee jurisdiction over civil and criminal cases among its members. Federal licenses to trade were not granted without the approval of the National Council. The treaty abolished slavery and granted all former slaves "the rights of native Cherokees." It granted the right to the Cherokee to sell the products of their farms "without restraint," paying taxes only on items sold outside Indian Territory. It established a right-of-way for the construction of a railroad. It established the procedures for a general tribal council in the territory, including provisions for a federal census and for council representation to be determined by district population. It established lands for missionaries and schools. It ceded Cherokee lands in Kansas and provided for the survey and payment of the lands to the national fund; it also allowed the Cherokee to sell lands in Arkansas and "east of the Mississippi" with approval from the Secretary of the Interior. It allowed Cherokee "heads of families" residing on ceded lands to remove to the Cherokee Nation. It allowed the Cherokee to opt for the allotment of their reservation lands. It allowed for the construction of monuments to mark Cherokee borders with Arkansas, Missouri, and Kansas. It allowed the Cherokee to appoint an agent to review the tribe's accounts with the government of the United States. It established payments from the United States toward the interest of the nation's funds for the establishment of schools, an orphan fund, and salaries of district officers. It established a payment to Reverend

Evan Jones, who had worked as a missionary among the Cherokee for forty years. It paid moneys from all Cherokee veterans without heirs into a fund for an orphanage. It guaranteed protection against "domestic feuds and insurrections, and against hostilities of other tribes," and "against interruptions or intrusion from all unauthorized citizens of the United States who may attempt to settle on their lands or reside in their territory." It granted the United States the right to establish military posts in the Nation. And it provided for the United States to reimburse the Cherokee Nation for provisions and clothing given to the U.S. Army in the past, for diplomatic expenses for traveling to Washington, and to missionaries who lost property as a result of being ordered out of the Nation by federal agents.

The treaty represented "compromise" on both sides (Wardell 1938, 203). The "Southern Cherokee" were able to secure a repeal of the Nation's confiscation laws but were unable to prevent the Council and the United States from abolishing slavery and granting rights of "native Cherokees" and lands to "former slaves" and "free negroes." The Council was able to prevent the United States from including a provision for initiating statehood out of Indian Territory and for separating the Southern Cherokee as a distinct tribe. But the Council was not able to prevent the United States from granting the railroad rights-of-way through Cherokee lands or dissuade the United States' interest in relocating additional tribes into their territory (Wardell 1938, 203–4).

To secure the latter point, the treaty set out very specific provisions. First, it provided that the United States would relocate only "civilized Indians, friendly with the Cherokees and adjacent tribes." It identified "unoccupied lands east of 96°" as that area to which said tribes would be relocated. It then established a difference between those tribes that would relocate under the terms and conditions of "abandonment" and those of "preservation" and defined those terms as follows.

Those tribes who "abandon[ed] their tribal organization" were required to pay the Nation "a sum of money which shall sustain the same proportion to the then existing national fund that the number of Indians sustain to the whole number of Cherokees then residing in the Cherokee country." After said payment was made, the members of the tribe would "be incorporated into and ever after remain a part of the Cherokee Nation, on equal terms in every respect with native citizens" (Article XV).

But should a tribe "decide to preserve their tribal organizations, and to maintain their tribal laws, customs, and usages, not inconsistent with the constitution and laws of the Cherokee Nation," they would have "a district of country set off for their use by metes and bounds equal to one hundred and sixty acres, if they should so decide, for each man, woman, and child of said tribe." For that land, the relocated tribe would make a payment to the Nation for an amount based on the total acreage as negotiated between the tribe, the Cherokee, and the president of the United States. After said payment, "they shall enjoy all the rights of native Cherokees" (Article XV).

The land issued from the Nation to the relocated tribe was to be "conveyed in fee-simple" and "held in common or by their members in severalty as the United States may decide." The Cherokee Nation, however, "retain[ed] the right of possession of and jurisdiction over all of said country west of 96° of longitude until thus sold and occupied, after which their jurisdiction and right of possession to terminate forever as to each of said districts thus sold and occupied" (Article XVI). The treaty expedited federal negotiations with tribes for their relocation into Cherokee territory.[4] These negotiations included the Delaware Tribe.

During the 1700s, the Delaware were methodically forced out of their original territories in Delaware, New Jersey, Pennsylvania, and New York by English, Swedish, and Dutch colonists. The expulsions happened by fraudulent land deals (the infamous "Walking Purchase" of 1737) and armed conflicts that angered the Delaware, particularly toward the English and their individual allies like the Seneca and Mohawk among the Haudenosaunee, or Six Nations Confederacy (including the Cayuga, Mohawk, Oneida, Onondaga, Seneca, and Tuscarora). In response, the Delaware aligned with other tribes like the Shawnee and intermittently with the French against the English in violent raids and massacres. English colonies in Pennsylvania and Ohio declared war against the Delaware and their allies and sought reprisal. In fear, subgroups of the Delaware migrated away from the conflict into Arkansas, Oklahoma, Texas, and Ontario. After French withdrawal from the colonies and through the American Revolution, the Delaware refrained from official alliance with either the English or the Americans, though they would negotiate in 1778 with the United States for its safe military passage through Delaware territory to fight the English and their allies among the Haudenosaunee in the north (Weslager 1978).

After English withdrawal, the Delaware found themselves on shaky ground with the United States. Government officials adopted much of the English colonists' perceptions of the Delaware as a "hostile" and "unfriendly" tribe. The United States responded by chopping away at Delaware governance and territorial rights. In treaties ratified by Congress in 1785, 1789, and 1795, the Delaware's territories were reduced to lands in the Ohio River Valley to which they had been most recently removed. At once, the United States pressured them for land cessions that resulted in their removal out of the valley and into the territories of Indiana, Missouri, and Kansas. Repeatedly, the Delaware were "settled" in areas that later became states. They would then have to deal with federal and state officials pressuring them for land cessions in order to facilitate homesteading, railroad, and other corporate interests. By the mid-1800s the Delaware Tribe was without the collective means of fighting back. They had been wiped out — from an original population of about 25,000 to one of about 1,100 — by relentless military conflict, disease, and raids against their properties (Weslager 1978; Brown and Kohn 2008).

In 1854, the Delaware Tribe signed and ratified its twentieth treaty with the United States, then agreeing to remove from their lands in Missouri to Kansas on the strict provision that they would secure a permanently undisturbed reservation. Once relocated, however, federal agents and railroad representatives pressured them to remove again to Indian Territory (securing partial land cessions from them in 1860 and 1861). The Delaware resisted. Under intensifying pressure, and reassurances that the new reservation would be permanent and undisturbed by either the United States or other tribes, the Delaware agreed to talk. It would not be until 1866 that the tribe ratified a treaty agreeing to remove into Indian Territory, but not all Delaware people agreed with the removal.

The 1866 treaty was signed by Captain John Connor, Captain Sarcoxie, Charles Journeycake, James Ketchum, James Connor, Andrew Miller, and John Sarcoxie. It provided for the sale of the tribe's lands in Kansas by the Department of the Interior (DOI), which would mediate the sale and transfer of the funds to the tribe's trust account. It commissioned a survey and appraisal of the lands and their improvements to determine the value "at a fair price." Articles IV and V provided that the money earned would be paid to the tribe as a whole. The money would then be used to purchase lands in the Territory under the following conditions.

ARTICLE IV. The United States agree to sell to the said Delaware Indians a tract of land ceded to the Government by the Choctaws and Chickasaws, the Creeks, or the Seminoles, or which may be ceded by the Cherokees in the Indian country, *to be selected by the Delawares in one body in as compact a form as practicable,* so as to contain timber, water, and agricultural lands, to contain in the aggregate, if the said Delaware Indians shall so desire, a quantity equal to one hundred and sixty (160) acres for each man, woman, and child who shall remove to said country, at the price per acre paid by the United States for the said lands, to be paid for by the Delawares out of the proceeds of sales of lands in Kansas, heretofore provided for. *The said tract of country shall be set off with clearly and permanently marked boundaries by the United States;* and also surveyed as public lands are surveyed, when the Delaware council shall so request, when the same may, in whole or in part, be allotted by said council to each member of said tribe residing in said country, said allotment being subject to the approval of the Secretary of the Interior.

ARTICLE V. The United States guarantee to the said Delawares peaceable possession of their new home herein provided to be selected for them in the Indian country, and protection from hostile Indians and internal strife and civil war, and a full and just participation in any general council or territorial government that may be established for the nations and tribes residing in said Indian country. (Emphases added)

The language of Articles IV and V indicated that the Delaware Tribe was to remove *as a tribe* to their new lands. Once there, the United States guaranteed them protection from "hostile Indians and internal strife and civil war" as well as "full and just participation" in the general tribal council the United States proposed to establish in Indian Territory (a council likewise referred to in the 1866 treaty with the Cherokee and treaties with the other Five Civilized Tribes, including the Choctaw, Chickasaw, Seminole, and Creek).

The Delaware treaty also provided that the tribe would not be asked to relocate until homes were ready for them in Indian Territory. It required the creation of a "registry" of all Delaware who chose to remain in Kansas and those who chose to remove as the treaty did not require all Delaware Tribe members to be removed. Foreshadowing the provisions of the General Allotment Act of 1887, "adult Delaware Indians" who chose to remain in Kansas would be allotted individual tracts of land (at eighty acres each), "dissolve their relations" with the tribe, and qualify to become "citizens of the United States." To become a U.S. citizen, a Delaware was required to prove, within five years, that *he* [*sic*] was "sufficiently intelligent and prudent to control his own affairs and interests" and "that he has adopted the habits of civilized life." Upon doing so, *he* would "receive a patent, in fee-simple, with power of alienation, for the land heretofore allotted him." *He* would also receive, in "his just proportion, in cash or in bonds, of the cash value of the credits of said tribe, principal and interest, then held in trust by the United States; and also, as the same may be received, his proportion of the proceeds of the sale of lands under the provisions of this treaty, when he shall cease to be a member of said tribe." The treaty allowed minor children to be included in a share of the tribe's assets and, upon becoming adults, they could choose whether or not to remain or remove with the tribe. All unallotted lands and abandoned buildings ("surplus lands") were to be sold on behalf of the tribe and the money put into a national fund held in trust by the BIA.

The treaty guaranteed that within thirty days of its ratification the Secretary of the Interior would give notice to the Missouri River Railroad Company "that he is authorized to contract with them or other responsible party or parties for the sale of said lands on the terms specified in this treaty" to expedite the purchase and transfer of money to the tribe's trust account. It provided that the money would not be used to settle individual member debt and that trade in Delaware country would be monitored by the chiefs and council and "the salaries of the chiefs shall henceforward be four hundred dollars per annum." It granted a right-of-way to railroads through the Delaware's new territory. It settled at $30,000 all property damage and theft in Kansas against the tribe.

Article XI provided that "the Delawares acknowledge their dependence upon the United States, and again renew their pledges of devotion to the Government thereof, and ask its protection; and the United States agree to protect, preserve, and defend them in all their just rights" (Treaty with the Delaware 1866, in Kappler 1975). While seeming to protect their rights to self-government and territorial integrity upon removal, the treaty had to have made clear — had to have reminded the Delaware — that the interests of the United States would continue to override their own. Repeatedly, the Delaware had been asked to cede and remove from treatied lands. In fact, by 1867, for all purposes the United States had acquired the contiguous forty-eight states and Alaska and was well on its way to laying down railroads and telegraphs from coast to coast in order to facilitate interstate trade and communications. It was also reinforcing its military presence in Hawai'i that would lead to an illegal annexation of the Hawaiian kingdom in 1893 endorsed by the Congress in 1898 (Trask 1993; Kauanui 2005); the United States was also looking to establish colonies in central and south America as well as in the Pacific (which would be effected by a treaty with Spain in 1898). The United States, then, was not merely a colonial but an imperial power. Its negotiations with the Delaware reflected its global ambitions. Being recognized as a tribe afforded the Delaware — as it had the Cherokee — the right to negotiate treaties with the United States but the legal integrity of the rights so treatied was subsumed under the ambitions of the United States.

The Tribes in Agreement

The disciplining of tribes to the interests of the United States by treaty did not mean that all tribes were treated equally. Overwhelmingly, tribes were only able to secure treaties or good relations with the United States when treaty provisions aligned with or benefited the agendas of the United States. This was certainly the case for the Cherokee and Delaware. As reflected in their respective 1866 treaties, their individual political concerns were irreconcilable. Clearly, both expected their independent and autonomous rights to self-government and territorial integrity to be affirmed and protected. But there was simply no way for the United States to honor both treaties *and* achieve its goal of removing tribes into Indian Territory, establishing statehood out of the Territory, and then dissolving tribal rights therein. The irreconcilability would be mediated by the United States to favor its interests, which in this particular instance meant that the Cherokee Nation would benefit while the Delaware Tribe would not.

Federal negotiations with the Delaware for their relocation started before the tribes' respective treaties were ratified in 1866. Initially, the negotiations failed because the Cherokee National Council refused to allow the Delaware Tribe to remove into their territory under the only conditions that the Delaware would consider — that they remain an autonomous, self-governing tribe with a distinct territory bounded under the terms of their

1866 treaty with the United States (Haake 2002). The challenge for federal agents, then, was to appease the tribes' very different agendas—or at least to appear to have done so—to secure their cooperation.

An intertribal agreement was signed and witnessed by federal agents on April 11, 1867, in Washington, D.C. However, before the Delaware signatories to the agreement—Chief Charles Journeycake, Isaac Journeycake, and John Sarcoxie—left Washington, they complained that the agreement had been modified without their approval, to the tribe's detriment, and in contradiction with the provisions of their 1866 treaty (similar to *Lone Wolf*). They believed that the agreement had been changed by federal agents to favor the Cherokee Nation. They immediately expressed to Cherokee and federal officials that they were not signing the agreement that the tribe had approved and that in doing so were acting contrary to the tribe's wishes. Many scholars and Delaware people have speculated to different and unsure ends about why the leaders signed the agreement in spite of their profound concerns about its terms (Haake 2002, 420–22).

What is sure is that the agreement advanced the interests of the United States for Indian Territory. It directly drew from the Cherokee's treaty of 1866, particularly Articles XV and XVI. This violated the Delaware's treaty of 1866, particularly Articles IV and V and the provisions that the tribe would be removed to Indian Territory *as a whole* and to bounded, bordered lands held in common.

The 1867 agreement begins by promising that once an agreement had been reached between the tribes, the United States would work to select the specific lands for the Delaware in Cherokee territory (the fact that specific lands had not already been defined had caused the Delaware delegates some concern). The agreement provided that the Cherokee had agreed to accept a payment "to sell to the Delawares" lands "for their occupancy." It guaranteed that the lands would total 160 acres for each individual who "elects to remove" (based on a registry produced by the tribe and federal agents) and determined the amount of money the Delaware would pay for the lands in question: "a sum of money equal to $1 per acre for the whole amount of 160 acres of land for every individual Delaware who has already been registered upon the aforesaid list." It required the Delaware to pay the Cherokee "the same proportion to the existing Cherokee national fund that the number of Delawares . . . sustains to the whole number of Cherokees residing in the Cherokee Nation." The total number of Delaware registered or added within four months would be the basis on which the payment was to be determined.

The agreement also guaranteed that the lands the Delaware purchased would not be allotted as part of any future agreement with the Cherokee Nation without the consent of the Delaware Tribe. But here is where the language gets especially difficult for the Delaware. The agreement referred to those individual Delaware who "elect to remove" to the Cherokee territory as being "incorporated by these articles into the Cherokee Nation" and guaranteed their participation in decisions about the Nation's lands in the future as any other "native citizen" of the Cherokee Nation, practically duplicating Article XIV of the Cherokee's 1866 treaty. It explained that once the Delaware had paid the agreed-upon amounts for the lands and a sum based on the number of individuals to remove, "all the members of the tribe registered as above provided [those listed on the registry of those who have "elected" to remove], shall become members of the Cherokee Nation, with the same rights and immunities, and the same participation (and no other) in the national funds, as native Cherokees, save as hereinbefore provided. And the children hereafter born of such Delawares so incorporated into the Cherokee Nation shall in all respects be regarded as native Cherokees."

Upon the Delaware delegates' return from Washington and before and after the Tribe's relocation to Cherokee territory, many Delaware leaders and people made public their opposition to the agreement and the way that it undermined their 1866 treaty rights (Haake 2002). In fact, several hundred or about one-third of the tribe stayed behind in Kansas in protest. In response, federal agents withheld funds through the winter of 1867 in order to exasperate the conditions of their then homelessness and starve them into submission (Nichols-Ledermann and Rementer 2008). It worked. In the end, only twenty-one remained behind.

The Tribes in Court

The Cherokee negotiated an amendment to Article 17 of their 1866 treaty in 1868 (concerning the sale of about eight hundred thousand acres of Cherokee lands in Kansas) before treaty making with tribes was unilaterally ceased by the Senate in 1871 (Prucha 1994, 289). The 1866 treaty would be the last for the Delaware. All subsequent negotiations between the United

States and tribes would be designated "agreements" or "compacts" and would no longer carry the constitutional weight of "treaties."[5]

This shift reflected broader policy changes aimed at eradicating tribal cultures and identities and transforming Native people into citizens of the United States. The General Allotment, or Dawes, Act of 1887 encapsulated these efforts.[6] The act provided for selected reservations to be broken up in severalty and issued to enrolled members as parcels ranging from forty to six hundred acres each, based primarily on the value of the lands and the tribal members' marital status (Carlson 1980; McDonnell 1991). Surplus lands or those lands unassigned to tribal members were sold to non-Indians. The immediate result was the radical reduction of total reservation lands—from 148 to 48 million acres—but other effects included the exasperation of reservation and rural Indian poverty, unemployment, malnutrition, starvation, despair, alcoholism, and crime (Debo 1940; Perdue 1981; Harring 1994).

Section 8 of the General Allotment Act exempted the lands of the "Five Civilized Tribes" in Indian Territory because of the provisions of their respective "removal treaties" with the United States.[7] For instance, as stipulated in the Cherokee's Treaty of New Echota (1835), "The United States hereby covenant and agree that the lands ceded to the Cherokee nation in the forgoing article shall, in no future time without their consent, be included within the territorial limits or jurisdiction of any State or Territory." But immediately following the passage of the General Allotment Act, Congress pushed its agenda on transforming Indian Territory into a state and commissioned delegates to negotiate agreements with all of the tribes in the territory for allotment.

The tribes initially refused to negotiate. The United States responded by applying severe political and economic pressure on them to do so, including a rather aggressive public relations campaign that blamed the tribes for not controlling immigration and crime in the Territory (Debo 1940). In response, negotiations between the tribes and the United States proceeded despite much opposition within the tribes against allotment and statehood (Perdue 1981; Harring 1994). These negotiations reached "agreements" (Bledsoe 1909) that resulted in allotment, statehood, and the virtual liquidation of tribal landholdings by 1934.

Within the Cherokee Nation, armed and passive resistance occurred while their elected leaders negotiated an agreement to allot that would be solidified in 1902 (Bledsoe 1909; Debo 1940; Perdue 1981; Harring 1994). The Cherokee National Council excluded Delaware officials from the negotiations. The Cherokee and Delaware would go to the Supreme Court twice — in 1894 and 1904 — to address the question of Delaware land rights. As with the 1866 treaties and 1867 agreement, the Delaware would find themselves at the mercy of those interests within the United States that would affirm Cherokee rights at their expense.

In 1893, the Delaware filed suit against the Cherokee in the U.S. Court of Claims. In the Cherokee's 1866 treaty, their "strip lands" and "neutral lands" were ceded to the United States. The money earned from the sale of these lands and the lease of other lands was deposited into the Cherokee's national fund held in trust by DOI. When the Cherokee National Council decided to make payments from these funds to "native Cherokee," they excluded the Delaware. The Delaware sued the Cherokee "involving not merely the right to share in these proceeds, but also the interest of the Delawares in the reservation and the outlet" (*Cherokee Nation v. Journeycake* 1894). With the suit, the Delaware Tribe attempted to assert its claims in the terms of their 1866 treaty. They sought participation in the Cherokee Nation *as a tribe* with legal and economic interests in any decisions regarding the Nation's lands because they had been relocated within the Nation's borders.

Anticipating the conflict, Congress had passed an act in 1890 allowing the Delaware to file suit against the Cherokee in the U.S. Court of Claims. The United States was made co-defendant as trustee. Citing the Cherokee's 1866 treaty and the 1867 agreement, the court concluded that the "Delawares were incorporated into the Cherokee Nation, and, as members and citizens thereof, were entitled to equal rights in these lands and their proceeds" (*Cherokee Nation v. Journeycake* 1894). It determined that the Delaware had rights as "native Cherokee" ("as members and citizens" of the Cherokee Nation) and so no longer held rights or interests *as a tribe* in Cherokee territory. Consequently, the Court ruled that the Delaware were entitled to rights in the Nation as any other "native Cherokee."

But the Cherokee National Council did not want to treat the Delaware as "native Cherokee." It appealed the decision to the U.S. Supreme Court. There, both tribes reiterated their positions: The Cherokee did not see the Delaware as Cherokee citizens with rights of government participation or economic shares in the Nation; the Delaware wanted to participate *as a tribe* in the decision-making processes of the Nation per the provisions of its 1866 treaty.

The Supreme Court's ruling rejected the relevance of the Delaware's 1866 treaty and focused on the 1867 agreement, interpreting it through the provisions of the Cherokee's 1866 treaty. The court reasoned that two options for relocation had been provided to the Delaware — "abandonment" or "preservation." It decided that the Delaware had chosen to "abandon" their government and "absorb" themselves into the Cherokee Nation "on equal terms in every respect with native citizens." Therefore, the task before the court was to determine what kinds of rights "native citizens" held within the Cherokee Nation and specifically in regards to land management decisions. It looked to the Cherokee Nation's Constitution of 1839 to do so.

> Not only does the Cherokee constitution . . . provide that the lands shall be common property, but also the legislation of the Cherokee Nation from 1839 on to the present time abounds with acts speaking of these lands as "public domain" or "common property" of the Cherokee Nation. . . . Now, if these lands be the public domain, the common property of the Cherokee Nation, all who are recognized as members and citizens of that Nation are alike interested and alike entitled to share in the profits and proceeds thereof. Given, therefore, the two propositions that the lands are the common property of the Cherokee Nation, and that the registered Delawares have become incorporated into the Cherokee Nation, and are members and citizens thereof, it follows necessarily that they are, equally with the native Cherokees, the owners of, and entitled to share in the profits and proceeds of, these lands. (*Cherokee Nation v. Journeycake* 1894)

The court concluded that the Delaware had been assigned individual tracts of land and not contiguous lands *as a tribe*. No mention was made of the Delaware treaty of 1866 which provided that the lands to which the tribe would be removed were "to be selected by the Delawares in one body in as compact a form as practicable."

Attorneys for the Delaware argued that despite the tribe's relocation into Cherokee territory the DOI continued to maintain a separate trust account for them in order to manage their financial assets as a distinct tribe; in other words, the DOI recognized and treated the Delaware as legally dis-

tinct from the Cherokee Nation. The court disagreed. It maintained that
the tribe's funds were reserved for them to make improvements to their
new homes in the Indian Territory and that the funds did not indicate their
having preserved their autonomous status as a tribe. The court concluded
that it saw "nothing in the matters suggested by counsel sufficient to overthrow the plain import of the language used in the agreement," which it
found to confirm that the Delaware had become "incorporated into the
Cherokee Nation" and "became members thereof" (*Cherokee Nation v.
Journeycake* 1894). As the Court of Claims, the Supreme Court ordered the
Cherokee Nation to make financial restitution to the Delaware as they had
to "native Cherokee" from the funds earned on the sale and lease of said
lands, and by implication, to include them in any future land management
decisions and revenue sales.[8]

The Cherokee reached an allotment agreement with the United States in
1902 (Bledsoe 1909; Debo 1940).[9] Anticipating legal conflict with the Delaware Tribe over its terms, Congress passed An Act for the Protection of
the People of the Indian Territory and for Other Purposes in 1898. In
itself, the act suggested that the language of the 1867 agreement had not
settled the legal questions it raised between the tribes or in their relations
with the United States in so clear a fashion as the Supreme Court decision
of 1894 claimed that it had. To address the conflicts, Congress provided for
the segregation of Delaware Tribe lands before any allotment was carried
out with the Cherokee Nation. This implied that Congress recognized not
only a legal distinction between the tribes but the legal relevance of the
Delaware's claims to self-government and lands in the Territory under the
provisions of their 1866 treaty with the United States. This acknowledgment contradicted or overrode the Supreme Court's 1894 decision since
otherwise it would have meant that the Delaware lands in the Nation were
to be allotted as the same as other "native Cherokee." The 1898 act provided that the Delaware Tribe was "authorized and empowered" to sue the
Cherokee in the U.S. Court of Claims "for the purpose of determining the
rights of said Delaware Indians in and to the lands and funds of said nation
under their contract" with the Cherokee in 1867. The suit was pending in
the U.S. Court of Claims when the Cherokee reached an agreement to allot
in 1902. It would go before the Supreme Court as *Cherokee Nation v. Delaware Tribe* in 1904.

Before the Court of Claims, the Delaware asserted its independent tribal status from the Cherokee through an assertion of collective land tenure. The Delaware argued that they had incorporated into the Cherokee Nation *as a tribe* and not *as individuals* owing to three factors: (1) they had not abandoned their tribal organization, laws, customs, or identity; (2) they had been assigned to 157,000 acres of land that functioned like an "estate," which was held in common by the tribe and was not composed of individually assigned tracts of 160 acres each; and (3) they had been assigned lands that would be passed on to their descendants in common and not as individual inheritances as provided within the General Allotment Act. The Court of Claims disagreed. It cited the Supreme Court's decision in *Journeycake* (1894): The Delaware had equal shares in Cherokee lands and proceeds as the 1867 agreement had granted them the status and rights of "native Cherokee."

The Cherokee Nation appealed to the Supreme Court on the same grounds as it had in *Journeycake* (1894). The National Council did not perceive the Delaware to possess the legal status or rights of "native Cherokee." They did not want the tribe via its members granted shares in the assets or lands of the Nation. They did not want the tribe via its members participating in Cherokee governance.[10]

Following *Journeycake*, however, the Supreme Court ruled that the Delaware had been "incorporated" into the Cherokee Nation as individuals and not as a tribe under the terms of the 1867 agreement. The court argued that this was represented by Delaware people having been assigned specific lands or homes "in severalty" and not as "held in common" by the tribe. It maintained that the Delaware relocated as individuals with rights to occupy certain homes within the Nation as "native Cherokee" did. Therefore, like other "native Cherokee," the Delaware would share in any proceeds issued to citizens of the Nation but no more or differently.[11]

But as if to acknowledge the difficulties and implications of their ruling, the justices reflected out loud that "it is unnecessary to speculate as to the nature of the Indian title derived from the United States by treaty." This is incredibly odd given that the grounds on which they based their decision were the 1866 treaty between the United States and the Cherokee and its translation into the 1867 agreement. They basically asserted that they did not have to "speculate" on the kind of land title "derived" from such legal compacts — that is, it did not need to consider the "nature" of the land title by treaty or agreement in the context of the broader questions the case raised about treaty law in the United States. This alleviated the court's responsibility to consider the provisions and status of the Delaware's 1866 treaty in light of the 1867 agreement, to give it due consideration in understanding the agreement as it had with the Cherokee's treaty. The court refused to reconcile these provisions as it refused to consider Delaware interpretations of the significance of their treaty and the agreement. In doing so, the Supreme Court violated its own precedent. It had established a precedent for at least appearing to interpret the provisions of tribal treaties from the perspectives of those who had entered into them. This was done to ensure that the courts upheld the principles and intents of the treaties from the perspectives of those who had signed them since oftentimes tribal representatives were not fluent in English — the language the treaties were written in — and so depended on full disclosure from federal representatives and interpreters about the provisions they were agreeing to (F. Cohen 1940; Prucha 1994).[12] In this case, the court reversed this precedent. It rejected the need for oral testimony from Delaware people in interpreting the significance of the agreement because, it maintained, the language of the agreement was clear enough and that it would only need to consider said testimony if the language was confusing or vague. This affirmed the Cherokee's argument that the Cherokee held the land in common and that, beyond the right to use and occupy assigned homes as other Cherokee citizens under the Constitution and laws of the Nation, the Delaware had been granted no other provision — even while maintaining that the Delaware did not possess the citizenship or property rights of "native Cherokee."

The Supreme Court rejected outright the Delaware's insistence that its representatives *never* would have signed away the tribe's rights to self-government and lands. To support this argument, the Delaware offered testimony from tribal officials and elders about the conditions under which they signed the 1866 treaty and 1867 agreement and their interpretations of what they were agreeing to. The court insisted that the clarity of the agreement negated the need for such evidence. Whether they liked it or not, the court insisted that being incorporated as "native Cherokee" was what the tribe had agreed to do. To prove it, they accepted oral testimony from a federal agent who had served at the Delaware agency when the agreement was signed.

The agent, John G. Pratt, was received by the court as impartial, and therefore credible, because he was not Native and had served for the Delaware agency in Oklahoma during the 1867 negotiations:

> Q. Do you know whether or not the agreement frequently referred to in your testimony was read over to the two delegations representing the Delawares and Cherokee tribes of Indians?
>
> A. It was read over repeatedly; read over and corrected and altered and read over again several times, and each party put in his suggestions, until they finally harmonized.
>
> Q. Then, as I understand, the agreement, as finally signed, expressed the wishes of both sides, and both sides were fully satisfied with all it contained?
>
> A. No; the Delawares were not satisfied, but they signed because it was the best they could do. They wanted to own the land outright.
>
> Q. They did not contend at any time afterwards that the agreement did not fully express what they intended to express, did they?
>
> A. No, sir; I did not hear anything of that kind. (*Cherokee Nation v. Delaware Tribe* 1904)

The court concluded,

> We can perceive no room in this case for a departure from the familiar rules of the law protecting written agreements from the uncertainties of parol testimony. The testimony offered [by the Delaware] was, in the main, that of interested persons nearly thirty years after the agreement had been reduced to writing and signed by the parties thereto. Nor can we find a latent ambiguity in the terms of the contract which requires the admission of parol testimony to explain its effect. In the light of the circumstances and the language used in the writing, its construction is not rendered difficult because of latent ambiguities. (ibid.)

As a result of the decision, the Delaware were enrolled as "Cherokee Delaware" on the Cherokee rolls produced to administer the allotment of Cherokee lands. They were allotted lands at 160 acres each within the 157,000 acres they had been assigned under the 1867 agreement. Likewise, they shared in the proceeds of the sale of the "surplus lands" of the Nation under its agreement to allot with the United States (Bledsoe 1909).

Despite the objectives of allotment—to dissolve tribal governments and landholdings in Indian Territory toward statehood—the Cherokee Nation was able to protect its national headquarters in Tahlequah and was granted "jurisdictional service authority" over all Indians living within the fourteen counties that were created out of its lands when Oklahoma became a state in 1907 (Carroll 2002/2003). This had the effect of establishing its property rights to the exclusion of all others from those rights—including the right to administrative control within its "jurisdictional service area" and access to federal programs and funding.

The Delaware Tribe continued to operate as an independent government though twice dispossessed—by the United States and by the Cherokee— from their rights to self-government and territorial integrity. Following the death of Chief Charles Journeycake in 1895, "the tribe began directing its business under the leadership of a business committee. Though it was composed mostly of men from historically leading families, the committee members were approved by the U.S. government. Together, the business committee and the tribe's general council made decisions affecting the Delaware Tribe" (Brown and Kohn 2008, xxvi). The United States government's approval of the leadership of the business committee affirms that despite the Supreme Court opinions about Delaware legal status in 1894 and 1904, the BIA continued to recognize the Delaware as an independent tribe and maintained government-to-government relations with it. The only real immediate change, then, after the court's decisions—and it was a significant change—was that the Delaware Tribe did not hold land in common and could not apply for federal funds or services independent of the Cherokee. The Cherokee Nation controlled the administration of all federal funds and services reserved for Native people within its "jurisdictional service area," then including the "Cherokee Delaware" (Carroll 2002/2003).[13]

The Rearticulated Tribe: Back to Court

The 1866 treaties, 1867 agreement, and 1894 and 1904 Supreme Court decisions do not provide an exemplary account of the serious conflicts that have characterized Cherokee and Delaware relations since the 1860s. These conflicts were evident not only in the courts but also in incidents of violence and property-related crimes (theft, damage, etc.) that came to characterize their relations (Burton 1995, 86–87). But they do indicate the diametrically opposed political agendas between the Cherokee and Delaware as they indicate United States interests in those agendas. For while the United States related to both tribes as tribes with legal standing in negotiations over matters of government and territorial integrity, its interests in Indian Territory were more directly furthered by supporting the Cherokee than the Delaware. In fact, the Supreme Court's decisions in 1894 and 1904 empowered the Cherokee over the Delaware — marked by a dramatic shift in the Nation's claims about the Delaware as its citizens.[14]

Before and during the 1894 and 1904 cases, the Cherokee did not treat or represent the Delaware as citizens with rights in Cherokee governance and resources. It appealed hard to the court against the Delaware's "incorporation." But after 1904, the National Council shifted its strategy. It mobilized the court's language to claim the Delaware (and relatedly the Loyal Shawnee) to be citizens under Cherokee jurisdiction.

The Delaware Tribe did not respond well to these changes. Delaware people responded by refusing to participate in Cherokee governance — some refused to be enrolled as "Cherokee Delaware" or to register afterward (a separate process for voting or running for tribal office). Later, many refused to accept allotment certificates issued to them by the BIA as "Cherokee Delaware."

Concurrently, the Delaware Tribe continued its government operations — holding elections and general assembly meetings, passing and enforcing laws and amendments to its Constitution, establishing and operating a business committee, and conducting formal relations with the BIA. The Cherokee Nation did not interfere with any of these operations. But the difficult questions about the legal status and rights of the Delaware Tribe would be redressed by the Supreme Court in 1977 and then again by the Cherokee and BIA in 1979.

Legally, the "Cherokee Delaware" were distinct from the "Absentee Delaware" and the "Kansas Delaware." The "Absentee Delaware" never joined the main group in their relocation from Missouri to Kansas in 1854; instead, they split off in 1789 and migrated through Missouri into Texas. They moved again into Indian Territory in 1859 to settle in Anadarko near the Wichita and Caddo tribes. In 1958 they adopted the designation Delaware Nation of Western Oklahoma and in 1959 reorganized under the Oklahoma Indian Welfare Act of 1936. In 1973, they adopted a constitution and in 1999 changed their name to the Delaware Nation. The "Kansas Dela-

ware" were the twenty-one registered adults and their descendants who remained in Kansas under the terms of the 1867 agreement. Their affiliation
with the Delaware Tribe was dissolved in 1867 and they were issued allotments in Kansas and U.S. citizenship (Weslager 1978).

The Indian Claims Commission (ICC) settled a claim in 1977 that had
been filed by the Delaware Tribe for violations of its 1854 treaty with the
United States. The Delaware claimed that the United States had failed
to secure a fair price for the lands that the Delaware had ceded in Missouri upon their removal to Kansas. The ICC agreed and awarded the tribe
$1,199,763.20 in compensation. The funds were to be distributed to both
the "Cherokee Delaware" and the "Absentee Delaware."[15] The descendants
of the "Kansas Delaware" filed a suit against the United States, the "Cherokee Delaware," the "Absentee Delaware," and the Secretary of the Interior
in the District Court for the Western District of Oklahoma for being excluded from the claim and its settlement (*Delaware Tribal Business Committee v. Weeks et al.* 1977). The District Court ruled in their favor, finding a violation of due process. Each defendant appealed separately to the Supreme
Court.

In 1977 the Supreme Court reversed because it found that the "Kansas
Delaware" had severed their ties in 1867 and so had relinquished any rights
to share in the collective assets or lands of the tribe. From the perspective
of the Delaware Tribe, what was most important about this decision was
that it affirmed their independent status as a federally recognized tribe:

> Indeed, the Indian Claims Commission is not empowered to hear indi-
> viduals' claims, but may only adjudicate claims held by an "Indian tribe,
> band, or other identifiable group." . . . As tribal property, the appropri-
> ated funds were subject to the exercise by Congress of its traditional
> broad authority over the management and distribution of lands and
> property held by recognized tribes, an authority "drawn both explicitly
> and implicitly from the Constitution itself." . . . This authority of Con-
> gress to control tribal assets has been termed "one of the most funda-
> mental expressions, if not the major expression, of the constitutional
> power of Congress over Indian affairs." . . . In 1904 Congress appropri-
> ated $150,000 to settle claims of the Delaware Tribe of Indians, one of
> them arising out of another injustice done to the Delawares under the
> 1854 treaty, unrelated to the breach which forms the basis for the dis-

tribution under Pub. L. 92–456. . . . The 1904 Act directed the Secretary
of the Treasury to pay the settlement to the tribe known in this suit as
the Cherokee Delawares "as said tribe shall in council direct." (*Delaware
Tribal Business Committee v. Weeks et al.* 1977)

Because the ICC had accepted and rendered a decision on their claim, it
acknowledged the Delaware Tribe as an "Indian tribe." Because Congress
managed Delaware lands in Kansas and appropriated funds on behalf of
the Delaware Tribe, it, too, had acknowledged and exercised its "constitutional power" over the Delaware as an "Indian tribe." This finding fundamentally reversed the Supreme Court rulings of 1894 and 1904 by finding
for the independence of the Delaware Tribe from the Cherokee. For the
Delaware, it was an affirmation that they had never given up their sovereign
status even in the contested context of their respected leaders' signatures
on the 1867 agreement (Brown and Kohn 2008).

The Cherokee National Council understood the implications of the
Weeks decision. Formally recognized by the Supreme Court as an "Indian
tribe," the Delaware had a legitimate claim to seek separation from the
Cherokee—jurisdictionally and territorially. Anticipating Delaware plans
to do just that, the Cherokee lobbied hard with BIA officials. The result was
issued on May 24, 1979, when the BIA sent a memorandum to the Delaware
Tribe informing them that all direct relations with the BIA would cease,
that they were under the "jurisdictional service authority" of the Cherokee Nation, and that the Cherokee Nation would administer all relations
of individual Delaware tribal members with the BIA as they would their
other citizens. The Delaware Tribe was instructed that they could register
as "Cherokee" and participate in Cherokee governance with equal status
and rights as "native Cherokee." Very few did so, understanding that registration to be a violation of their 1866 treaty and the 1977 finding for their
independence, as well as an affirmation of their termination.

Back to the BIA

Delaware efforts to be reinstated were initiated formally in 1992. While they
would be successful in securing reinstatement in 1996, a Cherokee lawsuit
in 1997 resulted in their second termination by the U.S. Court of Appeals
in 2004. The 1997 lawsuit and its results were made very public through

several news forums, spurred on primarily by an intense interpersonal exchange between Chad Smith, the Cherokee Principal Chief, and Dee Ketchum, the Delaware Chief, within their Letters to the Editor, which were published in the *Cherokee Phoenix and Indian Advocate* and the *Delaware Indian News* and then picked up in several local, tribal, and national news forums (Haake 2002). What becomes particularly apparent in these exchanges is not that the tribes have different political stakes in how they interpret their treaties and common law (obviously) but that they never really question federal authority to decide the terms and conditions of their legal status and rights. On the contrary, both consistently marshal recognition discourses to challenge the other's political motives and actions. As a consequence, recognition functions as a kind of discursive weapon in their criticisms of one another.

It began in 1992. The Delaware Tribe submitted a letter to the DOI stating its intent to apply for acknowledgment under "Part 83 procedures" (for recognition to be established by BAR, as discussed in chapter 1). The DOI informed the Delaware that it would not consider such an application because the tribe had "not existed as an independent political identity since 1867, and have been absorbed into the Cherokee Nation of Oklahoma for general governmental purposes since that time" (*Cherokee v. Delaware* 2004). In response, the Delaware requested instructions for filing an appeal. The BIA explained that the tribe was not prevented from applying through the Federal Acknowledgment Program (FAP). But having been told that the BIA would not receive the application well the Delaware Tribe chose to formally request that the BIA "reconsider and retract" its 1979 decision (*Cherokee v. Delaware* 2004). To support this request, the tribe submitted extensive documentation to support its claims of possessing and so maintaining a legitimate, legal status and rights as a tribe independent of the Cherokee Nation since 1867.[16]

Under the direction of the Assistant Secretary of the Interior, Ada Deer, the BIA reviewed the Delaware's documentation and relevant laws and concluded that the 1979 decision should be rescinded. On June 27, 1996, the Federal Register published Deer's Notice of Intent to retract the decision and invited public comment. On September 23, Deer issued a notice of the BIA's decision to reinstate the Delaware Tribe: "Notice is hereby given that the Delaware Tribe of Indians is a tribal entity recognized and eligible for funding and services from the Bureau of Indian Affairs by virtue of its status as an Indian tribe" (A. Deer 1996). The Notice reviewed the few public comments that the BIA had received, including concerns from the Delaware Tribe of Western Oklahoma (now the Delaware Nation) about the potential confusion of tribal names and the implications to its recognition status should the eastern tribe be reinstated. The Delaware Tribe responded by clarifying its designation; the notice explained that no such impact would take place. Comments from the Cherokee Nation were brief but important:

> This comment concerns the Cherokee Nation's jurisdictional service area, its court system, law enforcement, Indian child welfare services and civil jurisdiction. Referencing 105 Stat. 990 (1991) and 25 C.F.R. 151.8, the tribe states that it cannot responsibly share its jurisdictional land base, and provides that if the Delawares "concede that their actions will not result in any diminishment of the Cherokee's present funding, its service area or jurisdictional base, then separate recognition would be agreeable to the tribe." (quoted, A. Deer 1996)

In other words, the Cherokee made their support of the Delaware's reinstatement contingent on the Delaware not challenging Cherokee jurisdiction or inadvertently diverting federal funding reserved to the Cherokee Nation for managing programs to Natives within its "jurisdictional service area." Not finding a viable complaint on point, Deer's Notice concluded that, based on a "comprehensive legal analysis of the pertinent treaties and agreements," "the 1979 letter should be retracted because it was not consistent with federal law" (A. Deer 1996).

On September 23, 1996, the Delaware Tribe was reinstated and added to the BIA's list of federally recognized tribes. Almost immediately, the Delaware applied for federal grants to rebuild their government infrastructure, including programs for child services, a health and wellness center, a museum and cultural complex, and renovated headquarters. They sought to purchase and take the lands into trust on which the buildings would be built. They also looked into legal action to remove its roughly eleven thousand members registered as "Cherokee Delaware" from the Cherokee rolls to be reregistered with the Delaware Tribe. To both the Delaware and the Cherokee, this was especially important because BIA funding of tribal programs and services is contingent on tribal population counts.

These actions incited the Cherokee. In October 1997, the National

Council filed a lawsuit against the DOI (naming Bruce Babbitt, then Secretary of the Interior), the BIA (naming Kevin Gover, then Assistant Secretary), and the Delaware Tribe in the District Court of Washington, D.C.
(*Cherokee Nation v. Delaware Tribe et al.* 1997). The Cherokee argued that
the BIA's reinstatement of the Delaware violated the Administrative Procedure Act of 1946. They asserted that the Delaware had "willingly" and
"knowingly" given up their independence and autonomy as a tribe by pur-
chasing land and citizenship rights within the Cherokee Nation under the
terms of the 1867 agreement.[17]

In response to a motion from the DOI, the District Court dismissed the
suit because "the Delawares were an indispensable party that could not be
joined because of sovereign immunity." The Circuit Court reversed, "holding the Delawares could not assert sovereign immunity because they relinquished their tribal sovereignty when they entered into an agreement
with the Cherokee Nation in 1867." The Circuit Court, however, "limited
its holding to the joinder issue" and remanded the case back to the District
Court to decide the "proper interpretation of the 1867 agreement with the
Delaware Tribe as a party to the proceedings and in light of the full administrative record." The District Court transferred the case to the Northern
District Court of Oklahoma because it found that it lacked jurisdiction
(summarized in *Cherokee Nation of Oklahoma v. Delaware Tribe of Indians
et al.* 2004). The Northern District Court of Oklahoma would take until
2002 to render its decision.

Because the conflicts between the Cherokee and Delaware were fundamentally over the interpretation of the law and its mediation of their relations, it is probably no surprise that they ended up being vetted publicly.
During the five years that the 1997 suit bounced back and forth between the
district and circuit courts, these conflicts would gain international attention, focused by a rather heated public debate between Chad Smith and
Dee Ketchum over their very different interpretations of their tribes' legal
status and rights.

It started the year following the suit's initial filing, in the midst of tribal
elections that would put Ketchum into office in 1998 and Smith in 1999.
During the campaign, Smith had apparently reassured Ketchum and the
Delaware Tribe that he would withdraw the lawsuit and work toward an
amicable agreement for the Delaware's reinstatement. After the elections,

however, he refused to withdraw the suit. He and Ketchum, along with several council members on both sides, began debating the matter through local and tribal newspapers that were often posted and commented upon on many popularly visited news sites, including Indianz.com and *Indian Country Today* (indiancountry.com). Repeatedly, Smith attempted to control the representations of the issues and the criticisms of himself and the Nation by affirming the cultural authenticity of the Delaware people and separating that issue from the matters involved in Delaware tribal status and rights. To Smith's apparent surprise, his remarks only intensified criticisms among other Native peoples and particularly tribal governments who understood one of their central responsibilities to be the protection and preservation of their tribal cultures. Carrying on a lawsuit that would result in the Delaware's termination was perceived by most as undermining the abilities of the Delaware to preserve their culture and identity as a tribe.

It began with an editorial in the *Delaware Indian News* in which Ketchum criticized Smith for "reneging" on his promise to withdraw the suit and instead maintaining the Nation's efforts to "terminate" the Delaware (Ketchum 2001).[18] Smith replied in the *Cherokee Phoenix* that the accusations were "patently false" and that he intended to "take [the] opportunity" to update his readers on the history between the tribes (C. Smith 2001a). He explained that the Cherokee had never had anything against the Delaware people, that the Delaware chose to become Cherokee citizens, and that the Nation's intent was solely to protect its sovereignty.

> The Delaware people in question are those whose ancestors chose to become members of the Cherokee Nation according to a Delaware treaty with the Cherokee Nation in 1867. Since that time, Delawares have been full members of the Cherokee Nation, received allotments and service benefits under the Dawes Commission Rolls as members of the Cherokee Nation, voted in our elections and served in our government. The Cherokee Nation has never said that the Delawares are Cherokees. Delawares are citizens of the Cherokee Nation with the same rights and privileges of Cherokees and the adopted Shawnees. The Cherokee Nation never has and never will make an effort to terminate the Delaware language, culture and identity. By law, the Cherokee Nation recognizes these citizens as Delawares, though citizens of the Cherokee Nation. (C. Smith 2001a)

Smith insisted that his and the Nation's efforts were merely to "retain all rights of sovereignty within . . . jurisdictional boundaries," which they were forced to do because of the efforts of "many bogus 'Indian' groups, and another Indian tribe" to attack Cherokee sovereignty. He "recommended that the Delaware should "acquire land outside [Cherokee] jurisdiction and to assert any and all sovereignty rights they may have there" (C. Smith 2001a). He then lamented the failure to reach an agreement with the Delaware but blamed Ketchum and the Delaware council's ambitions for it. More specifically, he claimed that Ketchum and the council withdrew from the negotiations because he and the Nation refused to dismiss the suit "with prejudice" (C. Smith 2001a).

Smith's assertion that the Delaware were "incorporated" willingly and equally into the Nation as citizens was an assertion of the Nation's jurisdictional authority over the Delaware Tribe as an aspect of its tribal sovereignty. It folded into Smith's attempts to divorce his and the Nation's respect for the cultural authenticity of the Delaware from the implications of the lawsuit's arguments about Delaware legal status and rights. This seems to be a response to the nationwide criticisms that Smith and the National Council gathered in their legal actions against the Delaware. Beginning in local and tribal news forums, the criticisms swelled to include the National Congress of American Indians, who represented the Delaware as the first treatied "grandfather tribe" and outright condemned the Cherokee's efforts (NCAI Resolution #SAC-06-063 2006). By insisting on Delaware cultural authenticity, Smith attempted to deflate these criticisms.

As with Smith and the Cherokee National Council, Delaware leadership never challenged federal recognition authority or the public terms of cultural authenticity through which it was framed. Instead, their efforts were focused on reinstatement, invoking their cultural distinction from the Cherokee to solidify their legal legitimacy as a tribe. Ketchum's response to Smith began by refuting Smith's claim that the Cherokee Nation's efforts were not "seeking to terminate the Delaware Tribe": "As Chief Smith is aware, 'termination' is a legal term referring to the loss of recognized sovereign tribal status. In *Cherokee Nation vs. Secretary of Interior and Delaware Tribe*, the Cherokees have requested that the court find that the Delaware Tribe has not existed since 1867, is not a sovereign entity and that the Bureau of Indian Affairs stop recognizing them as a tribe" (Ketchum 2001).

Rejecting Smith's assertions as a denial of his true political aims, Ketchum then refuted Smith's characterizations of Delaware objectives and the historical review of the relationship between the tribes:

> Chief Smith states that the Delawares chose to become members of the Cherokee Nation. This, again, is not true. The Delaware people never chose to be citizens of the Cherokee Nation. We bought the same rights and privileges as other Cherokee members. The Delaware Treaty of 1866 promised the Delawares a new reservation of their own in Indian Territory. When the Delawares were moved to Oklahoma, within the boundaries of the old Cherokee Nation, two payments were made to the Cherokee Nation. The first payment of $279,000 was made into the Cherokee National Fund, providing the Delawares with full privileges and rights in the Cherokee Nation. This payment was much like buying stock in a corporation. The second payment of $157,000 was to pay for a land base so the Delaware Tribe could continue to function as a tribe with our own tribal government, which we have done since the beginning of time without interruption. (Ketchum 2001)

Ketchum claimed that the Delaware purchased the "privileges and rights" of Cherokee citizens and a "land base" for "tribal government." While this furthered his argument that the Delaware never *willingly* became Cherokee citizens, and while this is certainly true, it does not fully engage the 1867 agreement or the way it was interpreted by the courts. The payments were supposed to provide funds for the Cherokee Nation for infrastructure support for the Delaware Tribe's relocation and to compensate the Nation for the loss of the use of its total land base. The payments were not intended to be a purchase of citizenship "privileges and rights." Rather, the Delaware's arguments to the Supreme Court in 1894 and 1904 were predicated on the assumption of its 1866 treaty rights to a reserved and bounded land base within Cherokee territory that would enable them to maintain self-government.

Ketchum turned to the Delaware's 1866 treaty to insist that the United States had guaranteed them rights to self-government and lands within Cherokee territory: "Chief Smith advocates that the Delawares are seeking to 'carve out' a part of the Cherokee Nation. This is false. . . . The Delaware Tribe only seeks to have jurisdiction over its own lands. In the treaty of 1866, Article 11, with the federal government, the Delaware Tribe is guaranteed to have its just rights preserved, protected and defended. These just rights include having a land base" (Ketchum 2001). From there, Ketchum demanded an apology from Smith for seeming to equate the Delaware Tribe with "'bogus Indian groups' attacking the sovereignty of the Cherokee Nation." Ketchum again asserted the cultural authenticity of the Delaware Tribe and attacked Smith for suggesting that the Cherokee can set the terms of Delaware culture and identity: "Neither the federal government nor Chief Smith has the ability to take our language, culture and identity. So Smith's offer to allow the Delawares to keep our language and culture is insulting at best" (Ketchum 2001). Ketchum concluded by addressing Smith's narration of the tribes' negotiations, which he claimed were based on the Nation's refusal to recognize the legal rights of the Delaware Tribe to self-government and lands as guaranteed to them by treaty:

> In reference to the commissioners appointed to attempt settlement negotiations . . . Two of the three Cherokee commissioners refused to recognize the Delawares' federal recognition, therefore, the Delaware commissioners found it impossible to proceed with the negotiations. Chief Smith falsely implies that the Delawares have requested that the BIA take federal funds from the Cherokees for the Delawares. But in fact the Delaware Tribe has agreed to provide its current programs on the $241,000 that it has already received from the federal government; without taking any funding from the Cherokee Nation. This is in contrast to the $50 million in federal funds received by the Cherokee Nation. I have been involved in the Delaware tribal government for 16 years, with 12 of those years serving with my brother when he was chief. The Delawares have tried in vain to negotiate an agreement to live harmoniously with the Cherokees. However, we will continue to fight anyone inferring that the Delawares, who are sovereign in nature, are not federally recognized. In conclusion, let me reiterate that we will continue to fight Chief Chad Smith against his lawsuit to terminate the Delaware Tribe. Who stands to lose in this issue? The Cherokee people do by spending millions of dollars on this lawsuit. (Ketchum 2001)

Throughout Ketchum's letter, tribal sovereignty and federal recognition status were elided into one another as are Delaware cultural authenticity and legal legitimacy. Nowhere does Ketchum directly question or challenge federal recognition authority or how the authenticity of Delaware culture is measured and by whom. While this is understandable given that the sovereign status and rights of "Indian tribes" are equated with recognition status, the avowal of recognition inadvertently upholds an unequal relation of power between the United States and the Cherokee and Delaware as (un)recognized "Indian tribes." Instead of antagonizing the legal terms and social conditions of that relationship, Ketchum mobilizes recognition and its link of cultural authenticity to legal legitimacy to condemn Smith and the National Council for not properly respecting either.

The exchanges between Smith and Ketchum immediately backfired for Ketchum. Ketchum and several council members were seen by many Delaware people as being too stubborn and arrogant, criticized especially for underestimating the power of the Cherokee and for ruining Delaware relations with the Nation's leadership and chances at reinstatement. In November 2002, Ketchum and several council members were voted out. The new chief, Joe Brooks, however, would suffer a similar fate in 2005—for failing to reach an agreement with the Cherokee, likewise aggravated by and then defiant of Smith and the Cherokee National Council's perspectives about Delaware legal status and rights.

Meanwhile, the Northern District Court of Oklahoma issued its ruling in December 2002. To the shock of Smith and many on the National Council, the court extended "great deference" to the BIA and "concluded its retraction of the 1979 letter did not violate the APA." The court reasoned that "the Delawares were a federally recognized tribe prior to 1979 because (1) a claims statute appropriated funds to the 'Delaware Tribe of Indians,' and (2) 'the Supreme Court explicitly and unambiguously declared that the Delaware Tribe of Indians was a federally recognized Indian tribe in *Delaware Tribal Business Committee v. Weeks.*'" The Cherokee Nation appealed, explaining in a news release that it would challenge the BIA "ignoring its own requirements" and granting federal recognition to the Delaware Tribe "which has been an integral part of the Cherokee Nation since 1867" (*Cherokee Nation v. Delaware et al.* 2002).

In 2004, the Court of Appeals agreed. As the Supreme Court had in 1894 and 1904, it focused its decision on the 1867 agreement through the provisions of the Cherokee's treaty of 1866, ignoring altogether the Delaware's treaty of 1866. It claimed that the lower court had failed to take into due consideration these earlier decisions: "The Supreme Court has twice interpreted that contract [the 1867 agreement]. We must decide in this case whether the Department of Interior's ("DOI") interpretation of that contract and concomitant decision to extend Federal recognition to the Delawares is contrary to the Supreme Court's reading of the same document" (*Cherokee Nation v. Delaware et al.* 2004). It argued that the laws governing recognition were clear, as provided by the Federally Recognized Indian Tribe List Act of 1994. It reasoned that the district court had deferred too much to the DOI's legal review and found that the review had not adequately considered the 1894 and 1904 judgments as having "consistently" interpreted the Delaware's "incorporation" as Cherokee under the terms of the 1867 agreement. It found that the DOI and BIA had thereby "contravened" Supreme Court precedent by accepting the Delaware's argument.

Finally, the court challenged the reliance of the DOI and BIA on its interpretation of the significance of the *Weeks* decision. In a glaringly incongruous argument, the court stated that *Weeks* offered a different conclusion about Delaware tribal status than in 1894 and 1904 but that there was no legal conflict and so no obligation of the court to consider whether or not the Delaware's status had been changed by *Weeks*. It explained that this was because the Delaware had been allowed to reconstitute itself for the sake of filing or appealing claims decisions but for no other purposes or consequences that the Court of Appeals was obligated to consider:

> At most, *Weeks* stands for the proposition the Delawares reconstituted for claims purposes. Whether the Delawares were reconstituted be it through Act of Congress or administrative practice sometime after 1867 is not before us. The present case, instead, turns on the DOI's interpretation of the 1866 Cherokee Treaty and 1867 Agreement. We thus have a duty to follow *Journeycake* and *Delaware Indians* because they directly control our interpretation of the agreement. Even assuming *Journeycake* and *Delaware Indians* conflict with the dicta in *Weeks* (which they do not), we nevertheless would be bound by those decisions. (*Cherokee Nation v. Delaware et al.* 2002)

While acknowledging the departure of *Weeks* from the previous rulings, the Court of Appeals found there to be no incongruity or inconsistency within

Supreme Court decisions about Delaware tribal status that it was obligated to consider. While not "unsympathetic" to the Delaware's situation, the Court of Appeals set aside the DOI and BIA's 1996 decision. In October 2006, the Supreme Court refused to hear the Delaware Tribe's appeal. The Delaware were removed from the BIA's list of federally recognized tribes in March 2005.

Disciplined Tribes

The impact of the 2004 decision was immediate and real. The Delaware Tribe lost close to $7 million in federal grants, which included funds for a Community Child Development Center, a Health and Wellness Center, and the employment of about one hundred individuals including those in the tribal headquarters in Bartlesville, Oklahoma (Adcock 2009). Delaware people throughout the United States were devastated. They blamed the tribe's leadership for being arrogant and uncooperative, the Cherokee Nation for being vindictive and hypocritical, Smith for being untrustworthy, and the DOI and BIA for being incompetent. These criticisms seemed to embolden Joe Brooks and the tribal council.

In August 2005, the Cherokee Nation proposed an agreement with the Delaware mirroring the terms of a 2000 agreement and congressional bill that supported the independence of the Loyal Shawnee from the Cherokee Nation. Brooks and the tribal council refused. That November, the Delaware people held a recall election and replaced the then openly agitated Brooks — "I will fight the chief of the Cherokee Nation until hell freezes over!" (Staff Writer, *Bartlesville Examiner-Enterprise* 2004) — with the more reserved Jerry Douglas.

In January 2006, Douglas and several other council members went to BIA headquarters in Washington and met with officials to seek counsel on how to proceed. They were directed to negotiate an agreement with the Cherokee Nation and encouraged that if such an agreement was reached the tribe would be reinstated (as the Loyal Shawnee had been in 2000). In July, Douglas and the council announced that they would submit to the Cherokee Nation's conditions for reinstatement. In August, the Cherokee National Council and the Delaware Tribal Council independently approved the agreement as a Memorandum of Understanding (MOU). The MOU was forwarded to the BIA for approval. Meanwhile, the Delaware

Tribe sought sponsorship on a recognition bill from John Sullivan, who was Oklahoma's First District Congressman (Ruckman 2006). The Cherokee Nation endorsed the bill, promising that they had worked with Douglas and the new council to put years of intertribal conflict to an end (Snell 2006).

While the Delaware's council approved the MOU, Delaware people and their allies voiced serious concerns about it. Many demanded a tribal election to vote on it before tribal ratification could be considered legitimate. The vote never happened. Instead, the MOU was moved easily through the tribal ratification process, including the following provisions:

▷ the restoration of federal recognition status for the Delaware Tribe;

▷ the affirmation that Delaware members are entitled to all federal and state services and programs reserved for Indians with recognition status;

▷ the fact that within the "jurisdictional service area" of the Cherokee Nation (the fourteen districts of northeastern Oklahoma), the Delaware Tribe must seek consent from the Cherokee Nation to take lands into trust, conduct gaming activities under the Indian Gaming Regulatory Act, or receive many types of federal and sate funding provided to recognized tribes;

▷ the affirmation that the Delaware Tribe may continue to operate the Elder Nutrition, Childcare, Light and Heat, 8(a) contractor status, Language, and HUD maintenance programs as already established; and

▷ the affirmation that the Cherokee Nation maintains full jurisdiction within the "jurisdictional service area" of the Cherokee Nation, including jurisdiction over Delaware allotted lands and tribal businesses. This includes the power to regulate and tax existing Delaware tribal businesses on the tribe's fee lands in Bartlesville. (summarized from Peckham 2006)

Through the November 2006 tribal elections (Douglas was reelected to a four-year term), criticisms of the MOU's implications for Delaware sovereignty were muted by an overwhelming expression of relief in the promise of reinstatement. Still, criticisms percolated through media coverage of the issues confronting the Delaware:

It's not the best deal for us, but it's the best we can do under the circumstances. We had no bargaining power. When you get down to it. We had nothing. . . . We're not going to get what the treaty of 1867 promised us. That's all water under the bridge. In order to progress, we have to come to terms. (Edna Havens, Delaware of Bartlesville, Oklahoma, in Robinson 2006)

It's time that we share this information. . . . There's a lot of skepticism and a lot of rejection for what we are hearing. . . . The bill contains some concessions that we hope not to make. (Curtis Zunigha, former Delaware chief, in Hudson 2006)

[The tribe should] quit kissing up to the BIA and the Cherokees. (Ed Wilson, Delaware of Bartlesville, in Hudson 2006)

When you've got the BIA stacked with the Cherokees, the deck is stacked against us. . . . Right now the bill, as it stands, verifies the Cherokees dominance over the Delaware. . . . The Cherokees just spent three to four million dollars suing us and now they are going to throw us a bone. That just doesn't sit well with me. Why do we have to have the Cherokee go hand in hand with us in this? Why can't we go it alone? (Dee Ketchum in Hudson 2006)

Let me start by saying, I absolutely support the Delaware Tribe having our federal recognition restored; we should be actively pursuing all options that will not harm our people and/or our tribe. However, I am concerned with the avenue our current chief and council have chosen. Other options are available and after this legislation is marked up by Congress there is no guarantee the Cherokee Nation will continue to support it; which in my opinion is a good thing. I do not want this legislation to pass. In 1867, an agreement was made by the Delaware and the Cherokee, this agreement has been of much heated debate since its signing. The 1867 agreement specifically violates the Delaware Treaty of 1866. . . . Today, our Delaware chief and council are making yet another agreement with the Cherokee Nation and attempting to have Congress pass legislation restoring our federal recognition. As I mentioned, I am absolutely for the restoration of our federal recognition. We were the first Indian nation to sign a treaty with the newly formed U.S. government. We have fought many wars on the side of the U.S. government. We have retained our culture and our heritage through at least six major removals. We are a tribe; we are a nation. (Rusty Creed Brown, former Delaware tribal judge, in R. Brown 2006)

In response to the criticisms, the tribe's attorney, Tom Peckham, wrote an article entitled "Sovereignty Now or Sovereignty Later: Federal Recognition Legislation Proposed" for the *Delaware Indian News*. In it, he explained the difficult concessions with the Cherokee Nation as a necessary step in the process to reinstatement, as status he equates with sovereignty:

> The Tribal Council elected to support the proposed legislation despite its flaws. It is flawed. The Delaware Tribe should be recognized by the United States without any restrictions or concessions. But looking at the Tribe's options there is no clear path to that result. . . . The proposed legislation is far from perfect, but it does restore the full federal recognition of the Delaware Tribe. It does allow Delaware members to receive services as Delaware, without joining Cherokee. It places no restrictions on the Tribe outside the fourteen counties. Does it give up too much for what it brings? Is it too much like the Shawnee bill? The Tribal Council has answered those questions in the negative. The Tribe is in a position it should never have had to face. It was wronged by the United States repeatedly, including in 1867 and in 1979. But the Tribe must face the situation as it is. The Tribal Council has decided that, while the medicine is bitter, it is better than the disease when the disease is not being federally recognized for a year or more to come, maybe many more. Federal recognition could give the Tribe the resources and standing to keep working to build your own government and your own economic base. With creativity and hard work you likely will be able to do everything you were doing after 1996 and more. But my opinion on the ultimate question should not matter. No one can tell you what it means to be Delaware. You all have to decide that. (2006, 5)

In the subsequent issue of the *Delaware Indian News*, Brooks and council members pleaded with Delaware people to stop expressing public concerns and dissent about the MOU. But nowhere in these concerns have the Delaware people—whatever their differences on the strategies—publicly questioned recognition as the goal. Therefore, when a vote was called for on May 27, 2006, the Constitution and By-Laws and MOU were approved overwhelmingly (Adcock 2009).

Recognoscere

Recognition derives from the Latin word *recognoscere*—to recall to mind; again, to know; COGNITION. It implies not only a recollection—a bringing back to one's awareness what was forgotten or dormant—but an active state of knowing. So, there are no innocent or preordained *recognitions*. As Jacques Lacan aptly describes in *Écrits* (1977) as *anamnesis* (the construction of the present through our memories of the past), it is impossible to disentangle our interpretations of the past—the how and what is recalled or remembered—from the political web of social relations through which they are articulated.

In many ways, this chapter is about the politics of interpretation: the power of federal agents to translate political objectives into treaty provisions; the power of the U.S. Congress and courts to interpret those provisions into law; the power of the United States and tribal governments to recollect and so assign "original intent" to the texts of treaties, laws, and their amendments; and, all the while, the power of assigning intent and consequence to these various kinds of representational and interpretative politics.

Since there are no innocent or preordained ways of knowing, there are always ethical implications in the choices made about what and how the past is recalled. These choices define the political and interpersonal relationships that Native peoples (seek to) articulate with one another.

But it is not so easy as concluding that Natives are *either* disciplined and interpolated into national narrations as (un)recognized tribes (Foucault 1979; Althusser 1971) *or* that their remembrances are altogether revolutionary and transformative (Laclau and Mouffe 1985; Hall, in Grossberg 1996). The historical conditions that articulated Cherokee and Delaware subjugation to federal plenary power and of Delaware subjugation to the Cherokee suggest that it is all a little more complex than these kinds of binaries allow to be narrated.

The Cherokee and Delaware invited the terms of federal recognition because recognition affords tribes at least some measure of legal protection against ongoing anti-Indian political efforts (McCulloch and Wilkins 1995).

These efforts have focused on many issues including land rights, tax exemption status, hunting and fishing rights, and gaming. They have for the most part reified racist and paternalist discourses to try to divest tribes of their legal status and rights by configuring those rights as mere "special" benefits and privileges based on race that so discriminate against non-Indians, namely "whites" (Barker 2005/2006). Recognition status provides tribes with one of the only effective means available to Native peoples in the United States to secure some measure of protection against these efforts and the racist hostilities that fuel them (issues taken up again in chapter 5).

Given the stakes, recognition is deeply valued by tribes who have too often become defensive against one another in their efforts to protect it and all of the rights and services it affords (or, often, is *supposed* to afford). But what these difficult issues indicate is that (un)recognized tribes must not only navigate the heated terrain of national politics aimed often at undermining their legal status and rights, but they are confronted every day with choices about how they are going to treat one another given those politics. These choices reflect the viability of Native epistemologies of relationship and responsibility "on the ground" of how Natives chose to treat one another — often through how they choose to remember the past.

Part II MEMBERSHIP

membership [L *membrum*, flesh] **1** the state of being, or status as, a member **2** members collectively, as of an organization **3** the number of members.

Webster's New World Dictionary, Third College Edition

3 Of the "Indian Member"

In part 1, the "Indian tribe" was shown to be a construct of U.S. national narrations that furthers Native domination and reinvents U.S. democracy and humanism out of histories of colonialism and imperialism. This work depends on an especially racialized notion of Native authenticity, one that is *recognizable* by national narrations as valuably unique to the national polity and so *investable* with a unique set of legal rights. The "Indian tribe" that manages these configurations demands that Native peoples represent the authenticities on which their legal status and rights are contingent. How Native peoples chose to navigate these demands represents the complexities within their struggles for self-determination as well as the kinds of social relationships and responsibilities they seek (to make) with one another as (un)recognized "Indian tribes."

The "Indian member" is cut from the same cloth—*identifiable* and *investable* with a unique legal status and rights based on her or his cultural authenticity as a Native. Specific rights that issue from membership include voting in tribal elections; holding tribal office; sharing in tribal revenue; the use of tribal lands and natural resources such as for grazing, timber, fishing, and hunting; and housing, health care, and education (Goldberg-Ambrose 2002b). The provision of these legal rights implicate as well the social rights of enjoyment and reputation (Kauanui 2008, 22) and the power to exclude these rights from others (Harris 1993).[1]

Within federal law, the required measure of Native authenticity has been overwhelmed by blood degree. Blood degree measures the purity of genealogical descent and so the legal legitimacy of membership rights (Goldberg-Ambrose 2002a). But it also serves as a mechanism for a certain kind of racialization that is about making Native peoples the colonial-imperial (colonized-imperialized) subjects of U.S. power.

In "Whiteness as Property" (1993), Cheryl I. Harris maintains that the investment and protection of property rights by racialized inclusion implies that those same rights come with the power to exclude them from others. The United States has used this exclusivity to produce Native domination on the basis of multiple kinds of sociocultural "impurities"— measurable and quantifiable by blood. At the same time, blood has been a part of a whole host of subject-making practices that have brought "Indians" into and under the routine administrative control of the United States. As Philip Deloria writes in *Indians in Unexpected Places* (2004), the rolls on which blood was recorded standardized Native people's names by translating them into English with relevant demographic information used to administer federal policies. This was commensurate with the production of church documents that recorded "Indian" people's births, baptisms, lineages, marriages, and deaths. Together, "this knowledge could be translated into power over Indian people. To be known by name, date and location of baptism, rations drawn, and enrollment number was to be intimately visible to the colonial bureaucracy. It made it easy to locate a particular person in time and in space and to determine the need for education, discipline, containment, or shunning" (16).

Yet another imprint left by the blood of the "Indian member" is on tribal constitutional and common law (Pommersheim 1995; Yellow Bird 2005). This law has been made to navigate its jurisdictional limits by federal statute (F. Cohen 1940; Deloria and Lytle 1984; Wilkins and Lomawaima 2001). But tribal governments have asserted successfully through the courts their absolute jurisdiction over membership criteria as an aspect of both their rights to self-government and as an embodiment of the cultural traditions of tribes whose elected officials—as knowledgeable of those traditions—are charged with the responsibility of preserving and protecting (discussed further in chapter 4). The definitive link of "self-government" and "cultural tradition" means that those who are excluded from membership status are not merely excluded from its associated legal rights. They are excluded from status and rights based on their lack of cultural authenticity—based on the politics of those kinds of criteria that determine membership status as a reflection of the "self-government" of cultural tradition.

The "Indian member" manages the resultant links between legal legitimacy and cultural authenticity by suggesting that those who are not members are excluded naturally and inevitably because they are not authentic in the specific terms of knowledge, practice, and identity on which specific criteria are based. These terms include the race of blood quantum, the gender of descent, the kinship of lineality, and the cultural knowledge of ceremonial participation and community service. Chapters 4 (on tribal membership policies) and 5 (on tribal disenrollment practices) take up these issues in the context of intra-tribal politics. For here, I would like to provide an etymology of the "Indian member" that demonstrates its historically constitutive role in the production of tribal membership as a property right that is implicated in the inclusionary/exclusionary ideologies of race, gender, and sexuality.

The Property of . . .

Citizenship and property rights in federal law have always been racialized and gendered in ways that protect the privileges of those classified as "white" men (Frankenberg 1993; Harris 1993; Almaguer 1994; Crenshaw, Gotanda, Peller, and Thomas 1995; López 1996; Wing 1997; Lipsitz 1998). Almost two hundred years of civil war and social conflict resulted in the amendment of citizenship and civil rights for nonwhites and women (Thirteenth Amendment to the U.S. Constitution, 1865; Fourteenth Amendment to the U.S. Constitution, 1868; Nineteenth Amendment to the U.S. Constitution, 1920), but even then required legal action to secure their enforcement (President John F. Kennedy's Executive Order #10925 1961; Civil Rights Act 1964; Voting Rights Act 1965; President Lyndon B. Johnson's Executive Order #11246 1965).

The movements — and those against them — that informed these legislative interventions in racial-gendered discrimination likewise informed the struggles of Native peoples for territorial rights. These struggles "began" with the United States' claim to an exclusive, proprietary right to acquire Native lands by "discovery" under the conventions of international practice (Anaya 1996; R. Miller 2006; Barker 2005a). These conventions were rationalized through racialized notions of Native inferiority. As discussed in chapter 1, the legal definitions of the "Indian tribe" that emerged from tales of U.S. superiority assumed that Native peoples lacked the essential qualities — such as belief in a Christian God or a capitalist, free-market economy — that would prove they possessed a status equal to that of the "civilized world" (Berkhofer 1979; Drinnon 1980; Dippie 1982; R. Green 1990; R. Williams 1990). These claims rationalized Native dispossession by any means necessary, including the genocidal programs conducted by the military that resulted in the virtual decimation of whole tribes, bands, or families and often with full public support and cooperation (Forbes 1982; Rawls 1984; Trafzer and Hyer 1999).

But the United States government also dispossessed Native peoples of their territories by inaction. It allowed its citizens to illegally immigrate and homestead treatied lands. It encouraged its citizens and banks to loan Natives large sums, thus saddling the latter with extravagant financial debts that could only be paid by land cession. It passed laws that confined Native political and trade activities to reservation borders and then significantly curtailed Native jurisdiction within them, particularly over those "whites" who were illegally homesteading (Debo 1940; Harring 1994). These and other inactions were done as well in the service of maintaining "white" men's privileges over Native property (see Berger 1997; Hogan 1998).

Into these histories fold the discourses and ideologies of gender and sexuality, which directly undergirded U.S. colonial and imperial aims (see Stoler 2002; A. Kaplan 2005). U.S. national narrations assumed heterosexist norms in evaluating Native savagery and sexual deviance to warrant and necessitate Native conquest and land dispossession. In fact, transforming Native gender roles and sexual identities was an immediate objective of the "Christianization" and "Civilization" programs instituted by Congress and the BIA, then located within the Department of War, in the early 1800s (Tinker 1993; Niezen 2000).

From the perspective of colonial-imperial authorities in Europe and the United States, missionaries were seen as central figures in the colonization process because of their role in language learning and reeducation, both of which facilitated trade and settlement (Van Kirk 1983; Tinker 1993). Further, under Papal bull and related Protestant doctrine, the introduction of Catholic and Protestant values to "heathens" and "infidels" redefined church-military aggression as both just and justified, absolving a host of sins committed against Natives in the name of conversion (Tinker 1993; Niezen 2000).

Colonial-settlers were particularly obsessed with issues of gender and sexuality in part because of the stark and much misunderstood differences they perceived between their own Christian social norms and those that they perceived to characterize Native societies (Leacock and Goodman 1976; Jacobs, Thomas, and Long 1997). They found Native gender roles and sexual identities to be barbaric and even dangerous to proper Christian norms and civil society, especially since women and "third gender," "two spirit" people occupied a very public significance and social equality with men and heterosexual people in Native governance, land tenure, and religious life (contrary, of course, to the prevalent stereotypes of Native women as sexually promiscuous and drudge laborers and of Native men as sexually aggressive and lazy [R. Green 1990]).[2] This prominence was seen to be counter to God's designs for the order of things between the sexes and so between the church and sinners. It was believed that a complete transformation was needed in order to secure Native conversion and subjugation to God's will (V. Deloria 1979). For colonial-settlers and their militaries, this conversion was seen as the easiest means to Native political cooperation and labor (Leacock and Goodman 1976; Holly 1990; Tinker 1993; Niezen 2000; Berger 2004; Prindeville 2004).

Concurrent with missionary efforts, colonial-settlers introduced a capitalism and free-market ideology that grossly disenfranchised women and "third gender," "two spirit" people (Allen 1986). In fact, colonial officials and traders often refused to sit at the proverbial negotiating table with Native women present (Van Kirk 1983; Perdue 1999). This refusal reflected government and military practice as within treaty negotiations. For example, when a Sauk Nation woman protested against removal and insisted that women had a right to be involved in the negotiations over the tribe's land rights as the tribe's agriculturalists, Edmund Gaines, the U.S. Army Major General sent to negotiate with the Sauk, responded that "the president did not send him . . . to make treaties with the women, nor to hold council with them" (quoted in Berger 2004).[3] Similarly, "third gender," "two spirit" people were abused and disparaged in virtually all official and military matters of relations with Native peoples. They were blamed for the social depravity and immorality of Native societies and were repeatedly the victims of harassment and violence (Roscoe 1989; Jacobs, Thomas, and Long 1997; Taylor 2008).

In *Cherokee Women: Gender and Culture Change, 1700–1835* (1999), Theda Perdue demonstrates that the impact of missionization and capitalist economies on Native communities — as fundamentally patriarchal, sexist, and homophobic social forces — was profound (though of course uneven). Native women's and men's identities and social roles and responsibilities went through significant, transformative changes even before the United States became the United States. These changes were manifest in women's political and economic subordination to men and their virtual absence (absenting) from public affairs but also their very real loss of control within tribal economies and land management (see Berger 1997; Perdue 1999). While not to underestimate the cultural "survivance" (Vizenor 1994) of traditional values and practices about gender and sexuality against these social forces (discussed further in chapter 4), it is also true that Native societies and social values were much changed by their exchanges with the ideologies and practices of the religions and economies that defined the United States.

Initiated by the Civilization Fund in 1810, federally sponsored "Christianization" and "Civilization" programs crystallized through coercively heterosexist norms of the assimilation policies of the latter part of the nineteenth century. The Congress and BIA dedicated themselves to "saving" Native peoples from genocide by integrating them into the great "melting pot" (as if genocide were some "out there" natural occurrence and not being directly facilitated by federal laws and military policies). To bring this integration about, Congress and the BIA criminalized Native religions and incarcerated spiritual leaders (in both prisons and mental institutions) as a way of curtailing those cultural perspectives and intertribal alliances

that would empower Native peoples against the social forces of colonization and imperialism (Niezen 2000). Concurrently, boarding schools
and allotment policies were developed to dispossess tribes of their governments, lands, financial resources, children, languages, and cultural knowledge under the guise of securing their social integration and economic self-
sufficiency through education and farming.

Assimilation policies sought to make Native men into good Christians,
heads of households, and hardworking, tax-paying farmers (believing them
to be lazy drunks living off federal welfare and Native women's labor).
These policies sought to make Native women into submissive Christian
wives and mothers (believing them to be too powerful and neglectful).
These kinds of Native men and women would form unambiguous heteronormative family units, paying taxes and submitting to federal and state authorities. Citizenship and economic opportunity were held out to Natives
as the proverbial carrots for those who successfully transformed themselves
into model Americans.

Of course, what actually happened was quite different from the promise. Boarding schools produced whole generations of soldiers (Loew 2007;
Denetdale 2008), field-hands, maids, seamstresses, and school staff (Lomawaima 1994). They contributed directly to the disproportionately high rates
of interpersonal violence, substance abuse, depression, and suicide within
Native communities that resulted from the physical and sexual abuse of
children at the schools (A. Smith 2005). Allotment was equally devastating. The General Allotment Act of 1887 provided for selected reservations
to be broken up in severalty and issued to enrolled members as parcels
ranging from 40 to 600 acres each, based primarily on the value of the lands
and the members' marital and dependent status (Bledsoe 1909; Carlson
1980; McDonnell 1991). "Surplus lands" or those lands unassigned to tribal
members were sold to nonmembers. The result was the radical reduction
of reservation lands—from 148 to 48 million acres—but related consequences included the exasperation of Native reservation and rural poverty,
unemployment, malnutrition, starvation, ill health, and crime (Debo 1940;
Perdue 1981; Harring 1994).

Into the myriad of social problems resulting from assimilation, the
"Indian member" emerged to codify the legal status and rights of Native
peoples not merely within federal but tribal law. This codification was
deeply embedded within the discourses and ideologies of race, gender, and

sexuality about what constituted a culturally authentic Native deserving of the unique legal status and rights reserved for Native peoples within the law. The "Indian member" that resulted shored up the power of inclusion (status) with the power to exclude (rights) on the racialized, gendered, and sexualized grounds of authenticity.

The Allotted Indian

Before the allotment period, the U.S. Census Bureau counted tribal populations by their "race" as "Indians" in more generic estimations of their totals (Snipp 1989). Individual Natives were specifically counted or registered on census rolls on the occasion of removals, asset liquidation, and per capita distribution (Foreman 1974). Neither of these types of counts have been considered especially reliable. What is rather interesting about them is the apparent lack of any federal or tribal regulation or accounting of tribal members before the allotment period. This seems to indicate a couple of things: (1) the United States had no real political motivation for needing to monitor tribal populations; and (2) tribes had no need to regulate it. The General Allotment Act changed all of this. Both the United States and tribal governments were motivated to establish membership criteria (and so account for their members) because the act provided for the allotment of reservation lands and the dissolution of tribal assets to members. Rampant fraud throughout the United States — with nonmembers claiming to be members in order to get access to the much-publicized oil and other riches of Indian lands (Debo 1940) — warranted the concerns and bore on the criteria that were generated. The General Allotment Act and its amendments by the Curtis Act of 1898, the Burke Act of 1906, and the Omnibus Act of 1910 provided the regulatory contexts in which these criteria were developed, initially within tribal "agreements" to allot signed in Indian Territory (Bledsoe 1909).[4]

The administration of allotment required that those individuals recognized by their tribal governments to be members were officially registered on census rolls that recorded their blood quantum paternally and maternally, marriage and dependency status, and age.[5] This information was used by the BIA to evaluate the "competency" of the individual to manage the demands of private property ownership and so earn the rights and privileges of citizenship that came with being issued full land title (F. Cohen

1940; Carlson 1980; McDonnell 1991). "Competency" was determined by theories of social evolution and human genetics that fused race, biology, and culture. The theories went that the *less* Native blood/biology a person possessed, the more socially assimilated into U.S. society she or he was; the *more* Native blood/biology a person possessed, the less she or he was socially assimilated (Morgan 1877; Bieder 1986). Apparently, fluency in English was also factored into the evaluation of "competency" (McDonnell 1991).[6]

Depending on the results of the competency evaluations, which were supposed to result from interviews, individuals were to be issued one of two kinds of land patents or title to their allotments: fee simple or trust (F. Cohen 1940, 109).[7] Patents in fee simple and U.S. citizenship were issued to individuals determined to be competent; patents in trust without U.S. citizenship were issued to individuals deemed incompetent. The term of trust was not to exceed twenty-five years or until that time that the individual demonstrated that she or he had learned the demands of private property ownership. At that time, they could apply for a fee simple transfer.

In the *Handbook of Federal Indian Law* (1940), Felix S. Cohen reports that 60 percent of the initial fee patents issued were sold within three years of the law's passage (by 1890). Uncritically, the BIA assumed that this was owing to the "misdiagnosis" of Native "competency"—that Natives were being given fee titles when they were actually incompetent at managing the demands of private property ownership.[8] But in response, BIA commissioners initiated a series of regulatory policies "requiring more rigid proof of competency" from agents administering allotment "in the field" even while Congress passed several amendments to the allotment act that suspended the issuance of trust patents altogether in order to expedite allotment and statehood out of Native territories (Bledsoe 1909, 25).

In the context of these incongruous BIA policies and congressional statutes, and while advancing the end of Native dependency on federal trust through full land ownership and U.S. citizenship, Commissioner Cato Sells issued a policy directive in 1917 that was meant to expedite the issuance of fee patents and protect allottee titles through stricter "competency" standards.

[A policy] of greater liberalism will henceforth prevail in Indian administration to the end that every Indian, as soon as he has been determined to be as competent to transact his own business as the average white man, shall be given full control of his property and have all his lands and moneys turned over to him, after which he will no longer be a ward of the Government . . . *Patents in fee.* — To all able-bodied adult Indians of less than one-half Indian blood, there will be given as far as may be under the law full and complete control of all their property. Patents in fee shall be issued to all adult Indians of one-half or more Indian blood who may, after careful investigation, be found competent, provided, that where deemed advisable patents in fee shall be withheld for not to exceed 40 acres as a home. (quoted in F. Cohen 1940, 25)

Sells initiated federal commissions to review the field agents' evaluations of Native competency. The agents were required to supply, along with their determinations, "a list of all Indians of one-half or less Indian blood, who are able-bodied and mentally competent, twenty-one years of age or over, together with a description of land allotted to said Indians, and the number of the allotment. It is intended to issue patents in fee simple to such Indians" (quoted in F. Cohen 1940, 25–26). The field agent determinations and blood reports were to be used by the commissions in conclusively ascertaining who among Natives were "able-bodied and mentally competent" against those who were not.

The extent to which blood was directly applied in competency evaluations at the field and federal levels is impossible to determine. Instead, it is important to note that the BIA's regulations of competency and land title by blood marks the constitutive role of race in Native dispossession. The census rolls produced during the allotment period provided a federal record of tribal members' blood and lineality and served as the administrative venue for the institutionalization of the identification of tribal members by blood as a not-so-subtle proxy for race. These practices were deeply entrenched within scientific discourses and ideologies of cultural authenticity that definitively linked blood, biology, culture, and identity (Haraway 1989). Blood degree could be used because it was thought to be an adequate measure of culture and identity — of degrees from or to authenticity. Blood's institutionalization on the census rolls, then, served as the mechanism for the racialization of a culturally authentic, rights-invested "Indian member" whom both federal and tribal governments would claim jurisdictional power over.

Of course, nothing is ever simple. The rolls were immediately caught up in legal contestations over their legitimacy and accuracy. There was intense resistance within tribes to allotment and the statehood that invariably followed. Many refused to be registered (enrolled), give up their names or the names of their families, provide personal information, or accept the patent certificates they received in the mail following the closure of the rolls (Debo 1940; Perdue 1981; Harring 1994). Further, federal officials were often grossly ignorant of tribal languages and social politics and so accepted information about individuals on the word of others, some of whom spoke from the context of intense family and interpersonal conflicts, providing false or incomplete information. This was evident in the fact that the rolls were replete with errors of every kind imaginable: from mistakes in the spellings of individual names to records of siblings with different blood degrees, to falsifying degrees and other information when unknown, to including nontribal people. Many were omitted from the rolls by fault, intention, or absence of documentation. Despite these issues, Congress passed two pieces of legislation in 1906 and 1908 that made the rolls produced by the controversial Dawes Commission in Indian Territory, and by implication everywhere else, "conclusive evidence" of tribal identity and lineality: "The rolls of citizenship . . . shall be conclusive evidence as to the quantum of Indian blood of any enrolled citizenship . . . and for all purposes the quantum of Indian blood possessed by any member of said tribes shall be determined by the rolls of citizens of said tribes approved by the Secretary of the Interior" (quoted in Bledsoe 1909, 75).

In addition to securing the land titles and leases that were issued on their basis, the legal validation of the rolls made them the baseline document within federal and tribal policy for determining tribal identity and descent (Goldberg-Ambrose 2002b). For tribes that did not go through allotment, related rolls produced either during the same period or shortly thereafter were treated likewise. It was thus possible to use the rolls to determine the legitimacy of membership claims and individual rights to participate in tribal governance and property.

Quickly, being enrolled and being able to document descent to someone on the rolls became the only mechanism within federal and tribal law by which individuals qualified for tribal membership status and rights (and were so counted by tribes when applying for federal funds that were dependent on population totals). These conditions tacitly perpetuated the racialization of tribal membership through the discourses and ideologies of cultural authenticity that served as the condition on which enrollment was determined. They defied the political contexts informing the production of the rolls, the use of the rolls in tribal dispossession, and the fact that tribes did not have an administrative history of keeping and preserving written documents like certificates of birth, marriage, and death that were required after the rolls closed. This forced Native people born after the rolls were closed—for instance, in Indian Territory in 1906—to go to federal, state, and local government offices and churches to secure documentation of their lineality. For those who could not do so—for whatever reason—they and their descendants were granted neither legal status nor rights in their tribes.[9] But then, that was the point.

The utility of the rolls in administering federal policy led to the BIA's establishment of the Certificate of Degree of Indian Blood, or CDIB, during the allotment period. (After the passage of the Alaskan Native Claims Settlement Act of 1971 and its extension of tribal status to Alaskan Native villages, the CDIB was renamed the Certificate of Degree of American Indian/Alaskan Native Blood.) Until the decision in *Santa Clara Pueblo et al. v. Martinez et al.* (1978), examined in chapter 4, an individual had to possess 25 percent Indian blood and be enrolled with a federally recognized tribe in order to register with the BIA and be issued a CDIB (the 25-percent blood requirement was set likewise for membership in Alaska Native villages by the 1971 act). The CDIB was required by federal and even some tribal agencies for proof of membership or for qualifications for services that are restricted to enrolled members, sometimes on the basis of blood degree, as with the Indian Health Service requirement of 25 percent. After 1978, the BIA has issued CDIBs irrespective of but maintaining the record of blood and lineality to all enrolled members of federally recognized tribes.

As discussed in chapter 1, these processes paralleled congressional actions for Native Hawaiians. The Hawaiian Homes Commission Act of 1920 promised to "rehabilitate" Native Hawaiians through renewed land tenure. As J. Kēhaulani Kauanui shows in *Hawaiian Blood* (2008), however, federal authorities introduced a 50 percent blood degree requirement not to facilitate Native Hawaiian "rehabilitation" but to undermine Hawaiians' legal claims to sovereignty and land. The assumption was that Native Hawaiians who qualified for membership would eventually "dilute" themselves into the U.S. mainstream by the natural and inevitable consequences of their cultural assimilation and social evolution. This anticipation was perpetuated by the Indian Reorganization Act of 1934, which included membership or a 50 percent blood degree for nonmember "Indians" to be considered "Indians" under the statute. In each instance, blood anticipated the inevitable "dilution" of Native populations by next-generation disqualification.

All of these processes were made all the more powerful by the constitutive role of gender and sexuality in federal rationalizations of its associated colonial and imperial efforts at Native dispossession, anticipating with sober resolve what was being left behind (the heathenism of Native gender roles and sexual identities) for what was being obtained (the promise of salvation, citizenship, and economic opportunity). In other words, the eventual "dilution" of Native populations by blood, and so of culture and identity, was anticipated as a good thing for Natives. The "dilution" would mean their progress.

The Reconstituted Indian

Congress passed the Indian Citizenship Act in 1924 as a way to "clean up" the administrative mess of allotment, which had tied citizenship to fee title, under the guise of awarding American Indians for their patriotism and service during World War I. The 1924 act extended citizenship to all "noncitizen Indians born within the territorial limits of the United States" irrespective of land title. It also made explicit that citizenship did not negate tribal membership: "That the granting of such citizenship shall not in any manner impair or otherwise affect the right of any Indian to tribal or other property."[10] These provisions continued, in other words, the fusion of tribal membership to tribal property rights and shares, all of which was made entirely contingent on the information of blood and lineality instituted on the census rolls.[11]

In between the General Allotment Act of 1887 and the Indian Reorganization Act (IRA) of 1934, which suspended allotment policy, tribal agreements to allot were developed in such a way as to encourage tribes to establish strict membership criteria so as to adequately restrict access to tribal lands and assets. These criteria, however, were not to be determined through Native customary governance practices or epistemologies of belonging, affiliation, and kinship (see Wilkins 2004; Kauanui 2008). These diverse customs and epistemologies would have required the re-centering of Native expertise in their development and administration. Instead, membership was standardized by the racialized criteria of blood quantum in the interests of federal objectives for Native government dissolution and land dispossession.

As said, within national narrations, blood was considered to be an objective measure of Native cultural authenticity and so legal legitimacy. It certainly proved a more expeditious means to deciding legal legitimacy than the complexities posed by Native customs and epistemologies—which offered alternative perspectives on belonging and kinship that would have included a generosity regarding intermarriage, adoption, and naturalization as well as alternative understandings of belonging and kinship that would have tied members back to their lands and governments as citizens with multiple kinds of responsibilities (LaDuke 1999; Kauanui 2008; Nelson 2008). Instead, the criteria reinforced racist ideologies of Native identity that served to warrant and necessitate Native land dispossession.

After allotment policy was suspended by the IRA in 1934, tribal membership criteria were reestablished in tribal constitutions developed under the IRA and again outside of and following the IRA (Deloria and Lytle 1984; Goldberg-Ambrose 2002b). Developed by John Collier, BIA commissioner, the IRA was borne of harsh congressional and public criticisms of the BIA and federal policy that were seen to have resulted in profound levels of social disparity for tribal people. The IRA had a stated purpose of reinvigorating tribal self-government through economic development and land reacquisition.[12] It allowed tribes the opportunity of reacquiring unallotted lands, established reservation schools, affirmed cultural rights to self-determination (particularly in language and the arts), and provided programs and grants to rebuild social infrastructures including administration, court systems, small business loans, and housing (Deloria and Lytle 1984; see Prindeville 2004, 102–3).[13]

In order to qualify for IRA programs and funds, tribes had to hold elections by 1936 and vote in favor of "reorganizing" themselves under the IRA. If accepted, they had to establish a constitution and by-laws defining the operations of their government that, once approved by the DOI, qualified the tribes to apply for the programs and funds the IRA reserved.

However, two restrictions applied regarding membership and governance which would have severe consequences to the kinds of membership criteria that were instituted by tribes during this time. First, the IRA restricted dual membership in tribes on the grounds that federal services and funding were provided to tribes on the basis of their total population. This restriction meant that tribes had to guard against dual membership within their criteria. This had important consequences in tribal prohibitions against such customary practices as considering to be members (by adoption or naturalization) those Native people who "married into" the tribe as well as their children (as discussed more fully in chapter 4). Second, only one tribal government could be constituted on a reservation, and that government had to conform to the particular electoral model provided within the IRA. A number of issues were raised by this restriction.

For those tribes who had been relocated together on a single reservation, they had to reorganize themselves under a single government with a single constitution and by-laws (such as the Alabama and Coushatta Tribes of Texas, the Cheyenne-Arapaho Tribes of Oklahoma, and the Three Affiliated Tribes of the Fort Berthold Reservation in North Dakota). Tribes were very critical of this restriction because of the impact it had on their different customary governance structures and cultural practices for determining leadership. Further, tribes expressed frustration with the way the model constitutions and by-laws forced them to operate essentially as business entities that could administrate federal programs and funds.

Overwhelmingly, tribes expressed that they did not feel the IRA treated them as truly self-governing polities, recognized their treaty and land rights, or allowed them to establish forms of government that reflected the uniqueness and diversity of their cultural perspectives and customary legal practices.[14] This all became particularly troubling for women and "third gender," "two spirit" people. Customary forms of government included such practices as decision making by consensus, a sometimes lengthy and complicated process but one that empowered women's and men's councils by obligating them to work together toward a decision for the good of the entire community (Lyons et al. 1992). Government structures also included practices by which women's councils could elect or remove leaders or members of men's councils, and vice versa, given the gravity of concerns about the integrity and honor of the individual in question (Albers and Medicine 1983; Perdue 1999; Mann 2000). In many cultures, women and men were also able to assume the role of the other — or even another gender altogether — and be an acknowledged participant in the political processes represented by the council system (Roscoe 1989; Jacobs, Thomas, and Long 1997). While all of these practices were no doubt very thorny within the context of family and interpersonal politics, they were based on the belief that women and men were both important, equal though different participants in tribal governance and society.

In the end, the IRA governments and those that followed suit standardized an institutional structure and procedure that ran counter to Native cultural perspectives and customary practices (Deloria and Lytle 1984). This included an electoral process for decision making and the selection of leadership that negated the customary roles of the council systems and so the full and equal participatory roles of women and "third gender," "two spirit" people within tribal governance. The electoral system made it difficult for tribal governments to be conducted in a way that reflected not merely the process but the cultural values that informed those processes and in which women and "third gender," "two spirit" people were empowered participants. The electoral process became a powerful venue for the articulation of sexism and homophobia in tribal communities, immediately evidenced by the fact that women were marginalized by the votes: "As late as 1990, the U.S. Department of the Interior, Bureau of Indian Affairs, reported that there were only 61 female tribal leaders for more than 500 tribes" (Prindeville 2004, 111). Additionally, no provision was ever made for "third gender," "two spirit" people to participate as nonheterosexually identified individuals in elected tribal leadership.

The membership criteria that were developed within and after the IRA were filtered almost entirely by the rolls—and so by blood quantum—as produced during the allotment period. While some criteria allowed for customary forms of membership (such as adoption and naturalization), they ultimately reserved a membership that anticipated the norms of U.S. property rights—privileging those of blood, men, and the heterosexually identified to the callous exclusion of those of mixed descent, women, and the non-heterosexually identified.

Conclusions

Those tribes who have amended their constitutions or established new ones since the IRA period have continued to use the rolls or censuses and blood quantum in particular as the filter through which the "Indian member" is settled (Goldberg-Ambrose 2002b; Yellow Bird 2005). Because of the definitive link of legal legitimacy and cultural authenticity, this eligibility judges in harsh and unforgiving ways the culture and identity of the unenrolled, exasperated by the fact that several tribes now include DNA testing in their membership criteria (Tallbear 2003). This has had the consequence of racializing membership status and rights *within tribal law and governance practices*. In turn, it racializes the kinds of tribal sovereignty, self-government, and cultural tradition that membership criteria are asserted by tribal governments to embody and reflect.

In other words, the "Indian member" that results from these articulations is not merely one who results from a racist system of identification imposed by the United States on tribes as part of its colonial and imperial aims for Native dispossession. While that is certainly true, it is also true that the "Indian member" has always been co-constituted by tribal law. Since the *Martinez* decision by the U.S. Supreme Court in 1978 (analyzed in chapter 4), tribal jurisdiction over membership has been affirmed as an expression and protection of tribal sovereignty, self-government, and cultural tradition. Tribes now possess the absolute rights for amending membership criteria toward affirming their own unique cultural epistemologies and practices for determining belonging, affiliation, and kinship. While this may be a desired affirmation of tribal sovereignty and self-government, too many tribal officials and members have shored up the legal status and rights of the "Indian member" to protect and secure their own entitlements and reputations to the exclusion of others they racialize as culturally inauthentic (discussed more fully in chapter 5). Consequently, as simultaneously embedded within the sexist and homophobic anticipations of the assimilation and evolution of Native peoples to patriarchal, compulsory heterosexual, religiously conservative, and capitalist norms, the "Indian member" enacts a complex series of discriminations and disenfranchisements based on racist, sexist, and homophobic practices from within.

4 In *Martinez v. Santa Clara* (and Vice Versa)

The Indian Civil Rights Act (ICRA) of 1968 was driven by congressional hearings in which tribal members and nonmember Natives on reservations reported abusive exercises of power by tribal officials (including those in government, courts, and police departments).[1] Amending the Indian Reorganization Act (IRA) of 1934, the ICRA applied to all tribes irrespective of whether or not they had "reorganized" under the provisions of the IRA. It required tribes to conform their governments, courts, and police actions to the principles of the U.S. Bill of Rights regarding the rights of all Native people to free speech, religious freedom, due process, double jeopardy, self-incrimination, just compensation, speedy and just trials, fair sentencing, equal protection, and habeas corpus review.[2] It was amended in 1986 to increase the fines and prison terms that tribes could impose at sentencing, and in 1991 to overturn the U.S. Supreme Court's decision in *Duro v. Reina* challenging tribal jurisdiction over nonmember Natives on reservation lands. The first complaint to go before the Supreme Court under the provisions of the ICRA was in 1978.

In 1975, Julia Martinez and her daughter Audrey filed a civil complaint against the Santa Clara Pueblo in the District Court of New Mexico (*Martinez & Martinez v. Romney, Santa Clara Pueblo, & Tafoya*).[3] They claimed — on behalf of those similarly situated at the reservation—that the Santa Clara Pueblo Membership Ordinance of 1939 discriminated membership in the pueblo against women who married nonmembers, but not against men who married nonmembers, and that this gendered difference violated their equal protection rights.[4] Originally, the lawsuit also named George Romney, the secretary of the Department of Housing and Urban Development. The department had approved a housing project on the reservation; the Santa Clara Pueblo Council set qualifications for the new homes and their beneficiaries against women who had married nonmembers and their children but not against men who had married nonmembers and their children. These restrictions were amended in the pretrial period to allow the women to be issued homes (Julia Martinez's application had been originally denied but was then approved). However, the restriction remained that the women could not name nonmembers, including their children and husbands, as beneficiaries. Still, that aspect of the complaint was dropped before the trial. Originally, the lawsuit also named Paul Tafoya, governor of the Santa Clara Pueblo. It claimed that he and other tribal officials and their families were given special privileges. But before the pretrial period that aspect of the complaint was dropped. What went forward, then, was solely the complaint about the discrimination of membership status and rights against the children and husbands of women who married nonmembers.

In *Santa Clara Pueblo et al v. Martinez et al* (1978), the U.S. Supreme Court ruled that the ICRA required tribal governments to adhere to its civil rights protections. However, the court also found that Congress had not extended federal jurisdiction over resulting complaints except in habeas corpus procedures. It claimed that this was owing to two reasons. First, Congress had recognized by the IRA and the ICRA that tribes possessed sovereign immunity. Second, tribes were best suited to evaluate the "internal matters" of civil issues like membership as not only an aspect of tribal self-government protected by the ICRA and the IRA but because they were charged with the responsibility of protecting and preserving the unique cultural traditions on which tribal governments and laws were based. Ac-

cordingly, the Martinez complaint was remanded back to the tribe for review where it was summarily dismissed. The Ordinance remains unchanged
today.

The literature that has addressed the importance of the *Martinez* decision
is exhaustive.[5] For my purposes, it seems important to mark a couple of the
many kinds of assumptions and inquiries that have characterized it.[6] The
purpose is to understand the way that the literature has and has not considered the co-constitutive relationship between Native legal status and rights
and Native culture and identity, particularly as that relationship is articulated through notions of authenticity. This chapter will then provide a brief
historical contextualization of Pueblo cosmology and land rights struggles
before turning to a close reading of the district court trial transcripts and
the three court decisions. My intent is to show how the righted, propertied
"Indian member," disarticulated by the Santa Clara Pueblo Council from
the children and husbands of women who married nonmembers, are rearticulated by Santa Clara people to assert a particularly authentic culture
and identity and so legal legitimacy as Santa Claran. This work has grave
ethical implications to the kinds of social and interpersonal relationships
and responsibilities that Santa Clara people seek to (un)make with one
another as "Indian members."

The literature on *Martinez*, particularly within Native studies, has overwhelmingly assumed the legal righteousness of the Supreme Court's finding for tribal self-government and sovereign immunity. This assumption
has affected inquiries of many kinds into the implications of the *Martinez*
decision. A great deal of effort is made in reconciling tribal sovereignty
with the Santa Clara Pueblo's gendered discrimination of membership
status and rights. Many, tendered primarily from feminist scholarship, have
wondered why, assuming that the Santa Clara are a traditionally matrilineal and matrilocal society, the council would have chosen in 1939 to reverse
the tribe's traditions and institute a decidedly patrilineal—read patriarchal—membership requirement.[7] Advancing a strong argument for Native
women's right to equal treatment under tribal law, several have examined
the ideological differences between sovereignty and civil rights (Guerrero
1997), the primacy of sovereignty in Native women's political concerns and
efforts (R. Green 1980; Shanley 1984), the need for tribal governance to be

more accountable to civil and human rights principles (MacKinnon 1987), and the challenges of reconciling tribal governance with dominant notions of democracy and liberalism (Riley 2007).

Other types of inquiries follow from the first. Given the perceived gravity of the Santa Clara's choice to reverse their matrilineal traditions, the concerns go to the reasons for it. For example, Gloria Valencia-Weber (2004) argues that

> the Pueblos' long historical struggle to retain its land, the source of culture and identity, has not been included in the available analysis of why the Santa Clara Pueblo passed its ordinance. . . . The critical value of land, not as property but for cultural continuity, was not acknowledged in the three *Martinez* decisions. It does not appear in the law literature surrounding the case. Through the three "foreign" sovereigns in New Mexico—Spring in the 16th century, then Mexico in 1821, and the U.S. in 1846–1848—all the pueblos had to resist outsiders' schemes to obtain Pueblo lands. These schemes included marriage with Pueblo women; unconsented occupancy by outsiders led to adverse possession claims, enabled by the 1924 Pueblo Lands Act; counterfeit documents; and other forms of trickery allowed outsiders to extract fee simple pieces of land. The Santa Clara struggle clearly affected how it structured its membership laws. . . . Outsiders who critique the Santa Clara people and their laws should at least appreciate how the losses of land as a threat to culture have animated the Pueblo's choices. (56–57)

Out of respect for tribal sovereignty, many scholars such as Valencia-Weber refuse to make too-quick judgments of the Santa Clara Pueblo's Ordinance as a clear example of sexist or patriarchal ideologies and instead insist on its location within Pueblo struggles for sovereignty and territorial rights. But while acknowledging the need for a careful historical contextualization of the Ordinance within Pueblo cultural perspectives and land rights struggles, the literature has failed to actually provide this context, continually differing because of their complexity.

As a result of these deferrals, the Ordinance becomes a kind of tragic departure from the true cultural values of the tribe; its profound and even mysterious importance is its radical opposition against further land dispossession that only the Santa Clara Pueblo can truly understand. So, in the same instance that the Santa Clara are narrated as having lost or compromised their matrilineal traditions by a patrilineal criterion, they are reclaimed as having justly protected and preserved their traditions against further loss as an exercise of their sovereignty. The Supreme Court is represented as having done the right thing by deferring the serious questions of membership to the cultural knowledge that tribal officials have of their traditions and what they need to do to protect them (Berger 2006). The contradictions within these claims are continually deferred—it never seems to matter which "traditions" the Santa Clara are protecting or what kind of sovereignty they assert and the court affirms.

What is so compelling about the *Martinez* decision in understanding the articulatory politics of Native legal legitimacy (sovereignty) and cultural authenticity (membership) within these kinds of narrations is the way that the Supreme Court's verdict actually facilitated the recovery of a Santa Clara legitimacy and authenticity by suppressing matrilineality and matrilocality for patrilineality, patrilocality, and patriculturality. In other words, the Supreme Court accepted and advanced as legally legitimate and culturally authentic a tribal sovereignty that was male-centric, and it then resituated matrilineality as an "outside" feminist ethos imposed on the tribe by women's righters. *Martinez*, then, reinforced a definitive link between a heteronormative patriarchal culture to a legitimate sovereignty for tribal governments, rendering all other cultural forms of gender (and sexuality) inauthentic and illegitimate.[8]

Historical Contextualizations: Cosmology and Land

Each of the three colonial-imperial regimes that sought to subjugate Pueblo peoples—Spain (from the 1600s to 1821), Mexico (1821 to 1848), and the United States (1848 to the present)—shared characteristics of military aggression, economic exploitation, and missionization programs aimed at seizing Pueblo lands, controlling Pueblo alliances and trade, and taking over Pueblo social and cultural norms. These efforts involved physical and sexual violence, enslavement, and land fraud and dispossession, resulting in the staggering loss of life among the Pueblo and a fairly significant loss of territories and resources that became engulfed by the jurisdictions and borders of the United States in 1848. It also resulted in complex and uneven patterns of forced cultural change and transformation. These difficult issues are examined by Alfonso Ortiz in *The Tewa World: Space, Time, Being, and Becoming in a Pueblo Society* (1969).

A San Juan Pueblo, Ortiz provided a critical intervention with *The Tewa World* into the established scholarship on Pueblo worldviews and social organization. This intervention got him into trouble with some Pueblo for revealing too much of their religious teachings to outsiders,[9] but it also earned him much regard from many Pueblo and anthropologists.

In *The Tewa World*, Ortiz rejected the theoretical work of his predecessors within anthropology, notably Claude Lévi-Strauss and David Maybury-Lewis, to argue for the viability of dualisms between religious ritual and social organization. In order to make this argument, Ortiz had to "correct" much within the existing scholarship on Pueblo culture, particularly the works of John Peabody Harrington, Elsie Clews Parsons, and Florence Hawley Ellis.[10] While drawing from their respective descriptions of religious rituals and social structures, Ortiz was sharply critical of the way that their interpretations forced Pueblo beliefs and societies to conform to the terms of European and North American anthropology and archaeology. This, he found, too often paid attention to only one "side" of the dualisms (namely the human at the expense of the spiritual) and so assumed a stability, lineality, and structural permanence where there was dynamic and flexible interchange.

Ortiz begins *The Tewa World* with a skeletal outline of Tewa creation stories and tells how the two main divisions or moieties—Winter and Summer—are related and organize all resulting relationships, rituals, prayers, songs, and cultural symbols (13–28). Next, he defines the six categories—three human and three spiritual—"into which the Tewa classify all existence" (121). He shows how each of the categories are divided first into two parts (Winter and Summer) and then linked into three pairs—"that is to say, the spiritual categories represent counterparts of the human categories, and at death ... each human category becomes a spirit of its linked supernatural category" (121–22). "The supernatural categories are identified with three tetrads into which the Tewa divide the natural world" (122). Those spirits "who are the ancestral souls of the common Tewa dwell at the four shrines that are located outside the village, one in each cardinal direction" (122). Those spirits who are "counterparts of Tewa political officials dwell at earth navels which are located on the top of four sacred hills and four sacred mountains, also of the cardinal directions" (122). These four mountains represent the outer boundaries of the Tewa world "while the hills are located about midway between the mountains and the village" (122). The spirits who are the highest deities dwell in the lakes located near the four sacred mountains (122).

Ortiz then analyzes the six rites of passage that the Tewa undergo from birth to death. First is the naming ceremony at which time the child passes from the spirit world into the community as a whole (122). Second to fourth are the water giving, water pouring, and finishing ceremonies at which time the individual is recruited and initiated into either the Winter or Summer people, following no particular rules of descent but conforming to various cultural norms about maintaining the equality between the two divisions (123–24, 130). Ortiz is careful to observe that individuals have the option of changing their moiety by going again through the three requisite ceremonies of initiation. Fifth is the rite of marriage at which time a wife is initiated into her husband's division if it is not the same as her own but which otherwise serves to solidify ritual roles and responsibilities of the married couple (123). And sixth is the rite of releasing or death, at which time a person passes from the entire group back to the spirit world (123–24).

Ortiz marks several specific rituals within these rites of passage and related social practices that have been either entirely or partially derived from Spanish Catholic tradition. This includes such diverse matters as the imposition of social controls, a unilineal reckoning of descent and moiety membership (130), and norms for marrying out of the tribe (130). Several specific Tewa ceremonies also supplement Catholic rituals—from baptism to marriage to death—or are complete substitutions of Catholic rituals for Tewa ones (46–49, 50–52). Despite these influences, Ortiz maintains that the Tewa have been able to negotiate the relevance, vitality, and adaptability of their rituals and social relations.

For this study, two issues are important about Ortiz's work. First, while not directly about kinship, *The Tewa World* reflects a much more nuanced system in Pueblo reckoning of identity, kinship, and social responsibility than "matrilineality" or "patrilineality" can afford. In fact, something that characterizes the literature about Pueblo culture, including the Santa Clara, is that there is a great diversity of opinion about how lineality matters, ritually and socially. What I find particularly important about *The Tewa World* in relation to the *Martinez* case is that even though Ortiz identifies several moments within Pueblo rituals where women and men seem to be on un-equal footing—such as the rituals pertaining to moiety membership upon marriage—he does not use "patrilineality" or "patriarchy" to describe it (words that were readily available to him and used in other anthropological work on Pueblo culture). In fact, Ortiz completely rejects the notion that there is a unilineal reckoning of descent—either matrilineal or patrilineal—among the Pueblo and is critical of the way that existing anthropological work assumed its primacy.

Similarly, other anthropologists were not comfortable with describing Pueblo society through unilineal descent norms, most notably Edward P. Dozier, who was an adopted member of the Santa Clara Pueblo. In *The Pueblo Indians of North America* (1970), Dozier writes that while other Pueblo societies such as the Navajo and Hopi were "matrilineal," such an organization does not apply to the Tewa. Dozier insists that "bilateralism" is a better term because it allows for an understanding of the complex ways in which the Pueblo define a separate but reciprocal relationship between men and women within their cultural traditions. Dozier is critical of his predecessors, particularly Parsons and Ellis, who described the Tewa as patrilineal, patrilocal, patriarchal, or a combination of these.

Second, *The Tewa World* reflects a much more complex cosmology and epistemology than is afforded by the claims, particularly in the literature about *Martinez*, that the Pueblo hold "the land" to be sacred above all other things, therefore justifying and even necessitating that the Santa Clara forfeit their matrilineal and matrilocal customs to protect it. Ortiz demonstrates something else. While the land—and specific places—is certainly a central part of Pueblo worldviews and cultural practice, it can in no way be objectively reduced to or extrapolated from its interdependencies on other beings and realities.

Part of the challenge in understanding this concept of land is in dealing with how Pueblo territorial rights and cultural practices were bludgeoned through violent histories of colonialism and imperialism dating back to the early 1600s (Niezen 2000). By the 1920s "the land" had become a particular kind of political object within Pueblo opposition, alliance, and legal action. One instance of this is their land grant struggles.

Spain recognized the Pueblo's rights to self-government and territorial integrity by the issuance of twenty-two communal land grants to them, including the Pueblo of Jemez, Acoma, San Juan, Picuris, San Felipe, Pecos, Cochiti, Santo Domingo, Taos, Santa Clara, Tesuque, San Ildefonso, Pojoaque, Zia, Sandia, Isleta, Nambe, Santa Ana, and Zuni (F. Cohen 1940, 386). While the Pueblo were perceived to be "wards" under Spanish law (ibid., 383), the grants protected Pueblo jurisdiction and borders against settlement and secured Pueblo water and other natural resource rights within the granted borders (Brayer 1939).

The legal validity of the land grants was recognized by Mexico in a treaty with Spain in 1821 (F. Cohen 1940, 384–85). It was again recognized by the Treaty of Guadalupe Hidalgo and the Protocol of Querétaro of 1848 when Mexico ceded the territory to the United States (ibid., 385) and within the Gadsden Purchase agreement when the United States acquired additional lands from Mexico in the area (General Accounting Office [GAO] 2001b, 8–9).

In 1854, the United States established the Office of Surveyor General in New Mexico territory to evaluate land grant claims. The surveyor general required those to whom land grants had been issued—individuals, towns, tribes—to document the legitimacy of their claims. After review, the surveyor general recommended to Congress which grants should be considered legitimate. If approved, Congress directed the DOI to issue land patents in fee simple to the grantees (GAO 2001b, 9). In the end, the surveyor general reviewed 180 claims and Congress approved 64 of them. The surveyor general and Congress also reviewed and confirmed the twenty-two land grants issued to the Pueblo (ibid.).

But conflicts around land grants continued. As a result of public criticisms of the failure of the United States to honor the grants, Congress established the Court of Private Land Claims in 1891. The court operated until 1904 and arbitrated over 300 cases involving more than 36 million acres of land. It approved 155 additional grants and issued 142 land patents. However, these approvals represented only 6 percent, or three million acres, of the total acreage claimed (GAO 2001b, 11).[11]

Amid the controversies surrounding congressional recognition of the grants, Pueblo grants in particular were challenged in the courts and to Congress—sometimes with falsified documentation, sometimes in challenges of their validity, and sometimes in disputes over their boundaries. One of these challenges ended up before the U.S. Supreme Court in 1913, one year after New Mexico was granted statehood.

Julian Sandoval filed a petition in the Court of Private Land Claims for the confirmation of title to 315,300 acres in an area covered by the San Miguel del Bado Grant of 1794. The grant was issued by Governor Chacon to Lorenzo Marquez and fifty-one other men to form a settlement known as the Town of San Miguel del Bado. The descendants of Marquez, the fifty-one men, and other settlers of the town claimed to have held the land in common under the terms of the grant. Their claim was upheld by the Court of Private Land Claims. The United States appealed. In *U.S. v. Sandoval* (1913), the Supreme Court ruled that Mexico and not the local community held the title because it was ceded to the United States in the Treaty of Guadalupe Hidalgo. In other words, following the logic of *Johnson v. M'Intosh* (1823), the court ruled that Mexico was the sovereign over the lands in question and that it had ceded that title to the United States in the treaty of 1848. This title superseded all "communal" land grant claims.

The decision threw all land grants into question and fueled efforts within New Mexico to go after Pueblo lands (F. Cohen 1940, 389–90; GAO 2001b, 11). In 1922, Senator Holm Bursum (a Republican) from New Mexico introduced legislation that would have greatly reduced Pueblo landholdings by reestablishing their boundaries in light of non-Pueblo grant claims. The bill would also have impacted Pueblo water rights and religious freedom outside of grant borders. Nineteen Pueblo, however, responded quickly by establishing the All Indian Pueblo Council (AIPC). Successfully mobilizing protest from around the country and lobbying in Washington, D.C., the AIPC was able to defeat the bill.

In its stead, the AIPC lobbied legislation with the help of the Indian Rights Association, a group founded by John Collier in Washington before his term as assistant secretary of the BIA. The result was a much-compromised Pueblo Lands Act of 1924 (amended in 1933 and 2005). The act established the Pueblo Lands Board (PLB), composed of the secretary of the interior, the attorney general, and a third member appointed by the president of the United States. Its commission was to award compensation to the Pueblo for lost lands and to settle non-Pueblo claims to Pueblo lands. But much to the disappointment of the AIPC, the PLB approved almost 80 percent of non-Pueblo claims (F. Cohen 1940, 390–91; Briggs, Briggs, and Van Ness 1987; Klein 1996; Lorenzo 2005).

Pueblo land dispossession continued well after the 1920s. Significant sites within Pueblo cosmology were heavily restricted or transferred completely outside of Pueblo jurisdiction. The frustrations of the Pueblo were exasperated by the denial of their voting rights in New Mexico, Arizona, and Utah: "These states claimed that since Indian tribes and reservations were subject to federal jurisdiction, Indians were not citizens of the state and, therefore, were not eligible to vote in state and local elections. It was not until 1948, after lengthy litigation, that Indians finally won the franchise within these states" (Prindeville 2004, 102).

Given hundreds of years of efforts by Spain, Mexico, and the United States to dispossess the Pueblo of their lands, it is understandable how "the land" would become a unique kind of political object within Pueblo opposition, alliances, and legal efforts. It is also understandable that each Pueblo would have cultivated their own strategies to prevent further land loss, strategies that would have functioned within many different kinds of sociopolitical divisions within the pueblo. These strategies would have been a part of a shared or competing set of perspectives about what or who was responsible for the continued loss of territorial rights as well as perspectives about the significance of cultural change.

This is not the same thing as saying that Pueblo cosmology is all about "the land." As Ortiz's *The Tewa World* demonstrates, the land was not such an object within Pueblo cosmology, defined in relation to collective rights. It was seen to be interconnected and interdependent with the life of other places, beings, and realities.

What I find especially important about the *Martinez* decision and the literature that has followed it is its tacit acceptance of a notion that the land meant all things to the Santa Clara Pueblo, so much so, or in such a way, that it warranted and necessitated the council's complete reversal of the matrilineal and matrilocal customs in order to protect it. The assumptions being that the women who married nonmembers were complicit with the loss of territorial rights and culture, specifically that they were marrying "white" men, including Spanish and Mexicans by legal definition, who were then appropriating Pueblo lands for themselves (Berger 1997, 2004). And, that all of this loss was happening in a drastically different, proportional way than what was happening when men married nonmembers. The incongruities in the arguments—i.e., more men than women were marrying nonmembers, and there was much intermarriage of both men and women with other Natives—remain continually deferred to the mysterious importance of the land in Pueblo culture.

The Ordinance

In 1935, the Santa Clara Pueblo ratified their Constitution and By-Laws to "reorganize" themselves under the provisions of the IRA. The purpose of the Constitution was to "establish justice, promote the common welfare and preserve the advantages of self-government" for its members. It was approved by John Collier, the assistant secretary of the BIA, and by Harold L. Ickes, the secretary of the interior, on December 20, 1935. Article II concerned the tribe's requirements for membership.

> Section 1 (a) All persons of Indian blood whose names appear on the census roll of the Santa Clara pueblo as of November 1, 1935, provided that within one year from the adoption and approval of this constitution corrections may be made in the said roll by the pueblo council with the approval of the Secretary of the Interior. (b) All persons born of parents both of whom are members of the Santa Clara pueblo. (c) All children of mixed marriages between members of the Santa Clara pueblo and nonmembers, provided such children have been recognized and adopted by the council. (d) All persons naturalized as members of the pueblo.
>
> Section 2 Indians from other pueblos or reservations who marry a member of Santa Clara pueblo may become members of the pueblo, with the assent of the council, by naturalization. To do this they must (1) go before the pueblo council and renounce allegiance to their tribe and declare intention of becoming members of the Santa Clara pueblo. They shall swear that from that date on they will not receive any benefits from their people, except through inheritance. (2) A year later they shall go before the pueblo council again, swear allegiance to the pueblo of Santa Clara and receive membership papers; provided, they have kept their promise from the time of their first appearance before the pueblo council.

The Ordinance of 1939 amended Article II of the Constitution as follows:

> 1. All children born of marriages between members of the Santa Clara Pueblo shall be members of the Santa Clara Pueblo. 2. . . . . [C]hildren born of marriages between male members of the Santa Clara Pueblo and non-members shall be members of the Santa Clara Pueblo. 3. Chil-

dren born of marriages between female members of the Santa Clara
Pueblo and non-members shall not be members of the Santa Clara
Pueblo. 4. Persons shall not be naturalized as members of the Santa
Clara Pueblo under any circumstances. (footnoted in *Santa Clara Pueblo
et al. v. Martinez et al.* 1978)

The council restricted new memberships to "children born of marriages between members of the Santa Clara Pueblo" and "between male members of
the Santa Clara Pueblo and non-members." Children born to women who
were members but who married nonmembers did not qualify for membership, and children born to unmarried women did not qualify for membership. The Ordinance barred naturalization "under any circumstances."

During the District Court trial in 1975, several questions were addressed
to current and former council members who testified for the defense that
the tribe's Constitution and Ordinance reflected the cultural traditions and
teachings of the tribe. They said that they had been taught the tribe's traditions by their elder male relatives and that the Constitution and Ordinance
conformed to those teachings except in two areas. First was in regard to the
establishment of elections for council officials. Traditionally, the selection
of officials was conducted by the leaders of the Winter and Summer People.
They were not "voted upon" by the general membership. Second was in
regard to the institutionalization of council offices for the representatives
of the Winter and Summer People. Traditionally, the representatives were
considered cultural leaders who operated "behind the scenes" of the political life of the tribe.

Various reasons were given at trial for these changes. One was that the
separation of secular and religious leadership was owing to Spanish influence. The military and church had imposed a hierarchy on the Pueblo —
secular offices above religious ones — in efforts to negotiate with the Pueblo
over their lands and resources and to undermine the authority of Pueblo
religious leaders and teachings. Another reason was internal factionalism, wherein two subdivisions within the Winter and Summer People had
emerged along "progressive" and "conservative" lines. The attempt was to
provide for the representation of these factions on the tribe's council.[12]

While these and other changes within the Pueblo were addressed at the
trial, no attention at all was given to the specific differences in the requirements for membership within the Constitution and the Ordinance. This

was in spite of the fact that each defense witness asserted that they both reflected the traditions of the tribe.

Judith Resnik (1999) argues that the DOI applied severe pressure on the Santa Clara Pueblo to conform their Constitution and membership requirements to the "boilerplate provisions" it supplied. She argues that the DOI sought restrictive membership requirements because membership was tied to federal services and, therefore, dollars. But it was the council that chose to change its membership criteria. In fact, during trial testimony no mention was made at all of federal officials having anything to do with the passage of the Ordinance.

Instead, former and current council members testified that the Ordinance was passed for two reasons. First, its restrictions reflected the tribe's traditional beliefs and teachings about patrilineal descent and male authority. Second, the council was concerned about its ability to support the current membership given the tribe's limited assets.[13] The council even considered requiring a fee from new members to help support operations and other infrastructure expenses. Connecting the two, current council officials testified that their predecessors had decided that the best way to limit new memberships was to limit it to those children whose fathers were members.[14] This was not only in line with the traditional teachings of the tribe but it was a good option because the children of the women who married out would not be taught the traditions by their nonmember fathers, or they would move away to live in their fathers' communities.

All this did little more than raise questions about the differences within the Constitution and Ordinance that would go unaddressed at trial or in any of the three court opinions. Was it customary to determine membership by the marriage status of one's parents? Was it traditional to restrict membership differently for men and for women based on marriage? Was naturalization considered traditional—or not? If marriage and patrilineal descent were such central features of the traditional teachings and practices of the tribe, why were they not included already in the Constitution of 1935?

The literature examining Pueblo history and culture has placed the lines all over the proverbial map, marking the boundaries around what counts for Pueblo traditional culture and what counts for the norms, identities, and practices of the dominant cultures of Spain, Mexico, and the United States. Depending on where the lines are placed, the Pueblo are either described as traditionally matrilineal, bilateral, or patrilineal—as the result of their own traditions or those imposed by a colonial nation-state (Parsons 1939; Ellis 1951, 1967; Ortiz 1969; Dozier 1970). In almost all accounts, the Pueblo are described as having been acculturated to the heteronormative ideologies of colonialism and patriarchy. Pueblo women, once powerful and respected figures, are described as having been irrevocably disenfranchised and dispossessed under structures of domination that have taken Pueblo lands and resources, transformed Pueblo society from being agriculturally based to wage-earning, and imposed social hierarchies subordinating women to men (Jacobs 1995). In some accounts, Pueblo women are described as occupying a place—secretly—where they retain matrilineal or some other kind of women-centered or feminist sensibility (Prindeville 2004).

Putting on hold for a bit these kinds of cultural mappings, it is important to mark the way that the Santa Clara Pueblo Council represented its perspectives, experiences, and concerns at trial. As noted above and discussed more fully in the review of the testimony below, council members contended that the Ordinance reflected the cultural traditions and teachings of the tribe, which they named explicitly as patrilineal, patrilocal, and patricultural and asserted as necessary to the tribe's very survival.

These categories and the larger narratives that they called upon were never countered by the plaintiffs. Neither attorneys nor witnesses for the Martinez women insisted that there were any other cultural perspectives and values defining the gender roles of the Santa Clara Pueblo. Instead, they focused on their experiences of discrimination as owing to the fact that they had married nonmembers or were the children of mothers who had. While on point of the complaint, the absence of a counternarrative rendered the discriminatory policies and actions of the council practically mute in the face of cultural authenticity. The result would be a lingering question—sometimes explicit—about the cultural authenticity and so legal legitimacy of Martinez and her children, and so of all of those similarly situated at the Pueblo.

To return to the cultural mappings, how they are drawn depends on the conclusions that result about the *Martinez* case. Scholars who believe that the Pueblo were forced to acculturate from a once matrilineal or bilateral society to a patriarchal one have concluded that the Pueblo punished women for marrying nonmembers by treating their husbands and children as irrelevant to the life of the tribe — carrying on a second or even third line of discrimination against them as a reflection of ideologies of patriarchy and sexism (MacKinnon 1987; Christofferson 1991; Guerrero 1997). Scholars who believe that the Pueblo were patrilineal all along have contended that the council merely made explicit an ideology governing tribal culture that has been grossly misunderstood by outsiders.

The point here is not to get at the "truth" about Pueblo traditions. It is to think through the ways that Pueblo culture has been articulated within the context of the case and to what political ends. As Louis Owens argues so powerfully in *Mixedblood Messages* (1998), meaningful understandings of Native culture have been undermined by colonial, racist, and assimilationist ideologies that pretend all cultural change and transformation are tragic and that all mixes are anti-Indian and anti-sovereignty. He finds the challenge is to respect the difficult choices Native peoples have had to make in the impossible political situations they have had to confront as a direct legacy of U.S. colonialism and imperialism over their governments, lands, and bodies.

So it seems important to reconsider the questions raised by the differences within the Constitution and Ordinance from the context not of how they are situated within and so settle the truths about Santa Clara culture but how they were narrated (or not) at trial in assertions of cultural authenticity and legal legitimacy. As "both sides" laid claim to defining the "Indian member," they marked the kinds of social and interpersonal relationships they sought with one another in ways that mattered both politically and ethically to the kinds of rights they asserted as their own.

Testified

During the District Court trial, the plaintiffs were represented by the attorneys Alan R. Taradash, Robert B. Collins, and Tim Vollman from Window Rock, Arizona.[15] Julia Martinez and Audrey LaRose Martinez were called to represent themselves and Julia's husband, Myles H. Martinez, was called as a witness. After the defense presented its case, Patrick Gutierrez (a former governor), Herbert Alton Martinez (the son of Julia and Myles H. Martinez), Floripa Northcutt (a woman who married a nonmember), and

Alcario Tafoya (a representative of the Winter People ousted from the council for supporting the Martinezes' claim) were called as rebuttal witnesses.

The defense was represented by the attorneys Marc Prelo and Richard J. Grodner from Albuquerque, New Mexico. Paul Tafoya, the Santa Clara Pueblo governor, as well as the former council members Jose Gene Naranjo (the community director), Amarante Silva (the director of social services), Bill Baca (a former lieutenant governor), and Juan Chavarria (a former governor) were witnesses for the defense. Florence Hawley Ellis, a retired anthropologist and archaeologist from the University of New Mexico (UNM), was also called to testify for the defense.[16]

Testimony was heard on November 24 and 25, 1975. Judge Edwin L. Mechem delivered his verdict on December 20.

The plaintiffs made no opening statement and instead moved to call their first witness. The line of questioning for all three witnesses—Myles, Julia, and Audrey Martinez—focused on their efforts to get the council to reconsider the Ordinance's restrictions. The consequences were discussed primarily in terms of access to free medical care and educational programs, such as free hot lunches at local schools. Julia and Audrey Martinez also talked about the denial of their rights to participate equally in tribal governance and property—owing to the Ordinance but also to broader discriminatory practices by the council against women who married out and their families.

Myles H. Martinez testified first. He was born in January 1918 as an enrolled member of the Navajo Nation. He married Julia, an enrolled member of Santa Clara, in December 1941. They lived at Santa Clara and by the time of the lawsuit had borne ten children, eight surviving. While Myles did not speak but could understand Tewa, his wife and children were fluent in both Tewa and English. Their home was bilingual.

Myles's testimony was a chronicle of the failed attempts he and Julia made to get their children enrolled as Pueblo and for him to become naturalized. These efforts began after he was discharged from the U.S. Air Force in 1946 and they had their first child. Following protocol, he and Julia went first to her uncle, Pasqual Tafoya, who served as the representative of her division of the Summer People on the Council.[17] They discussed the issues at length with Tafoya, who said that he would take the matter to the council on their behalf. However, it appeared to Myles that that never happened, so they dropped the issue.

Their efforts resumed in 1963. Myles explained that they were given a copy of the Constitution by Paul Tafoya, the governor of the Santa Clara, and that they met with him to discuss his and his children's membership statuses. Tafoya explained that the matter had to be brought before the entire division first, before going to the council, and that that could not happen at that time.[18] The following year, the Martinezes spoke again to Tafoya, who then gave them permission to go before the council. They did so and requested that their children be enrolled. According to Myles, the council was not "in favor of it" but said that it would "study the matter" (10).[19] The council members also told the Martinezes that the resolution could not happen "overnight" and could take up to ten years to be granted (10). So the Martinezes attended a general meeting of the Pueblo to present their concerns to the membership. Again, they were told that "it would take quite some time to settle the issue" (11). Afterward, they attended a second council meeting and presented their concerns again but nothing had been done to move the claim forward.

In 1965, the Martinezes began to make several trips to Albuquerque to meet with representatives of the All Pueblo Agency. As Myles described it, they wanted to find out why they were not able to receive "free medical treatment" for the children and also to discuss issues with the public school and enrollment. The agency told them to return to their council.

Myles and several other nonmember Native men who had married Santa Clara women and lived at the Pueblo followed up with council representatives and were told that naturalization might be an option, and that their children would be automatically enrolled if the men became members, but only if they were willing to "renounce" their tribes. It would not be until 1971 that they were informed that naturalization was in fact not an option due to the same Ordinance that had established the patrilineal criterion.

Myles then testified that he did enjoy certain "privileges" irrespective of his membership status. These included "using irrigation water, farming, wood hauling, fishing, hunting, and stuff like that" (15). However, because he and his children were not enrolled, they were unable to secure medical care and adequate educational opportunities. This became particularly serious in 1968 when one of their daughters suffered a series of strokes and required hospitalization. For the first admission, hospital staff allowed her to go in under Julia's census number as the family could not afford the care. However, at the second admission, while the staff allowed them to use Julia's census number again, the Martinezes were informed that the hospital could not administer any additional free medical services to their daughter unless she possessed her own census number.

Myles scheduled an appointment with Francis Acoya, a state Indian commissioner. Desperate, Myles explained their situation and pleaded for help. Acoya told him to try to get a letter from the Pueblo affirming his child was a member and he would expedite obtaining a census number for her. Both Myles and Julia approached her council representative, Alfredo Tafoya, who promised to present the problem to the council. Apparently he either did not follow through or the council elected not to issue the letter because none was issued. The Martinezes followed up with several additional meetings with Francis Tafoya and Juan Chavarria, then the governor of the Santa Clara Pueblo. Tafoya and Chavarria deferred the issue and explained that it would take a long time to get the enrollment matters addressed by the council.

Upon cross-examination, Prelo pressed several key points with Myles, including the personal help he and his family received from council members and the governor. Prelo emphasized the fact that Myles was enrolled as a Navajo and so enjoyed medical, educational, and other benefits through the Navajo tribe. He suggested that the Navajo would allow the Martinez children access to those same benefits (an issue never confirmed one way or the other). Prelo also emphasized that the Martinez children were eventually issued census numbers though they were not enrolled. Consequently, they had access to all of the services and programs they seemed to care about—like free medical care and education grants—despite their membership status.

Upon redirect, Taradash drew out the legal distinctions between having access to social services and possessing rights to governance and property in the tribe. Myles explained that membership was the sole condition on which the right to run cattle, lease lands for agricultural or business purposes, vote in Pueblo elections, or hold office in the Pueblo government was based. Since he was not enrolled, he did not possess any of these rights.

While he enjoyed some access to things like irrigation, council members could rescind it at any time because he was not a member.

Julia Martinez testified next. She was born in October 1921 and both of her parents were Santa Claran. She agreed that she "participated in all the affairs and the functions of the Pueblo" (35), but mentioned quickly that she could not pass on her land or home to her children or husband because they were not enrolled. She stated that there were about forty other women similarly situated at the Pueblo.[20] She was asked to describe the process for bringing matters before the council and she said that first one had to go to the representative of their division and that he (*sic*) would take the issue to the council.

Like Myles's testimony, Julia's testimony focused on the several frustrated attempts they made to secure membership for their children and Myles. She said that they went to her uncle, Pasqual Tafoya, who was the representative of the Summer People, and inquired about getting their first child, Herbert Myles, enrolled. Tafoya explained to them that the Ordinance had "closed the enrollment" of all children born to women who had married nonmembers (37).

Julia's next attempt was in 1964. She and four other women, including Lydia Garcia (she could not remember the names of the others), went to Paul Tafoya and requested permission to go before the council. He granted it. At the council meeting, the women were told that their children could not become members even though "some of them are half—they are half Indian blood" in the Pueblo (39). Julia said, "And we had questioned before them, 'Why is it that on the men's side, automatic, that their children be enrolled in the members of Santa Clara even though they [are] married to non-members?'" (39). The women were told it was because of the Ordinance.

Afterward, the Martinezes and the women went to a general meeting. Julia described how Governor Tafoya held up a piece of paper before the assembly and said that that paper "starts the enrollment on the ladies' side" (40). They were not told what the paper was and they were not offered a copy. After the meeting, several women met at the Martinez home and discussed what to do next. Apparently, they had secured permission from Tafoya to go to the BIA in Albuquerque "to see if something could be done to have [the] children [become] members of the tribe" (41). They ended up meeting with Superintendent Peter Walz. Walz requested permission from Tafoya to meet with the council. He apparently did but without any of the women present. The women followed up with several additional meetings with Walz through the year. According to Julia, nothing was accomplished.

In 1965 the Martinezes received a letter from Walz telling them that the naturalization of nonmember Native men was an option. They met with Tafoya and the council, who likewise brought up the possibility of naturalization. After several discussions, the matter was dropped (the same Ordinance that established patrilineality prohibited against all naturalizations). In 1966 Julia met with another representative, Loretta Cruz Chavarria, again to no avail. In 1968, Myles and Julia met with Tom Lee, a Navajo who served as a New Mexico senator. Lee directed them to meet with Amarante Silva, a tribal judge, who wrote letters on their behalf to Santa Clara governor Juan Chavarria and to Lee. Again, no action was taken by the council.

Julia then described her daughter's hospitalizations for a series of strokes at the Bernalillo County Medical Center in Albuquerque. During the second admission, when Julia and Myles were informed that their daughter would no longer be allowed to receive free medical care, Myles requested a meeting with the local BIA agent and attempted to get help. They also went to the home of their representative, Alfredo Naranjo, and asked for help in getting a letter from the council to verify that their daughter was a member of the tribe (48). No letter ever came.

Also in 1965 the council formed a committee, chaired by Lawrence Singer, on the membership issues confronting the Martinez family. Julia and Myles met with Singer in 1968. Singer explained that it had been difficult getting the committee members to meet and so he had been working alone on their genealogical papers.[21]

According to Julia, the Martinezes met next with Clarence Acoya, a BIA agent, along with two BIA agents from Washington and Governor Chavarria. They brought a witness, a friend by the name of Joe Sanchez, who said that he could verify that the daughter was a member. In 1969, the Martinezes also met with a state senator in Albuquerque, who wrote a supportive letter to the council. These efforts did not result in any written verification of the daughter's membership.

On cross-examination, Prelo pushed Julia on the reasons why she and her husband elected to live at the Pueblo. He suggested that they could have everything they wanted by moving to the Navajo reservation (Myles was enrolled at the Navajo Nation, but because the Navajo had a matrilineal membership criteria, his wife and children did not qualify for membership there). Julia explained that they lived at the Pueblo initially because her mother was alone and had become paralyzed on one side after a severe stroke and could not take care of herself and that later they decided to stay (at no time had they lived elsewhere than at Santa Clara). Prelo asked if she knew whether or not they would qualify for membership at Navajo; she said she did not know and explained that they had never tried (a decision which conformed to the matrilocal customs of both the Navajo and Pueblo).

Next, Prelo asked Julia if she knew whether or not she could graze cattle on Pueblo lands; she did not and said that they did not own cattle and so had never made the request. Prelo asked if their children had census numbers and when they received them. Julia answered that they did in 1968. He inquired if they had received medical attention and other benefits owing to this fact (such as the free lunches in the public schools and a federal grant for Audrey to attend the University of New Mexico). Julia explained that they had but that it had been extremely difficult, often requiring Pueblo officials to intervene with hospital staff, school officials, and the BIA. Prelo made a point of the fact that tribal officials had consistently given them help and permission to go before the council to discuss their concerns. Julia countered that on one occasion they were turned away by a tribal official from picnicking at the Pueblo because Myles and the children were not enrolled.

The questions then turned to the Ordinance and tribal tradition. Prelo pushed Julia on whether or not she knew about the Ordinance's restrictions on children born to women who marry nonmembers. She explained that her uncle had informed her about the Ordinance and that that did not stop her from marrying Myles. She also testified that she did not know of any of the husbands being naturalized since 1939 but knew of about four that had been before that time. Prelo then questioned Julia about the relationship between the census number and enrollment. This turned into an inquiry about whether or not Julia considered herself to be a "traditional person."

Q: Did anyone ever tell you that your children had to be enrolled members of the Santa Clara Pueblo to get a census number?

A: Repeat the question.

Q: Did anyone ever tell you that your children, in order to get a census number, must be enrolled members of the Santa Clara Pueblo?

A: All I know is they have to have a census number so they can be verified by what the Government, Federal Government's benefits is to the Indians.

Q: That's not what I asked, Mrs. Martinez. But let me ask you this way. Do you know what the BIA requires before they will give a census number?

A: Yes.

Q: Would you tell us what this is? Is it one-fourth Indian blood?

A: That's right. You have to be—have to be recognized a fourth blood Indian to get the benefit of Federal grant or–

Q: And that's all, is it not? They don't have to be members of a given tribe?

A: That's my understanding.

Q: So the fact that your children are not enrolled members of Santa Clara did not prohibit them from getting medical services, is that right?

A: Still, we did have problems on that.

Q: But it wasn't because —

A: Even if it takes a fourth.

Q: I'm sorry?

A: Even if it did take a fourth blood Indian to be, still, we did have problems.

Q: But the problem was just with BIA officials in getting the right paperwork and documentation, is that correct?

A: I don't understand that question.

Q: I say, your problem was not getting the right paperwork from the BIA, convincing BIA that they had one-quarter Indian blood?

A: Yes.

Q: Is that right?

A: Yes.

Q: Do you know, Mrs. Martinez, do you consider yourself a traditional person in the Santa Clara ways?

A: Yes.

Q: You do? Do you know what the traditions are?

A: No.

Q: You don't. Were you raised in the tradition, do you think?

A: I was brought up.

Q: In the tradition of the Santa Clara Pueblo?

A: Yes.

Q: Do you know what the tradition is about women following their husbands wherever they marry? You know anything about that?

A: No.

Q: Other than the paper your uncle told you about, that's the only thing you know about that?

A: Yes.

Q: Did your uncle give you any other explanation about the paper at all?

A: No. . . .

Q: Do you know what the laws of inheritance are? Can your children inherit your property?

A: If they are members of the tribe.

Q: They can inherit your real property, the land?

A: A personal inheritance of mine.

Q: Do you know the distinction, Mrs. Martinez, between personal property and real property?

A: What my understanding, my knowledge, is in the homes of what I have, what I have.

Q: If I tell you that land is real property and that personal property is all of your other things, do you know whether your children could inherit personal property regardless of membership?

A: I don't know. (72–74)

Prelo insinuates that Julia and her husband could have, and even should have, moved to Navajo and enrolled their children there because they could get what they wanted, but even more so because it was the "traditional" thing for women to reside with their husband's tribe (advancing the argument that the Pueblo were traditional patrilocal). He suggests that her children's receipt of census numbers provides them with all of the rights and benefits of being an Indian—that there are no rights or benefits afforded to Indian people that she and her children have been denied by not being enrolled at Santa Clara. He then implies that Julia's claims to being traditional and having been raised in the traditions of the tribe are false at best because she does not answer affirmatively that she knows what the traditions are for "women following their husbands" when they marry or what the "laws of inheritance are."

By folding questions about her rights into questions about her authenticity, Prelo submits that Julia and her family are making erroneous claims to being legitimate members. Unfortunately, Julia responds by insisting on the family's legitimacy by blood, such as when she asserts her and her children's full-bloodedness (39). This recharges the council with discrimination while leaving race unchallenged as an accurate determinant of one's cultural and legal validity. What is important in Julia's responses is her refusal to engage Prelo on the question of tradition. Her answers are less an "I don't know" than a deferral on matters she would not find to be any business of the court. This would also be the strategy of her daughter.

Audrey LaRose Martinez testified next. She explained that she had been born in January 1946 and raised at Santa Clara, had four brothers and three sisters, spoke and understood Tewa fluently, and lived at the Pueblo except for her time at the University of New Mexico (where she was then completing a degree). She said that she was not enrolled and that there were more than one hundred children like her at Santa Clara. She answered that she and her siblings were all "eligible" to participate in all of the cultural and social activities that went on at the Pueblo if they chose to do so (77):

> Q: Are there any rights that members have that you do not enjoy?
> A: Yes. We don't have the right to vote, to hold office, the right to inherit any real property and the right to have been named as a beneficiary at the time that the housing projects came . . .
> Q: If something were to happen to your mother, would your brothers and sisters and your father have the right to remain in Santa Clara and live there?
> A: We don't know for sure. We can't be very definite or very sure in knowing that we could stay there if we wanted to.
> Q: Is it possible that you could be ousted from the Pueblo?
> A: Yes. (78–79)

Audrey explained that a housing project had begun at Santa Clara in 1968 and that initially women who married outside of the tribe were not eligible but that the rule had since been amended. However, she explained that the restriction remained in place that the women could not name nonmembers as beneficiaries — meaning that she and her siblings and her father could not be willed the home that was issued in her mother's name.

Audrey was then asked a series of questions about whether or not she had attempted to enroll herself. She explained then and upon cross-examination and redirect that the protocol was for her parents to handle her enrollment. So while she had spoken several times to council members and her representative about her situation, she had not attempted to enroll herself. She also stated that the family had hired an attorney in either 1971 or 1972 and that he had made efforts on her behalf but to no avail.

Upon cross-examination, Audrey was very respectful of Santa Clara leadership and protocol. She began by explaining that despite the lawsuit all of the women and their children were "quite willing to have this matter settled within the tribe" (83). She said that the governor, council members, and representatives had always been very "sympathetic" and helpful and had never treated them differently than enrolled members (85). She also testified that her grandmother — Placita Gutierrez — had been one of a few women who had married outside the tribe who had been granted an exception to enrolling her children after her divorce and when they returned to Santa Clara.

Audrey was also asked whether or not her participation in Santa Clara activities had been restricted differently than for men. She explained that women and men had different activities and that she was not barred from the activities she was eligible to participate in as a woman. "Is there any other way that you can think of that the Pueblo has denied you equal protection, anything else at all?" She responded, "No, other than the right to vote . . . and to hold office" (92). Upon redirect, the issue of land rights was flushed out so that Audrey explained more fully that her mother was not allowed to transfer title to any but enrolled members which excluded all of her children and husband.

After Audrey testified, the plaintiffs rested their case. But despite Julia's responses about whether or not she considered herself to be "traditional," both Audrey and Julia demonstrated that they and the entire family were not only fully involved in the cultural activities of the tribe but were respectful of tribal leadership and protocol. The task before the defense was to challenge their credibility on cultural grounds, which would implicate their legal legitimacy. This was first attempted through questions about the help they received from council members and Julia's understandings of tribal traditions. It would be carried through in the opening statement and course of testimony offered by the defense.

The defense began with a motion to strike Santa Clara governor Paul Tafoya as a defendant because they felt that the plaintiffs had failed to present any evidence that he, personally, had done anything but try to help the Martinez family and had done nothing, individually, to deny them equal protection. The motion was denied.

Grodner then made a brief opening statement, followed by calling Tafoya as the first witness for the defense. Tafoya was born in October 1928 at Santa Clara to parents who were both members. He had finished high school. He was married to a Santa Clara woman; they had four boys and three girls. He had served as governor in 1965, 1966, 1971, 1972, 1973, and 1974 and at various times as lieutenant governor, secretary, and interpreter.

Tafoya reported that the Pueblo was located about twenty-eight miles north of Santa Fe in Rio Arriba, Santa Fe, and Sandoval counties and covered approximately forty-eight thousand acres of mountainous, agricultural, and grazing lands. It had a membership of about twelve hundred.[22] He confirmed that the land was leased out to members and nonmembers for a variety of purposes, including grazing. He stated that the tribe's two main sources of income were from the leases and sand and gravel sales. The reservation had two schools through elementary; afterward, children went to public schools. Members and nonmembers attended the reservation schools. While the tribe received funds for education, they did not receive funds to provide other services. Tafoya was asked about the "cultural trademarks" of the Pueblo, which he identified as black and red pottery (104).

Questions then turned to the duties of his office and the structure of Santa Clara government. Tafoya said that his main responsibility was for the people and that his actions were governed by the council. He explained that the governor could not make a decision on his own and that it was the council that was responsible for making decisions in the tribe, such as those concerning membership. He explained that as governor he was charged with ensuring that "all the decisions made by the Council are in such a way that it is not harmful to the community, that it supports that community, it preserves the culture, the heritage, and it preserves the whole well-being of the Indian people" (105).

Tafoya was pressed on whether or not the Santa Clara political government was "closely related" to the religious part of the tribe (106). He answered that the leadership was coordinated between the two. He was then questioned about the Ordinance and whether or not the patrilineal rule had been followed before it. He remarked, "It was my understanding, in discussing these matters with the old people, that this was a rule that was carried on and it was my understanding that in the year 1939, it surfaced and, at that time, it became written guideline" (108). He clarified that the "old people" referred to the male leadership within his family.

Tafoya was asked to describe the status of men and women within the Pueblo regarding "religious privileges" (108):

> Well, I'm not really supposed to talk anything about religious matters when it involves my tribe. I've been restricted since the day I took office. Matters of this nature, I'm not supposed to discuss in the public. But I can state one thing: That the male Santa Clara Indian truly has that responsibility to teach and train and expose his family to the way of the Indian people, and this involves quite a bit within the Indian culture. Now, I'm talking about the Santa Clara Indian culture, and it is his responsibility, much more than it is the responsibility of a female member of the tribe. (109)

When asked if women had the same religious privileges as men, Tafoya replied that men had about twice as many. He also said that men were always considered to be the heads of households and that if a man was deceased or absent it would be the woman's male relatives who would fulfill the role.

The next line of questioning had to do with whether or not individuals could own or lease Pueblo lands. He explained that the land was communally held but that individuals were assigned to specific properties. Next, he said that there was no formal rule for individuals securing permission from the Pueblo's governor, council, or representatives before speaking to people outside of the tribe about tribal matters. But, he said, it was considered a show of respect if they did.

He then asserted that he did not believe that when Julia Martinez passed away the Martinez family would be "forced off the reservation." He felt that the council would help: "We like to protect them as much as possible, even though they might [not] be true members of the tribe. As long as they reside on the reservation, we are responsible and are concerned with their welfare. I'm sure they would not be chased off the reservation" (112). He said that he had never denied Julia Martinez, her children, or anyone else on the reservation any of their rights and that in fact he had worked hard to help them.

Next, he clarified that the census number did not mean tribal membership. Securing a census number entitled an individual to federally funded services for Indian people like medical care, education, and welfare—all services that the tribe could not afford to provide. He said that he had written letters for many Santa Clarans to support their efforts to secure census numbers but that the BIA required documentation proving blood quantum and that providing that documentation had proven difficult for some.

Tafoya was also asked to "describe the method by which the traditions and culture [are] passed down in the Santa Clara Pueblo." He responded, "I believe there's many, many different ways that this is passed down, but I do know that—again, I repeat and put the male on top, I think on the male side more of this is passed through the family from generation to generation" (115). He also said that it was traditional for the women to go with their husbands, meaning that if a woman married a non–Santa Clara man that it was the norm for her to leave the reservation.

Lastly, Tafoya was asked "what would happen to the Santa Clara culture" if the Ordinance were no longer enforced. He responded:

> It would tend to destroy the Pueblo as a whole because there would actually be no Government, no organization. It would take away a great deal of things that you have to have an organization for. You have to have a certain type of a Government in order to regulate the enforced rules and enforced laws and make laws. With it, we would have an influx of people that we don't know who they are. They would come in from all directions: Indians and non-Indians alike. So it would be a destruction on the Santa Clara Indian Culture. . . . My primary concern, as far as this lawsuit is that we like to keep our Government. We like to be a responsible people. We know what our community is all about. We know the people, the traditions and customs, the ceremonies, the religious life, the entire thing that makes the Indian and his way of life. That is, to me, is very important. Membership, at this point in question, is very important. I think the community is concerned very much about the general membership of the tribe, and I am sure that, eventually, they will work out their own problems. (116–17)

He testified that he knew of no exceptions to the Ordinance since 1939.

Upon cross-examination, Tafoya said that no one had been naturalized since 1939. He said that a child born to a Santa Clara woman who was not married became a member of the tribe. He explained that for a person to become a member of the tribe, he or she had to present all requested documentation to the council who had final authority to decide. He said he did not know or believe that Tewa language fluency was considered in the decisions about membership while it did figure in the requirements of holding public office. He stated that there were more mixed marriages than there used to be and that the unenrolled were afforded all of the same privileges as enrolled except voting and holding public office.

There was then some discussion about whether or not the issue of religion had been addressed during the pretrial period and whether or not Tafoya understood the traditions of the tribe regarding membership. He deferred to elders who knew better and said that he relied on their counsel. When pressed about who these individuals were and what information they had provided him with, he replied that it was his responsibility "to protect such individuals" and that he was not able to identify them (139). He was also pressed on his concerns for protecting the tribe's culture.

A: I am concerned about the culture. I don't want to destroy the Santa Clara Indian culture. We preserve it today. I like it. I want to live there and it is my responsibility to live by the rules, the regulations and the laws of the tribe. This is the only way we can protect and preserve our culture. If we let outside influences come in, that would tend to destroy what we now have. Then what's the sense of having a Tribal Government?

Q: Well, Governor, then why do you admit non-Indian wives of members to have their children enrolled? Isn't that an outsider?

A: Non-Indian wives to have their children enrolled?

Q: Isn't that an outside influence?

A: It is, but, again, I repeat, it is still the responsibility of the male member, who is the head of the family, it is his responsibility to teach his people the Indian way of life. (140)

Upon redirect, Tafoya testified that the tribe did not vote or have elected officials until the Constitution of 1935. He explained that unmarried women who bore children were allowed to stay in the tribe and enroll their children because the tribe felt that it was their responsibility to protect and care for them because they had nowhere else to go. He also claimed that the woman's male relatives would have the responsibility to teach the tradition to the children.

Jose Gene Naranjo was called next. He was born in 1911 to parents who were members. Except for a couple of years, he had lived on the reservation his entire life. He was married to Madeline Gutierrez Naranjo, a Santa Claran, and they had two boys and one girl. At the time, he was the community director but he had also served as a secretary (during the time the Constitution was ratified), a council member, and a representative.

Naranjo explained the tribe's government and how leaders were chosen by their divisions and voted into office. He said that the Ordinance was a reflection of the teachings of the tribe's elders that had been passed through generations and was merely codified in 1939. But he also provided two other reasons for the Ordinance's passage. First, there was an apparent increase in the number of mixed marriages, resulting in more children of nonmember men coming into the tribe. Second, the tribe had very limited lands and financial resources to support its existing membership. For these reasons, Naranjo said that the council was trying to preserve the culture and heritage of the tribe "by not letting too many people come in" (173). He said that the council recognized that there was a problem with enrollment and were studying it but that it would take time to resolve. Frustrated, he said that now they would have to wait for the outcome of the trial so it would only be further delayed.[23]

When questioned about who was responsible for teaching the traditions to the children, Naranjo described an equality between the father and mother—children needing to learn different things from each parent. During cross-examination, he stated again that both parents were equally involved in teaching the children. It was only upon redirect that he insisted the father was solely responsible for teaching the children. He also stated that men and women had unique religious activities and responsibilities and when pressed said that men had a little more.

Naranjo was asked about children born to unmarried mothers. In all cases, he said, owing to the tribe's sense of responsibility to the women and their children, the children were made members. In those situations, he said the male relatives of the women assumed primary care for the unmar-

ried mother and her children. The defense went further to call into question the moral character of the women by saying that they may not identify
the father by choice or that "sometimes, perhaps the mother doesn't know,
either?" (171). He agreed.

Upon cross, Naranjo was asked if he was baptized in the Catholic
Church. He said yes. When asked if he was "a good Catholic" the defense
objected to the question and said that they were only there to discuss "one
religion" (168). The judge agreed.

Provocatively, this would be the only time Catholicism was suggested
as a *present* influence at Santa Clara, otherwise situated as part of a far
distant past with modest impact confined to the structure of the tribe's
government. The court's rejection of the relevance of the question to a
discussion specifically about the tribe's traditions, however, marks an interesting anxiety that percolated throughout the trial. For both sides, tribal
"traditions" have an entirely assumed set of meanings to represent what
is authentically and legitimately Santa Claran. By refusing even the mere
suggestion that these terms might have significance in other contexts (like
Catholicism) or have meanings that are indeterminate (because of those
other significations), the evaluative link between the culture (authenticity)
and rights (legitimacy) of the Santa Clara can render its harsh judgment on
the cultural and legal credibility of the witnesses.

In other words, the court *had* to suppress any serious questioning of
what "traditions" meant in order to maintain a whole host of cultural and
legal integrities, including its own authority to evaluate the tribe's and so
its members' legal standing and rights. Naranjo's "slip" and the judge's suppression of it shows the extent to which the court could not tolerate an un-
settling of what Santa Clara "traditions" meant historically and culturally.

Amarante Silva testified next. He had lived many years away from the
Pueblo, as a boy at Santa Fe Indian School and afterward at the Navajo
reservation for purposes of employment and because he married a Navajo
woman. They had four girls and two boys. Since returning, he had served as
a secretary and on the council. He was then the director of social services.

Silva was asked and responded that he had instructed his daughters
about the consequences of marrying nonmembers so that they would be
"aware of this provision that the tribe has" (179). Three of his four daughters had married nonmembers. Because they understood the rules ahead

of time, he claimed, the two married to Natives from other tribes had enrolled their children on their husbands' sides and resided at their reservations with them. This, Silva suggested, was the traditional thing to do.

Silva was then questioned about his understanding of the Ordinance —
what it provided and why it was necessary. He answered that it originated
with the council as a rule that was "carried on for centuries" (182). When
asked, he said that the man was the head of the family, that it had been that
way for centuries, and that was the reason for the restriction of membership to a father's children. He claimed that he had been taught the rule by
the men in his family — his grandfather, uncle, father, and brothers.

Later, Silva was asked to describe the tribe's social organization in respect to the role of men and women. He said that the men were the heads
of household and were responsible for overseeing the family and for "teaching the cultural and traditional values" (185) to the children. Upon cross-
examination, he stated that his children spoke neither Tewa nor Navajo and
that he did not participate in the religious activities of the Pueblo but that
he was a part of the Summer People. Upon redirect, he was asked whether
or not his "home was run strictly under Santa Clara custom and tradition"
but he did not answer the question directly (185–86).

Silva was then pressed about the reason for the Ordinance. He testified
that it was because the "elders had foreseen the great numbers of outsiders
coming in" and that the tribe's limited resources would make it impossible
to support them (187–88). He was asked about children born to unmarried
mothers and situations of divorce and adoption. His answers conformed
to Tafoya's and Naranjo's.

Bill Baca testified next. Born in December 1903, he lived most of his life
at the Pueblo, finished only a couple of years at Santa Fe Indian School, and
worked as part-time security for a council member. He was married twice,
both to Santa Clara women, and by the first marriage had one daughter and
three sons and by the second one daughter and five sons. He had served as
lieutenant governor when the Constitution was adopted. Because of Baca's
age and difficulty in hearing, questioning was very brief. He testified that
he understood that the children of Santa Clara women who married nonmembers could not enroll following the Constitution. Asked if the women
who married out customarily lived on the reservation with their husbands,
he said he was not sure where they normally lived. He did say that the
man was the head of household and made the decisions about enrollment.

When asked about who taught the children the traditions and culture of the tribe he responded, "Well, I won't say because I don't know. I guess every individuals have their own way of teaching their children religious" (201).

Juan Chavarria was called last for the defense. He was born in 1907 and raised at Santa Clara. He was married to a Santa Clara woman in 1931 and had four boys and two girls. He had previously served as governor. He worked at the Institution of American Indians under the BIA in Santa Fe.

Chavarria was asked if he understood the rule regarding enrollment for daughters who married nonmembers. He explained that it had been "the rule of the tribe since immemorial" (208). He said he had been taught the rule by his grandfather, father, and great uncles and many other male elders of the tribe. He also said that there had been no exceptions to the rule since 1939.

Next, Chavarria testified that a man was the head of the family and responsible for teaching the children the culture and religion of the tribe. He said that it was customary for women to live outside the reservation if they married nonmembers but that in some cases they might not. He said that children of unwed mothers were enrolled by the council and that male relatives were responsible for their upbringing. "Do you know the reason for that rule?" He answered, "Well, it has been practiced for years and years, for generations and generations. That still applies today" (211). He also said that he was selected as governor by the religious leaders of the tribe, a practice that preceded and continued following the Constitution.

Upon cross-examination, he was asked whether or not his grandfather and other men had told him about the rules regarding whom he should marry. He said that it was so. He also said that he was taught that "it was forbidden to marry into the Navajo tribe" (217) and apologized to anyone offended by his revealing the religious teachings of the tribe in court. (Another moment in the trial when the instabilities of what tribal "traditions" mean for the Santa Clara, and the court, is marked without consideration.) He said the restrictions about women who married out were for the good of the tribe: "That, well, we like to keep things we have, our land, our culture, among our own people. For that reason, if we can marry our own people, that would be much more better for the tribe" (217).

He explained that nonenrolled members could participate in religious practices but only if they spoke and understood Tewa. He was also asked about the enrollment of illegitimate children and the central role of women in naming children. On this, he explained that the child received two names—one in Tewa and then one upon baptism in either Spanish or English. No further explanation was offered about the specific religious practices signified by the Spanish and English.

All of the defense witnesses to this point—all men and all having served or serving on the council—emphasized that patrilineality and patrilocality were the cultural norms of the tribe and that these norms were indicated by the men's political and religious leadership, their status as heads of household, and their responsibility for teaching the children. They indicated that they had been raised this way and had inherited the rules about membership regarding women who married nonmembers and other teachings from their elder male relatives (a role that they repeated with their children). When asked, they insisted that changing the Ordinance would threaten the integrity of the tribe's government and land base, its limited financial resources, and its culture. They all defined their responsibilities in terms of protecting the tribe against that happening. They all suggested that women who married nonmembers and their families were the primary threat to the tribe's cultural and legal integrity and financial and natural resources.

Of the 395 pages of testimony recorded over the two days of the trial, 109 pages (227–336) were given by Florence Hawley Ellis. Her testimony overshadowed the Martinezes, and even the other defense witnesses, as if to settle the "truth" about the tribe's traditions from the "objective" conclusions of a scientist. Ellis's remarks on the whole were wholly consistent with those of the other defense witnesses, some of whom she defers to as her informants. Standing as the sole "outside" and "scientific" expert during the trial, the plaintiffs conducted a rigorous cross-examination that attempted to tear apart the reliability of her methodology, sources, and conclusions.

Ellis graduated with a PH.D. in anthropology from the University of Chicago in 1934 and she taught there and then at the University of New Mexico, where she retired after thirty-seven years. She had received several awards and had written 162 articles and books, with 54 pertaining to ethnology in New Mexico. She had previously worked for other Pueblos on land claims and was currently working for the Santa Clara on a water claim. She said that she had been to the Santa Clara reservation "thousands of times" (232). Her research focused on historical patterns of cultural development, "with tying the old cultures, the prehistoric cultures, of a general area to that of the living cultures of the same general area" (232). She was hired by the Santa Clara Council to offer testimony at trial on the social organization of the tribe.

Ellis described the various languages of the Pueblo people, the different Pueblos and their locations in New Mexico, and the migration of the Santa Clara to their current location in approximately 1300 A.D. She described the centrality of pottery in dating and tracking various Pueblo through the region because of the specificity of the work and the rules about not borrowing or copying designs from one another because those designs were considered "territorial" (236–37).

She was asked to describe the tribe's two moieties. She said the Winter and Summer People provided the basic religious and social structure, that someone customarily became a member of his or her father's moiety with a ceremonial initiation that was religious in nature, and that each moiety had a *cacique* (chief) that was charged with all religious and secular affairs during the respective season.

Ellis then testified that, after 1620, the Spanish had imposed the secular and centralized form of government on the Pueblo in order to have leaders to deal with but also to break down Pueblo religion. The Santa Clara responded by having the secular leaders appointed by the religious leaders "who kept in the background" (239). She said that the Constitution of 1935 changed little in the tribe's organization. She described the Santa Clara as a "theocracy" but said that there was a lessening of the importance of religious leaders because "everything is becoming more secularized through acculturation" (241).

She was then asked how a child was introduced into the moiety. Ellis claimed that there were two ceremonies—one when the child was very young and one during puberty. If the father was known, the child was initiated into his moiety. She said the children were expected to participate in the activities of the moiety but that the participation of boys and girls was different: "The boy goes into much more esoteric matters in the Moiety than the girl is ever permitted to" (242).

She was then asked to define patrilineality in relationship to the Santa Clara. She said that they were a patrilineal people with such examples as the fact that a young married couple and their children would either live with the man's parents or be involved in the man's parent's household through economics and small ceremonial activities. She was asked who gave children their names. She explained that it was given by the two persons who had "first touched the child after it has been born" (244). She was asked to compare the "dominance" of men and women in a Tewa family. She responded that "there is no question but that the male is dominant in the Santa Clara household. . . . He is much more important an influence, he is much more important in decisions. He is supposed to support the family economically. He leads the family in religious matters, with the exception of a few small rituals in which a woman handles things, and he is supposed to see to the family on an overall basis" (245). Ellis described the women's functions to be within the home. She claimed that women used to be involved in the preservation of foods but that they were not, on the whole, "such farmers as they used to be" (245). She said women deal "with a few small rituals, but not major matters" (245). She stated that women who marry normally follow their husbands "to wherever his area of residence was" (246) and that a husband who married a nonmember would settle at Santa Clara. She reiterated that the father and the father's relatives were the ones responsible for teaching the children and that children born to an unmarried woman were taken into her family and moiety by her senior male relatives.

The final question concerned what would result if the Santa Clara "allowed their women to marry non–Santa Clarans, and if their children became members" (251). She answered, "Well, because of the importance of men in connection with carrying on of the culture, the training of the children in the socio-religious situation, the culture eventually would break down and be lost" (251).

The cross-examination was exhaustive. Apparently, Ellis had been hired by and prepared a report for the U.S. Department of Justice (DOJ) on the original complaint because the complaint had included the U.S. Department of Housing and Urban Development. The report was admitted by the plaintiffs as evidence and served as a starting point for questioning. Ellis was pressed about the content and sources of her report, which did not include references to Santa Clara membership records, which she explained she had not reviewed in its preparation (257). Primarily, her written sources addressed other Pueblo. She was then asked to identify her "informants" and named Cleto Tafoya, Severa Tafoya, Eugene Gutierrez, John Naranjo, Juan Chavarria, Lawrencito Tafoya, Amarante Silva, Jose G.

Naranjo, and Paul Tafoya. When pressed, she said that in respect to the case, she had spoken primarily to Paul Tafoya, Amarante Silva, and Jose Naranjo but that she had notes from the others from previous conversations about other matters.

Ellis was asked to clarify her sources about the religious life of the Santa Clara people and the availability and reliability of information about the traditional past in historical and contemporary writings. These questions were framed in terms of the tribe's proclivities for "secrecy." Ellis responded and reframed the issues in terms of accuracy and intergenerational knowledge, stating that older sources tended to be "much more detailed and accurate" because it was information taken down "before the culture broke down" (266) and because the older traditions were "not known by the young people of today" (267). The plaintiffs pointed out that Parsons, one of Ellis's key sources, wrote extensively about the impact of secrecy on the reliability of her data (Parsons was known for complaining that Pueblo informants often lied to her or gave her grossly incomplete information in order to protect it from outsiders). Ellis countered that what Parsons meant was that the secrecy made the resulting information incomplete and so that parts of it may be unreliable. On the whole, however, she maintained that it was reliable.

Ellis was then asked if she verified the information she received from her informants by observation. She was pressed about statements she had made during the deposition that she had not ever "done any serious work at Santa Clara" except recently on the water claims case (268). She clarified that she had relied on the work of others and had general observations owing to her frequent visits to the tribe over the years.

Ellis was asked about whether or not, in the context of the current dispute about enrollment, she had ever spoken with anyone of opposing views, especially given that all of her informants were men and of the same mind about the issues. She claimed that she had not but that she "was not talking to them about views" and so she could not fully answer the question (269). The inference in this line of questioning was that she had not spoken to any of the plaintiffs or other women and children similarly situated at Santa Clara. Therefore, her conclusions were skewed to favor the opinions of those she had spoken with and who were paying her for her testimony.

Next, Ellis was asked where she derived her sources about practices regarding mixed marriage and children of unmarried mothers. She had named three women in an article she wrote and was pressed about whether or not that was an adequate sampling given that the tribe included over twelve hundred members. She claimed it was. She then described the norm for extending enrollment to children of single mothers—that usually the first child was admitted without question but that all others were required to go before the council. It was pointed out that this contradicted earlier defense testimony and she said that the earlier testimony addressed generalities and not the specific process which she was clarifying.

Ellis was also pushed to explain the data she had included in an article that suggested a fairly low number of twenty mixed marriages among the Santa Clara, minimizing the impact of the Ordinance. This data originated in an appendix to a six-page paper Dozier had written when he had been her graduate student at UNM. Collins pointed out that, in the interrogatories, data were supplied by the council that indicated that there were eighty-two mixed marriages. He asked Ellis if she thought that figure was high or low. She responded that mixed marriages were "quite rare" among all of the Pueblo until after the Second World War, and that since then higher education and wage-labor opportunities off-reservation were the main contributing factors to the change in marriage patterns.

Ellis was asked about the relationship between initiation into a moiety and membership. She said it was possible that the two things were not dependent—that individuals could be recognized as members without having been initiated. The questioning then went to the point of those who had lost touch with the Pueblo and been formally evicted. She was asked whether or not this resulted from factionalism. She responded that she would not say because she thought there was a connotation to the question that was not true.

Collins pushed again on whether or not Ellis had done any specific study of Santa Clara membership traditions and the Ordinance. She said that she had not and that based on the fact that "Pueblo people characteristically think rather slowly about new problems" she did not imagine it would be an issue that would be resolved soon (292). Ellis then responded to Dozier's and Ortiz's descriptions of the Santa Clara as bilateral. (She did not explain that Dozier and Ortiz were specifically refuting her work when they used the term "bilateral" instead of patrilineal to describe the tribe's social organization.) She disagreed with this term because of the more central importance of the father and overall influence of men in Pueblo society (293).

Next, she explained the impact of the Spanish on Pueblo society and said that "there came to be a number of changes in material culture of the Pueblos, various matters that had been picked up from the Spaniards" (296). She also said that "there was a change to some extent in the governmental system because the Spaniards insisted that there be secular officers; but, these secular officers were primarily front men for the old religious hierarchy" (296). Interestingly, "Spanish" influence was not as threatening to the court as "Catholic."

Ellis stated that she felt the current dispute over enrollment had, as Collins phrased the question, "something to do with modern ideas of women's rights" (302). She said that that was her general impression, based on the fact that university students had gotten involved with the Red Power movement and its emphasis on "matters of equality" (303). She was asked if these students included Santa Clara Pueblo people and she said they did not.

Lastly, Ellis described a period of factionalism within Santa Clara Pueblo, between 1893 and 1934. She claimed that it had reached a point where the two moieties were not cooperating "except on rare occasions ceremonially" (307) and that otherwise one of the moieties withdrew from the political, public activities of the tribe. This was the period when the IRA was passed and the council decided that they would "reorganize" under its provisions as a way of bringing the moieties back together again. In previous publications, she referred to the factions at this time as "progressives" and "conservatives." Ellis claimed that the Constitution helped bring the factions together. She further claimed that despite the kind of factionalism that arose from "Spanish and Anglo influences" (313), the "general pattern" of the "traditional religious structure" of the Santa Clara was still "intact," but that the "total picture" of it was not (313–14).

Ellis's testimony did not wholly succeed in "proving" the "scientific objectivity" of her conclusions on Santa Clara cultural traditions and social organization as deriving from "patricultural" values and practices. Her sources and informants were shown to be less than objective. Of course, the issue is that all knowledge is inherently historical and political. But in the language and expectations of the court, the argument demanded a presentation of scientifically, objectively derived facts on which to base its decision. The fissures in Ellis's testimony about her work and conclusions made it difficult for the court to receive it as meeting these standards, particularly as she admitted that she had not interviewed anyone but defense witnesses in preparing her DOJ report or her trial testimony, that she had not reviewed Santa Clara documentation on the Ordinance or records of mixed marriages until preparing for her testimony, and that she had relied on materials by Parsons who had called into question the reliability of her own research and by Ortiz and Dozier who had disagreed with her conclusions about the patriculturality of Pueblo society.

But despite these limitations, the defense had offered a powerful narrative about the cultural authenticity of patrilineal traditions, customs, and practices—from governance and law through religion and kinship. This narrative positioned the Martinez family and by implication the other families at Santa Clara Pueblo like them as culturally inauthentic. Because of the ways that the "Indian member" holds cultural authenticity and legal legitimacy together, this inauthenticity implicated their legal legitimacy. They were thus represented as having contributed—however unintentionally—to the erosion of Santa Clara culture and so tribal self-government, land rights, and resources.

What would prove devastating for the plaintiffs was that, while several threads would be pulled out of the seamless shroud of the "patricultural" tale worn by the defense, they failed to offer a powerful narrative of their own about Santa Clara Pueblo traditions and teachings. Instead, their testimonies focused almost entirely on their personal experiences of discrimination by the council. A few things resulted.

First, the lack of an alternative narrative about Santa Clara traditions and teachings let rest the defense's claim that the tribe was historically patrilineal, patrilocal, and patricultural. As noted above, the Martinezes showed great deference to tribal protocol and leadership in their conduct of organizing for equal protection leading up to the trial and in their testimonies and manner at trial.[24] Julia Martinez even deflected questions about her traditional knowledge rather than engage issues she probably considered inappropriate to discuss in court (or with "outsiders"). She even accepted the insinuation that she was not culturally informed and engaged. These choices are incredibly honorable and respectful of the tribe. The Martinezes, as well as other women and their families like them at the Pueblo, were not culturally unknowledgeable and uninvolved. But by choosing not to offer a historical narrative about their traditional perspectives and practices, the defense's claims stood unchallenged. In other words, they could have drawn attention to the inconsistencies within defense testimony about the changes in membership criteria between the Constitution and Ordinance; they could have explained the fact that the Navajo were matrilineal and so Myles's enrollment status and rights could not be extended to his wife and children by law or custom; they could have explained that their living at the Pueblo was in line with the matrilocal customs of the Pueblo (which Myles supported, coming as well from a matrilineal tribe); or they could have un-settled the authority of defense testimony by calling out the influence of Spanish and Mexican Catholicism. The Martinezes chose not to take any of these actions, probably because such actions would have required that they describe the matrilineal and matrilocal heritage of the tribe, which they seemingly felt was inappropriate to do in court.

Second, at no time did the plaintiffs challenge the insinuation that it was women who married nonmembers and their families who were to blame for the cultural changes, loss of lands, and strained resources at Santa Clara (easily enough to question since the nonmember marriage rates appear to have been fairly even). Part of this insinuation was to link the women's alleged lack of cultural knowledge and participation to their being un-duly influenced by "outside" ideologies and values like "women's rights" and feminism. The women and their families were thereby situated within assimilationist paradigms as no longer really Santa Claran and so as not having a legitimate legal claim to membership status and rights. Narrating their matrilineal and matrilocal traditions and teachings would have chal-lenged these conclusions, but again, it would have required them to de-scribe things to the court that they apparently felt were inappropriate.

Instead, their strategy was revealed by the four rebuttal witnesses that the plaintiffs called to speak further to issues of discrimination at the Pueblo. Patrick Gutierrez spoke first. Born in 1905, Gutierrez had served as governor five times, including during the time when the Ordinance was passed. The point of his being called as a rebuttal witness, even though this aspect of the original complaint had been dropped in the pretrial period, was to show that exceptions were made by the council in enrolling the chil-dren of unmarried women when they were related to the tribe's leadership. Gutierrez testified that one of his daughters, Barbara, bore a child, Anita

Mae, while unmarried and then married the father a year later. The birth certificate was changed to make it appear that the parents were married at the time of birth. Anita Mae was retroactively enrolled. Gutierrez was also asked if he knew why the Ordinance was passed. He said that the council felt that there "were too many people coming in" and the tribe did not have "money to support all the people": "For that reason, we had to draw a line" (343).

Herbert Alton Martinez, the eldest son of Julia and Myles Martinez, testified next. The focus of his testimony was to call into question the defense's claims that members and nonmembers who resided on the reservation enjoyed the same rights and privileges within the tribe. He explained that, yes, both of his parents were "full-blooded" Indians but that he was not enrolled at Santa Clara because of the Ordinance. He said that he went to Santa Fe Indian School, Espanola High School, and then the University of Colorado in Denver. He spoke Tewa and had never lived on the Navajo reservation or attempted to enroll there: "I never thought about it because I was brought up Santa Clara, the traditional way, the religious way" (347). He was married to a Navajo woman and they had two boys. After his term in the military and work with the BIA in Denver, he returned to Santa Clara to live. He was staying on the lands of his aunt and in 1973 had applied for a land lease. He was denied and told that it was because he was not enrolled (348–49).

Floripa Northcutt testified next. Northcutt, an enrolled member of the Pueblo, was married and had two children. She was called to rebut the claims by the defense that women who married nonmembers and were residing at Santa Clara were treated equally and fairly as other members. She explained that she had applied for a permit to run cattle and been denied. Patrick Gutierrez was governor at the time. She was told by the council that she could not run cattle because she had married a nonmember: "That's what they told me at the Council. That I was given five days to take my cattle out, which was running with his [Gutierrez] sister's cattle, which his sister was married to a non-member, too" (354). Northcutt removed the cattle and then attempted to lease lands. She was not granted permission to lease lands and again was told that it was because she was married to a nonmember (354). She stated that she was a member of the Winter People and recognized Alcario Tafoya as her representative leader. The defense attempted to have her testimony stricken from the record on the grounds that she was a member and whether or not she could run cattle or lease lands was not relevant. The court disagreed.

The last rebuttal witness was Alcario Tafoya. Tafoya spoke in Tewa with an interpreter for the first part of his testimony and in English for the second (he preferred to speak in Tewa but concluded in English because of the late hour of the day). He identified himself as Fog Bird, So' Kho-wa Tsireh, and said he was seventy-four years old. He said that he was the representative for the Winter People but that the council had removed him from office for supporting a reversal of the Ordinance: "I was appointed by members of the clan along with another man as their listener" but that he had been removed because he "wanted to let these other children come in to be recognized in the village, and the other people didn't want this idea, so they removed me from office" (361). He said that this had occurred in 1968.

Tafoya then described how before the Constitution and Ordinance anybody who wanted to come in to the tribe had to go through the Winter People or Summer People and then to the council. He said that women and men who married out and their children were regularly accepted as members. He said that before the Constitution, leaders were selected by the elders of the tribe and that now they go through the election process. He also said that in the old days children did not necessarily go through initiation to their father's moiety but that it was discussed which way the child should go and it could go either way (367–68). He also said that people could switch moieties and that whether or not they were members they were free to participate in the religious activities of the tribe.

Tafoya was asked about Governor Tafoya's background and said that he did not recognize his leadership because the governor had never been initiated at Santa Clara Pueblo but was at San Ildefonso. He also said that fewer children were participating in the religious activities of the tribe but not because they were restricted from doing so—they seemed to have lost interest.

Upon cross-examination, Tafoya was asked how many grandchildren he had that were not enrolled. He said he had around twenty-six grandchildren and three great-great grandchildren (387). He was asked why, when he was governor in 1945, he had not challenged the Ordinance and he said that it was probably because he had not had such a large family—and so many unenrolled grandchildren—at the time. He was then asked about his two jail terms: The first one was because he tore up a foundation blocking his driveway that was built by one of the Summer People, and the second was because his wife was given a house by his father and he was repairing it and was arrested for trespassing (389). Upon redirect, he stated that the families of five of his seven children lived at Santa Clara and were initiated into the Winter People and participated in the religious activities of the tribe.

The rebuttal witnesses for the defense spoke powerfully to issues of discrimination for women who married out and their families and allies at Santa Clara. They also showed the privileges enjoyed by council officials and their families. But the witnesses were not so strong on challenging or undermining what had become the dominant narrative during the trial about Santa Clara "patriculturalism."

The Verdicts

On December 20, 1975, the District Court ruled for the defense.[25] It found that the Ordinance reflected the "traditional values of patriarchy still significant in tribal life." It also found that membership was "no more or less than a mechanism of social . . . self-definition" and as such was "basic to the tribe's survival as a cultural and economic entity." While the court identified a conflict between the "traditional values of patriarchy" and the ICRA's "equal protection clause" it maintained that "the balance to be struck between these competing interests was better left to the judgment of the Pueblo."

> The equal protection guarantee of the Indian Civil Rights Act should not be construed in a manner which would require or authorize this Court to determine which traditional values will promote cultural survival and should therefore be preserved. . . . Such a determination should be made by the people of Santa Clara; not only because they can best decide what values are important, but also because they must live with the decision every day. . . . To abrogate tribal decisions, particularly in the delicate area of membership, for whatever "good" reasons, is to destroy cultural identity under the guise of saving it.

The court remanded the complaint back to the tribe. However, it claimed federal jurisdiction over complaints filed under ICRA and so asserted that tribes did not enjoy sovereign immunity. On this, the Santa Clara Council appealed.

In *Santa Clara Pueblo et al. v. Martinez et al.* in 1977, the Tenth Circuit Court of Appeals asserted that the ICRA did provide a jurisdictional basis to federal courts over civil complaints against tribes. This was owing to the fact that the ICRA was "designed to provide protection against tribal authority, the intention of Congress to allow suits against the tribe was an essential aspect [of the ICRA]. Otherwise, it would constitute a mere unenforceable declaration of principles." However, the court disagreed on merits. It found that because the complaint involved discrimination on the basis of gender, the Ordinance could only be sustained if justified by a "compelling tribal interest." Because the Ordinance was only thirty-eight years old, and because "the rule did not rationally identify those persons who were emotionally and culturally Santa Clarans," the court held that "the tribe's interest in the ordinance was not substantial enough to justify its discriminatory effect." The Santa Clara appealed.

In *Santa Clara Pueblo et al. v. Martinez et al.* (436 U.S. 49) in 1978, the U.S. Supreme Court reversed the lower court findings on jurisdiction. The court found that the ICRA provided for federal review of tribal actions only in habeas corpus proceedings "given Congress' desire not to intrude needlessly on tribal self-government" and owing to Congress's recognition that civil matters "will frequently depend on questions of tribal tradition and custom which tribal forums may be in a better position to evaluate than federal courts." If federal review of civil complaints outside of habeas corpus proceedings were allowed, the court claimed that it could "substantially interfere with a tribe's ability to maintain itself as a culturally and politically distinct entity." In previous court decisions, it found that

> By not exposing tribal officials to the full array of federal remedies available to redress actions of federal and state officials, Congress may also have considered that resolution of statutory issues under 1302, and particularly those issues likely to arise in a civil context, will frequently depend on questions of tribal tradition and custom which tribal forums may be in a better position to evaluate than federal courts. Our relations with the Indian tribes have "always been . . . anomalous . . . and of a com-

plex character" (*U.S. v. Kagama*). Although we early rejected the notion that Indian tribes are "foreign states" . . . we have also recognized that the tribes remain quasi-sovereign nations which, by government structure, culture, and source of sovereignty are in many ways foreign to the constitutional institutions of the Federal and State Governments. . . . As is suggested by the District Court's opinion in this case, efforts by the federal judiciary to apply the statutory prohibitions of [ICRA] in a civil context may substantially interfere with a tribe's ability to maintain itself as a culturally and politically distinct entity. (*Santa Clara v. Martinez* 1978)

As many have observed, the serious ethical dilemma that has resulted from the *Martinez* decision is that civil rights complaints against tribal governments are remanded back to the same governments for review. Carole Goldberg-Ambrose (2002b) observes that because enrollment decisions are so often enacted through intensely familial, intratribal political factions, with those in power targeting their critics or longtime enemies for expulsion, very few remands to tribal jurisdiction have resulted in a reinstatement or reversal of the complaint (see also Wilkins 2004).[26] On the whole, tribes have merely reassured the relevant federal or state court that their membership decisions are rationally tied to their traditional values, laws, and customs. Under *Martinez*, no further explanation is required or legal review outside the tribe provided (issue addressed more fully in chapter 5).

Following the Supreme Court's ruling, the Santa Clara people have virtually withdrawn from public discussions of the case and its implications.[27] This silence has been discussed within the extant literature on the case as owing to Pueblo "inclinations" to not talk to "outsiders" about what are perceived to be fundamentally "internal" issues. Their silences are probably owing also to several factors entangled in their efforts to successfully navigate the mire of federal law to protect their collective rights to self-government, intratribal and intertribal debates about the case and its consequences, criticisms of the women for going outside the tribe with the suit in the first place, and their own interpersonal and community politics. Whatever the specific contributing factors, their withdrawal and resulting silence are stark features of the prolific scholarship about the case. It has certainly perpetuated misunderstandings and misconstructions of Santa Clara historical experiences and cultural values.

Membrum

member c.1225 (implied in *membered*), from O.Fr. *membre* (11c.), from L. *membrum* "limb, member of the body, part," probably from PIE **mems-ro* (cf. Goth. *mimz* "flesh"). Specific sense of "penis" is first recorded 1356, from L. membrum virile. In Eng., "member of the body" is the original sense; that of "person belonging to a group" is first attested c.1330, from notion of "constituent part of a complex structure." Meaning "one who has been elected to parliament" is from 1454.

— *Online Etymology Dictionary*

From the context of *Martinez*, there is something delightfully ironic about the fact that at the etymological heart of the "member" is the penis. Does this mean membership status and rights are fundamentally masculine? Affirming tribal sovereignty and self-government only after its masculinization? What kinds of social and interpersonal relationships do we erect by making members—by so defining one's belonging and representation of the body?[28] And what of those unmade, dismembered (dare we say made impotent or castrated)? What does that say about the body that remains?

It is not so ironic, however, for those Native peoples like the Martinez family. They must live every day with the real consequences not only of their exclusion from tribal political participation but also the myriad of social issues that derive from the kinds of sexist ideologies and practices that continually rationalize the cultural authenticity and legal legitimacy of that exclusion.

5 In Disenrollment

The *Martinez* case made raw the political intentions, passions, competitions, and ethics that swirl around the more viscous aspects of Native social politics and struggles for sovereignty and self-determination.[1] As discussed in chapter 4, motivations are often tied up in interpersonal, family, and community relations with results determined by whoever happens to be in power (Goldberg-Ambrose 2002a; Wilkins 2004).[2] But as shown in chapter 2, motivations are also informed by the efforts of tribal governments to maintain their legal status and rights within a system that has been unpredictable and punitive. Membership has been key within these social relations and political efforts because of its efficacy in linking tribal self-government (legal legitimacy) to tribal cultural tradition (authenticity). But the ethical principles on which tribal self-government and traditions are based, and so membership policies articulated, are opaque at best, having to negotiate both the power of U.S. national narrations and the complexities of Native cultural histories and knowledge.

These complexities are instanced again within tribal disenrollments following the passage of the Indian Gaming Regulatory Act (IGRA) of 1988. Though disenrollments occurred before the IGRA and have occurred in tribes without gaming (Wilkins 2004), there has been an explosion of disenrollments following the IGRA by tribes who game. And though disenrollments have involved numerous tribes in numerous states, they have become a particularly acidic feature of California Indian politics.[3]

For instance, the Pechanga Band of Luiseño Indians, in Riverside County, California, has disenrolled 223 individuals or a conservative 16 percent of its total membership. The decisions to disenroll were characterized by Pechanga Band officials as an exercise of self-government aimed at protecting the "integrity" of the tribe's culture and identity against frauds who merely wanted a share in gaming revenue. But disenrolled members have accused the Band's leadership of greed and corruption. They filed civil complaints in state court under the ICRA and Public Law 280 of 1953 against tribal officials, including those on the elected Band council and Enrollment Committee, for violating their rights to due process and equal protection. On the complaint of due process, the disenrolled asserted that the Band's actions failed to follow its own Constitution and By-Laws on process and violated a specific law passed by the general membership barring against disenrollments. But on the grounds of *Martinez*, the complaints were summarily dismissed by the court and remanded back to the tribe for review. The tribe quickly confirmed its decisions to disenroll.

It is tempting, indeed compelling, to accuse the Pechanga Band and other gaming tribes who have disenrolled of brass, economically motivated political interests and culturally hypocritical behavior. At the very least, the argument goes, certainly one of the most historically oppressed groups in the United States ought to know better than to oppress its own.

But it is more difficult to think through the work of disenrollment in how tribes have negotiated their political interests in the historical contexts of U.S.-Native relations. In California, these contexts "begin" with the state's history of Native genocide and land fraud and move through the legacies of that history in contemporary anti-Indian rights movements that have found renewed fervor over gaming. Including such organizations as the Citizens for Equal Rights Alliance and Stand Up for Californians, these movements have viciously racialized Native culture and identity—particularly of gaming tribes—in order to challenge Native legal rights not merely to gaming but to the opportunity for wealth and land reacquisition that it represents (Spilde 1999; Darian-Smith 2004; Cramer 2006). People from these organizations claim that real Indians would never be economically opportunistic, as a characteristic opposed to all of the ecological and spiritual values Natives are made to represent within these narrations. And, it goes, that if tribal cultures and identities are inauthentically Native, then their claims to possessing a unique status and rights under federal law are illegitimate. This is "proven" by how tribes take advantage of legal loopholes on the basis of race to discriminate for themselves lands, tax exemption, and development opportunities against other U.S. citizens. This is even more outrageous because—as the stories go—the racial identity of tribes is perceived as being at best convenient and at worst fraudulent (Kroft 1994; Benedict 2001; Barlett and Steele 2002a and 2002b).[4]

Unfortunately, many gaming tribes have reasserted the legitimacy of their legal status and rights as "Indian tribes" on the grounds of a cultural authenticity that leaves unchallenged the racist ideologies on which such authenticity is based. These assertions have deployed several different tactics—most profoundly disenrollment—to combat national and local efforts to undermine tribal rights. In claiming to disenroll the racially inauthentic, they have tacitly contributed to the re-racialization of Native culture and identity.

The important questions about political and interpersonal motivation, and the ethical principles of relationship and responsibility that have been raised by disenrollment, can only be understood in the context of these competing processes of social formation. And they are questions that need to be asked. Just what kind of tribal sovereignty, self-government, and tradition are articulated through disenrollment practices? What kind of sovereignty and self-government is constituted by the ideologies and discourses of racial authenticity?

Historical Contingencies in California

When Spain began its imperial efforts in the region where California was to become a state, it is estimated conservatively that the Native population was around 300,000. Forced into slavery and starvation by the Spanish military and Catholic church working in concert to bring about their power, about 100,000 Native people died between the first mission of 1769 and Spain's cession of the territory to Mexico in 1821. At the close of the U.S.-Mexican War and the "discovery" of gold in California's Sierras in 1848, another 50,000 died as slavery, starvation, and armed conflict characterized Native-Mexican relations as it had Native-Spanish relations. The result, then, of "contact" with Spain and Mexico was the genocide of at least half of the Native population in just under 80 years (Heizer and Almquist 1977; Forbes 1982; Rawls 1984; Thornton 1990; Tinker 1993; Almaguer 1994; Goldberg and Champagne 2002).[5]

After 1848, settlers from the United States quickly outnumbered everyone else in a rabid search for land and gold. Tribes were aggressively removed from their territories by state and state-funded public militia in violation of the Treaty of Guadalupe Hidalgo of 1848, which had provided that the United States would protect Native land grants in the treatied areas. Undeterred, settlers outright murdered Native peoples to gain hold of their lands (Forbes 1982; Rawls 1984; Almaguer 1994; Goldberg and Champagne 2002).

In 1850, California was admitted to the United States as a free state. But in 1851, the legislature passed the Act for the Government and Protection of the Indians, which allowed any "white" to force into work any "Indian" found to be "vagrant." Since Mexicans were then classified as "whites" by state law, this facilitated the enslavement of Native peoples by all property owners in the state (Almaguer 1994). Since "Indians" could not testify against "whites" in court, Natives had no recourse to challenge either their forced removal or enslavement or the physical and sexual violence that came with it. Despite its status as a free state, California permitted the open sale and trade of Native people for labor and sex trade purposes (International Indian Treaty Council and Project Underground 2003).

As if that was not enough, Governor Peter H. Burnett promised that "a war of extermination will continue to be waged between the two races until the Indian race becomes extinct" in his January 1851 message to the legislature (Trafzer and Hyer 1999). In 1853, the legislature officially ordered the "extermination" of all Indians. Reimbursed by the federal government, state bounties were paid per Indian scalp or severed head and were paid all expenses related to the efforts, such as for the cost of ammunition, guns, and horses (Forbes 1982).[6] Within two years, California paid out about one million dollars to individuals who submitted claims. It was inhumane. Whole tribes, bands, and families were massacred. Describing this campaign in *Native Americans of California and Nevada* (1982), Jack D. Forbes emphasizes that it was not merely military or state officials who participated in it: "The sequence of events [are] all the more distressing since it serves to indict not a group of cruel leaders, or a few squads of rough soldiers, but, in effect, an entire people; for the conquest of the Native Californian was above all else a popular, mass enterprise" (69).

By 1860, no more than twenty thousand of the Native population had survived. Those who did were almost entirely dispossessed of their territories and living in conditions of gross poverty and ill health. Many had begun to identify as Mexican to secure paid work as farmhands, passing into another analogously complicated status in hopes of survival.

Meanwhile, in 1851, the U.S. Congress sent a commission to California to negotiate treaties with tribes in order to secure land cession and tribal relocation onto reservations and under federal jurisdiction. By 1852, eighteen treaties had been negotiated with more than one hundred tribes. The treaties would have provided the tribes with approximately 8.5 million acres divided into eighteen reservations (Heizer 1972). However, California's governor and senate actively opposed the treaties, seeing them as excessively generous and cumbersome to the state's goals. They, along with several private citizens (mostly ranchers and miners), lobbied hard to stop the ratification process in Congress. As a result of their efforts, the U.S. Senate put an "injunction of secrecy" on the treaties, which held until 1905. But the tribes were never notified that the treaties had not been ratified. Federal and state agents and militia moved many Native people (often from several different tribes) onto smaller reservations (or "rancherias") under the auspices of carrying out treaty provisions while they seized the "deserted" lands for themselves.

In *Indians of California: The Changing Image* (1984), James J. Rawls describes what occurred after the recovery of the treaties in 1905. Several tribes and organizations including the Mission Indian Federation worked hard to try to secure a redress of the status of the treaties under constitutional law. As a result, the state gave its attorney general permission to represent the treatied tribes in a lawsuit against the United States for the nullification of the treaties (Rawls 1984, 210). As a matter of federal law, tribes had been forbidden to pursue complaints against the United States in court for treaty violations. But in 1928 the U.S. Congress passed the California Jurisdiction Act for just such a complaint to move forward in the U.S. Court of Claims (as *Indians of California v. U.S.*). The act also directed the BIA to produce a census of the members of those tribes who had signed the treaties. Approximately thirty-six thousand Indians were enrolled on the resulting census.

In 1944, the court recognized that a "promise" had been made to the Indians of California regarding their land rights "but the treaties were never ratified so the promise was never fulfilled" (Rawls 1984, 210). Therefore, the court ruled in favor of the plaintiffs and awarded them 7 cents per acre as compensation for the 8.5 million acres of reservation lands that would have been provided to them had the treaties been ratified. As Rawls observes, the award did not reflect the value of the land at the time that the treaties were signed (no public lands were being sold at the time for less than $1.50 an acre), nor any interest that would have accrued on the payment had it been made in 1852. The total award amounted to $17,053,941. The court then deducted $12,029,099 for the estimated expenses that the BIA had accrued in serving California Indians since 1852. Final judgment amounted to $5,024,842. In 1950, Congress authorized a payment of approximately $150 to each of the thirty-six thousand listed members (210). Meanwhile, California passed a few state laws that set aside some small tracts of land for some tribes. Termed "rancherias," about 117 of them were established by 1950, totaling less than ten thousand acres.

In 1946, Congress established the Indian Claims Commission (ICC) in an effort to settle escalating claims by tribes throughout the country against the United States for treaty violations. Until its expiration in 1978, the ICC received close to 850 claims and held 611 hearings. It settled the claims monetarily despite tribal protests for even a partial restoration of their treatied lands.[7]

Tribes in California pursued twenty-three claims for the government's failure to ratify the eighteen treaties. In 1963, the ICC ruled on their behalf, consolidating most of the claims into a single judgment. While recognizing tribal title to some sixty-four million acres of state land, the ICC claimed that title had been "extinguished" in 1853. It awarded 47 cents per acre, or about $29 million in compensation. The BIA updated the 1928 list of members to include about sixty-nine thousand individuals and issued per capita payments in the amount of less than $700 each (Rawls 1984, 211).

In 1953, California became part of Public Law 280 (PL 280) along with Minnesota, Nebraska, Oregon, Wisconsin, and later Alaska (Goldberg-Ambrose 1997). PL 280 transferred federal jurisdiction over reservation crimes between Indians to state authorities. It gave states jurisdiction over certain civil matters on reservations. It so required states to assume responsibility for the infrastructure necessary to enforce its jurisdiction over tribal criminal and civil matters.

Initially California refused and then unevenly assumed its jurisdictional responsibilities in relation to tribes, arguing that the federal government had failed to pass necessary legislation to fund the expense. As a result, police and even fire and ambulatory care as well as access to courts remained grossly inconsistent and often negligent among tribes. In many cases, criminal and civil matters went unaddressed. To exacerbate the situation, PL 280 also meant that tribes no longer qualified for federal aid and programs in criminal and civil matters since states had been given jurisdiction over them. This meant that tribes in California did not qualify for federal programs and support to establish their own police forces or court systems, furthering their dependence on a state that refused to comply with the law (Goldberg-Ambrose 1997).[8]

In 1958, California passed the Rancheria Act on fiscal grounds. The act terminated the legal status of thirty-eight tribes in the state and resulted almost immediately in the appropriation of their lands for public sale. In 1983, the decision was reversed for seventeen of those tribes.

As of the summer of 2007, there were 107 California tribes with federal recognition status (Marks and Contreras 2007, 2).[9] According to the BIA, as of September 22, 2008, seventy-four have petitioned for acknowledgment through the BAR. For both recognized and unrecognized groups, economics remain diverse and difficult. While a few recognized tribes have benefited from gaming (Goldberg and Champagne 2002; Riffe 2005) — there are fifty-seven operating facilities in twenty-five of fifty-eight state counties (Marks and Contreras 2007, 3) — others do not have any means to economic development. This is caused by a number of different factors including the fact that the modest amount of lands that tribes do possess are often "off the grid" of public highways, water, and power lines, and too small for any significant commercial or housing development (Marks and Contreras 2007).

Historical Contingencies in "Reverse Racism"

Conflicts over tribal gaming initially focused on questions about the extent of state jurisdiction over tribal lands[10] but quickly took on the scope of tribal sovereignty in relationship to states. If a state did not permit gambling, could tribes, as sovereigns, ignore state law and establish gaming facilities if they desired? In *Seminole Tribe of Florida v. Butterworth* (1981)[11] and *California v. Cabazon Band of Mission Indians* (1987),[12] the Fifth Circuit Court of Appeals and the U.S. Supreme Court said that they could (Tsosie 1997; Mason 2000; Washburn 2001; Goldberg and Champagne 2002; Darian-Smith 2004; Light and Rand 2005; Fletcher 2007; Cattelino 2008; Cornell 2008).

In response to state concerns resulting from these court decisions, and tribal concerns about protecting jurisdiction and economic development on reservation lands, Congress enacted the IGRA. The act mandates that states enter into "good faith" negotiations with tribes interested in opening high-stakes facilities (though many have refused [Cattelino 2008]), all of the provisions of which must be approved by the DOI.[13] Generally, resulting agreements or compacts allow tribes to establish facilities under existing or amended state constitutional law provided that the tribes pay a percentage of their profits to the state. The IGRA also regulates how tribes can spend gaming revenue. It must be used to fund tribal government operations, provide for the general welfare of the tribe, promote tribal economic development, donate to charitable organizations, or help fund local government agencies. Tribes can pay per capita amounts to members, provided that they prepare a plan to allocate the revenue, the plan is approved by the Secretary of the Interior, and the interests of minors are protected. To monitor compliance, the IGRA established the National Indian Gaming Commission (NIGC).[14]

By 2008, tribal gaming had grown to an almost $30 billion-a-year industry (from $8.5 billion in 1998).[15] Concurrently, antigaming perspectives and political efforts grew to include nontribal gamers, church groups, citizen and property rights groups, labor unions, and environmental agencies (Goldberg and Champagne 2002; Darian-Smith 2004; Cramer 2006; Barker 2005/2006). Despite the diversity of these constituencies, their arguments about tribal gaming have shared a "reverse racism" logic. Gaming tribes are racialized as "special interest groups" and minorities out to play the race card in order to "take advantage" of "unfair" federal laws that allow them to monopolize economic opportunities without threat of public accountability or taxation (Kroft 1994; Benedict 2001).

But these arguments ignore, among other things, the severe economic disparities that exist among tribes. In California, these disparities resulted in the Cabazon Band of Mission Indians and the Morongo Band of Mission Indians needing to turn to fairly modest gaming ventures—mostly bingo inspired by local churches—to provide some income. After the IGRA, tribes sought compacts to establish broader activities, all with the aim of achieving some measure of economic self-sufficiency (Lombardi n.d.; Goldberg and Champagne 2002; Darian-Smith 2004; Marks and Contreras 2007).

Following years of state refusals to negotiate the compacts (Lombardi n.d.; Goldberg and Champagne 2002), Governor Gray Davis signed the first fifty-eight in 1999. Under the agreements, which expire in 2020, tribes can operate facilities with each having up to two thousand slot machines. In 2000, Proposition 1A, the Indian Self-Reliance Act, amended the state's constitution to allow for other Class III operations. The act also created the Revenue Sharing Trust Fund administered by the California Gambling Control Commission. Tribes with more than 350 slot machines pay a percentage of their quarterly profits from the slots into the funds, which are then distributed to tribes without gaming facilities and tribes that operate fewer than 350 machines. Approximately 70 percent are eligible to receive payments because only about 30 percent operate facilities that require revenue sharing. According to the October 23, 2008, report by the California Gambling Control Commission about the quarter ending December 31, 2010, "All eligible tribes will receive a total of $275,000, which consists of $165,392.04 from license fees and interest income and $109,607.96 from shortfall funds. . . . The quarterly amount of the shortfall in payments to all eligible recipient Indian tribes for the quarter totals $7,782,165.16" (down from the $11,904,816.37 during the quarter ending September 20, 2006).

As a result of gaming, tribes have been able to reacquire a minor amount of lands, establish cultural centers and museums, expand businesses, support local governments, donate to charitable organizations, hire upward of two hundred thousand employees (the majority of whom are non-Native), and provide housing, education, and health care to their members (Lombardi n.d.; Goldberg and Champagne 2002; Riffe 2005). However, as has been the case throughout the country, while a few tribes have done extraordinarily well in gaming (less than 5 percent of the total), many more are still without electricity, water, phone, or cable lines, paved roads, or even access to emergency care or medical facilities. Despite this diversity, tribes have experienced a "backlash" against not only their gaming activities but all issues related to their land reacquisition, economic development, and increasing though still moderate clout in state and national politics (Wanamaker 2002a, 2002b, 2002c, 2002d; Adams 2000; Marks and Contreras 2007).

In 2003, California's gubernatorial recall campaign was focused by public outrage over the state's energy crisis and feelings of having been fleeced by Enron and politicians whose fraud contributed to if not directly caused the state's escalating budget deficit and bleak outlook.[16] (From the perspective of the 2008 recession, the crisis appears even more prophetic and complex.) Arnold Schwarzenegger, the Republican gubernatorial candidate, won quick popular support by promising to bring about a true, "no-nonsense" reform of state politics led by and for "the people." This came about as he was able to distance himself from Governor Davis and his Democratic opponent, Cruz Bustamante, on a number of key issues that Schwarzenegger focused rhetorically on tribal gaming (Werner 2003; Leduff 2003; Broder 2004a, 2004b; Bumiller and Stolberg 2004; Bartfield 2004b). Tribal gaming allowed Schwarzenegger to share in the moral outrage and righteous indignation that characterized the public debate over the state's escalating economic crisis while deflecting attention from his own circle of influence, including a number of President George W. Bush's advisors and Enron and other energy executives who were directing and funding the recall effort (McLean and Elkind 2003).[17]

Specifically, Schwarzenegger promised to put an end to what he characterized as the corrupt influence of gaming tribes on state politicians. As Bustamante was being denigrated and then discredited for taking contributions from some of the more affluent gaming tribes, Schwarzenegger used the 1999 compacts as an example of Davis's failure to make good economic decisions. He claimed that the compacts could have helped balance if not put into the black the state budget as they had in other states—

why, after all, had Davis not secured a 25 percent share of gaming revenue as had Connecticut from the Mashantucket Pequot and Mohegan Tribe (Coile and Feist 2003)? Instead, Davis and Bustamante allowed themselves to be bought off and manipulated by a powerful "special interest group" trying to skirt their civic, financial responsibilities to the state (Berthelsen 2003; Raine 2003). These assertions were encapsulated in a TV ad in which Schwarzenegger accused gaming tribes of not being willing to pay their "fair share" of taxes at a time when the state was facing a severe economic crisis. He then promised that if elected he would ensure that tribes were properly taxed (Matier 2003).

By representing tribes as greedy and selfish, and misinforming the public of the legal basis for tribal tax exemption status, Schwarzenegger presented himself as a powerful political player who would be immune to "special interest groups" and their money. Appropriating the discourse of public criticisms of Davis, Bustamante, Enron, and the entire state's energy industry, Schwarzenegger focused attention on tribes and tribal gaming revenue as the more insidious culprits in the state's economic crisis. This, in turn, allowed him to avoid addressing in any serious way the real causes for the state's situation, obscuring his own political alliances and corporate sources in his campaign financing (McLean and Elkind 2003).

The rhetoric was successful. Davis was removed from office and Schwarzenegger was elected. In his January 2004 state of the state address, Schwarzenegger dropped the talk about imposing taxes on tribes and claimed that he "respect[ed] the sovereignty of our Native American tribes" but "believed" that tribes needed to "respect the economic situation that California faces" (Editorial, Indianz.com 2004a). He wanted tribes to renegotiate their 1999 compacts to pay a greater share of their profits to the state. Aides echoed this by claiming that Connecticut earned upward of $400 million annually from their share in tribal gaming. In less formal settings, Schwarzenegger cavalierly stated that tribes were "ripping us off" by not paying higher percentages of their revenue to the state: "We want them to negotiate and pay their fair share" (ibid; see also Raine 2003; Matier 2003).

Schwarzenegger announced quickly his appointment of Daniel Kolkey, the former legal affairs secretary to Governor Pete Wilson, to renegotiate the 1999 compacts (Associated Press 2004a). In interviews, Kolkey identified Schwarzenegger's goal as securing $1 billion to $2 billion annually from the tribes, claiming that it was time for them "to pay their fair share" because they "have a monopoly on taking gambling proceeds from California citizens" (ibid; see also DeArmond 2004a). But in 2003, California tribes earned a total of $4.7 billion from gaming so $1 billion to $2 billion would have meant a much more considerable share of their revenue than 25 percent. With both tribes and some of the legislature criticizing the amount as unrealistic, Schwarzenegger quietly modified his goal to $500 million and later $300 million, promising to use the money on education and transportation (Editorial, Indianz.com 2004b).

In July 2004, Schwarzenegger signed renegotiated compacts with five tribes: United Auburn Indian Community, Rumsey Band of Wintun Indians, Pauma Band of Mission Indians, Pala Band of Mission Indians, and Viejas Band of Kumeyaay Indians (Riffe 2005). The compacts increased the tribes' payments to the Revenue Sharing Trust Fund ($2 million per year) in exchange for allowing the tribes to operate as many slot machines as they desired (paying on a progressive scale on their slots of up to $25,000 per machine). Additionally, the five tribes agreed to pay a $1 billion bond over eighteen years, amounting to about $150 million to $200 million per year, until the compacts expired in 2030 (Sifuentes 2004; Bartfield 2004a). The tribes followed up with an ad campaign of their own, heralding their willingness to share their revenues with the state as good citizens. The state then negotiated four new compacts with the Lytton Band of Pomo Indians, Buena Vista Rancheria of Me-Wuk Indians, Ewiiaapaayp Band of Kumeyaay Indians, and Fort Mojave Tribe. Under enormous political pressure over the question of off-reservation casinos, the Lytton compact was rescinded. The other three were quickly approved by the legislature and BIA (Sweeney 2005).

Schwarzenegger's negotiations with tribes, however, quickly stalled during the time leading up to the November 2004 elections. Card club and racetrack industries sponsored Proposition 68, which would have allowed them to install slot machines.[18] The Agua Caliente Band of Cahuilla Indians countered with Proposition 70, later co-sponsored by the San Manuel Band of Mission Indians and endorsed by the California Indian Nations Gaming Association. Prop 70 would have cancelled Prop 68 if both had passed, allowed slot machines at non-Indian card clubs and racetracks, and fixed tribal gaming revenue shares at 8.84 percent (Editorial, Indianz.com 2004c, 2004e; Sweeney 2004).

Schwarzenegger mounted a huge anti-Prop 68 and 70 campaign. In response, the sponsors of Prop 68 pulled their ads long before the November vote. So Schwarzenegger turned his attentions to Prop 70. He claimed it belonged in the "special interest hall of fame" (J. Ellis 2004). "For years, [tribes] have taken advantage of the state. . . . They've ripped off the state" (J. Ellis 2004; see also Editorial, Indianz.com 2004f). Now, the state was seeking "the right to open up those casino books" and betray tribal campaign financing and tax loopholes (J. Ellis 2004). He wanted Californians to trust him to negotiate compacts that would ensure "environmental protection, labor unions and audits, all while providing millions in revenue for state education, health care and transportation" (ibid.). He boasted that the five compacts he had already signed were going to garner upward of $300 million a year for the state, a figure he would later have to admit was closer to $16 million (Editorial, Indianz.com 2004g). However, the bravado worked and both measures were defeated (Wiegand 2004).

After the elections, Schwarzenegger invited gaming tribes back to the negotiating table. However, all of the more affluent tribes, including Agua Caliente and Morongo, ceased negotiations and demanded a public apology for Schwarzenegger's characterization of them during the campaigns. Schwarzenegger refused (Hermann and Miller 2004; Editorial, Indianz.com 2004c; J. Miller 2004a, 2004b; Yamamura 2004). With renegotiations stalled, Schwarzenegger issued a Proclamation on Tribal Gaming on May 18, 2005. The proclamation spelled out a strict policy regarding compacts with urban-based and landless tribes, which would then require a "buy in" of relevant local, state, and federal agencies.

Schwarzenegger blamed tribes for an economic crisis that was far beyond their influence or ability to reform. All things considered, there was a painful irony in the claim—that it was somehow the tribes who were enjoying illicit access to state property, business opportunity, and political clout. In some sense, that was the point. The maneuver fit well with national discourses in which gaming tribes were configured as "special interest groups" or minority groups taking unfair, opportunistic advantage of their race to find loopholes within the law to avoid their civic responsibilities to fellow citizens who were dumping billions of dollars into tribal economies. It proved an effective means to displacing the historical realities and legacies of colonialism and imperialism in California as well as the factors actually contributing to the state's steady economic decline on par with the nation's.

The real impetus in the economic blame game was to challenge the legitimacy of tribal status and rights. A myriad of constituencies—including gaming but even more so citizen and property rights groups who were taking on affirmative action policies throughout the country—aligned in aims to reverse Native rights on the grounds that they were based on race and were therefore unconstitutional. Gaming tribes served their ends by epitomizing just how much tribes were no longer really Indian enough—or the right kind of Indian—to be deserving or due of such status and rights. After all, real Indians would never be self-serving greedy capitalists (Spilde 1999; Darian-Smith 2004; Cramer 2006). And if tribes were no longer culturally authentic, then their rights were illegitimate.

This was most directly articulated through references to the revenue and growth of tribal gaming.[19] The unquestionably impressive numbers were an easy affirmation of the image of an all-powerful, rich, and fraudulent gaming Indian. It was an Indian selfishly and greedily living a life of luxury while states struggled against economic doom (as in Schwarzenegger's recall campaign) or while other Indians lived on in poverty (as in *Time* magazine's controversial special issue on tribal gaming and *South Park's* satiric episode "Red Man's Greed").[20] These images—misinformed, distorted, satirical, stupid—greatly distorted the economic reality confronting the majority of Native people in the United States, and so only further displaced ongoing patterns of Native domination facilitated by law. For instance, according to the U.S. Census of 2000 "American Indians/Alaskan Natives" reported a 24.5 percent poverty rate compared to the national average of 11.6 percent. But the point of the image was not to further historical understanding. It was to produce a particular kind of tribal culture and identity that served challenges of tribal rights. Essentially, that culture and identity had to be inauthentic if the legal challenge was to be effective. Nowhere was this more acidic than in public attacks of the Mashantucket Pequot (see Cramer 2006), epitomized by Donald Trump's infamous declaration before a Senate hearing on proposed amendments to the IGRA in 1992 that "when you go up to Connecticut and look—now [the Pequots] don't look like real Indians to me. They don't look like Indians to me, Sir. And they don't look like Indians to other Indians" (Kroft 1994).

Historical Contingencies Read Together

The deployment of racialized notions of cultural authenticity within anti-Indian (gaming) arguments is not an unfamiliar strategy in the politics of racialized dominance. In California, this has been enacted through a history of state law that has established and protected political and economic privilege for those classified as "white" (Heizer and Almquist 1977; Almaguer 1994; Lipsitz 1998). As Cheryl I. Harris argues (1993), the result is not merely the perpetuation of the legal protections and privileges for whites but the legitimation of the sense of entitlement and the enjoyment of status and reputation for those so classified.

The ideologies and institutions of white privilege have deeply informed the political perspectives and agendas of movements opposing tribal rights of which gaming is one of its venues. Linked up in powerful ways with anti-affirmative action and anti-immigrant efforts, the movements have re-articulated a discourse of civil rights to reassert the legal protections of whiteness. Therein, treaties and federal laws are defined as discriminating benefits, services, and funds for tribes against other U.S. citizens — coded as white — solely on the basis of race. As if treaty and federal law emerged out of a historical vacuum, the reverse racism argument reflects a gross level of ignorance about ongoing histories of oppression and discrimination. It also perpetuates a resentment and fear over the loss of privilege so firmly entrenched within the law for whites as to seem warranted (Barker 2005/2006; Kauanui 2002, 2008).

For instance, in 1999, Proposition 5, the Indian Casino Gaming Initiative, passed but was quickly challenged by hotel and restaurant labor unions and a consortium of self-identified "business and property owners." These groups filed two separate lawsuits claiming that the proposition was unconstitutional. The unions argued that the measure did not adequately address labor rights issues for tribal employees. The consortium of "business and property owners" argued that the measure was a form of racial discrimination because it provided a virtual monopoly of economic opportunities — and so the means and access to land acquisition — to Natives solely on the basis of race.

One of the more vocal organizations involved in that suit was Stand Up for Californians. Stand Up claimed that it "unite[d] over 30 grass roots, citizens' action groups from every corner of California and is widely supported by law enforcement, religious, environmental, business, city council members, county supervisors and other political leaders."[21] In its suit Stand Up maintained that Prop 5 violated the "constitutional rights of the property and business owners" to fair and equal access to land acquisition and economic development.

Prop 5 was overturned by the California Supreme Court. The court ruled that the proposition was illegal because it permitted forms of gambling that were not legal under the state's constitution. It did not respond directly to the complaint of racial discrimination, though Stand Up claimed victory on that point.

Californians for Indian Self-Reliance, a coalition of some forty tribes spearheaded by Mark Macarro, the chairperson of the Pechanga Band of Luiseño Indians, and Mary Ann Martin-Andreas, the chairperson of the Morongo Band of Mission Indians, was successful in getting Proposition 1A, the Indian Self-Reliance Act, passed in March 2000 by a strong majority vote (64.5 percent). The act amended the state's constitution to allow for gambling, affirm existing compacts, and allow for new compacts to commence. It also permitted union organizing at tribal businesses including casinos (Lombardi n.d.).

But in order to accomplish this, the tribes chose two political strategies to combat the anti-Indian gaming arguments.[22] First, they chose to distance themselves from the "undesirable" populations being targeted by other political campaigns—namely ("illegal") immigrants and criminals (particularly "repeat offenders")—by refusing to be similarly characterized as selfish welfare drains on the state's fraught economy. To do so, they mobilized a discourse of "self-reliance" to represent gaming not as an opposite of tribal culture and identity but as a means for small, isolated reservation-based tribal communities to achieve economic self-sufficiency. This, it was promised, would allow tribes to take care of their own people as well as the state in which they lived (through employment, support of local governments, and revenue sharing), so reflecting core social values of care and contribution as well as their sense of responsibility as state citizens.[23] This intended to separate tribes from *other* populations who had become drains on the state's financial resources and programs like public education and health care and who were skirting their civic responsibilities by not paying their fair share of taxes.

Second, tribes attempted to reauthenticate their cultures and identities and so their legal legitimacy by disenrollment. Disenrollment allowed tribes to assert the viability and relevance of their cultural traditions regarding membership—and the governments charged with its protection and preservation—against frauds and criminals. The strategy worked by suggesting that those members who remained were truly authentic, which in turn reinforced their legal legitimacy.

The Disenrolled

As of November 5, 2003, the California State Association of Counties reported the following about tribal gaming and reservations:

Number of Tribes/Compacts in California
- ▷ Total with Compacts, Request for Compacts, or Petitioning for Federal Recognition, or unknown status: 172
- ▷ Total that have Federal Recognition: 108
- ▷ Total Tribal-State Compacts: 65
- ▷ Compacted Tribes that have active gaming facilities: 52
- ▷ Compacted Tribes that are non-gaming: 13
- ▷ Total petitioning for Federal Recognition: 50
- ▷ Total withdrawn petitions or denied by the BIA: 7
- ▷ Total where their status is unknown: 39

Tribal Enrollment of Federally Recognized Tribes
- ▷ Total Enrollment (80 Tribes [out of 108]): 46,309
- ▷ Tribal Enrollment in Gaming, Compact Areas: 18,603
- ▷ Tribal Enrollment in Non-Gaming, Compact Areas: 6,644
- ▷ Tribal Enrollment in Federally Recognized, Non-Compact Areas: 21,062
- ▷ Tribal Population of Federally Recognized Tribes (96 Tribes [out of 108]): 51,385

Tribal Acreage of Federally Recognized Tribes
- ▷ Total Tribal Acreage in California (97 Tribes [out of 108]): 989,643

Indian Gaming Facilities in California
- ▷ Total number of fully operational casinos in California: 53
- ▷ Total number of casinos with Class II gaming: 1
- ▷ Total number of proposed casinos: 26[24]

It is more difficult to find solid, current statistics on tribal disenrollments in California. After comparing several different sources including federal, state, tribal, and nonprofit organization reports, it appears that of the 108 federally recognized tribes in the state, between fifteen and twenty have disenrolled four thousand to five thousand members. This is fairly significant in a state where the overwhelming majority of tribes have fewer than two thousand members each.[25] Since 1988, about 10 percent of the membership of California tribes have been disenrolled. But, for each of the fifteen to twenty tribes who have disenrolled, it has meant a loss of anywhere between 10 and 50 percent of their total membership.[26]

One of the most prominent tribes to disenroll members is the Pechanga Band of Luiseño Indians (also referred to legally as the Temecula Band of Luiseño Mission Indians and the Pechanga Band of Mission Indians). This prominence is owing to a hugely successful gaming, hotel, food, and entertainment complex begun in 1995 and boasting roughly $1 billion of the $9.1 billion annual gaming revenue statewide. This success has allowed the Pechanga to expand its economic portfolio as well as its political leadership in the state.[27] But its success and leadership mask—at least in popular media coverage of the issues—a difficult history. This history includes a grotesque massacre at the hands of the public militia in 1846, an unratified treaty with the United States in 1875, and a series of forced expulsions from their lands by local ranchers that culminated in 1875.

Over the next one hundred years, the Pechanga Band retained and recovered some of its original territories, confirmed by an Executive Order of June 1882 (2,680 acres), a trust patent issued in August 1893 (2,840 acres), a grant deed executed in March 1907 (235 acres), a trust patent issued in May 1931 (440 acres), and a trust patent issued in August 1971 (640 acres) (see Pechanga Band 1978). By 1971, the Pechanga Indian Reservation totaled an unusual, at least for California, 6,835 acres, anchored by a Spanish land grant issued to Temecula Headman and Chief Pablo Apis (also spelled Apish) in the 1840s and a land patent issued by President William McKinley to Paulina Hunter as a survivor of the 1846 massacre. The current reservation recovered the lands included within these two titles.

From their territorial base, the Pechanga Band ratified a Constitution and By-Laws on December 10, 1978, effective January 1, 1979. This ratification followed a short decade of the Band bringing electricity, a well and water system, telephone lines, and a sewage system to the reservation, resulting in an increase in member residency (Karshmer n.d.). The Constitution and By-Laws detailed the operations of Pechanga government, elections, the duties of elected officials, and the powers of the Business Council and other officials. It provided for a strict process of general membership meetings and majority voting on proposed amendments to the Constitution and By-Laws as well as of spending of the Band's money. Article II detailed the criteria for Band membership:

> Membership is an enrolled member documented in the Band's Official Enrollment Book of 1979. Qualifications for membership of the Temecula Band of Luiseño Mission Indians are: A. Applicant must show proof of Lineal Descent from original Pechanga Temecula people; B. Adopted people, family or band, and non-Indians cannot be enrolled. Exception: People who were accepted in the Indian Way prior to 1928 will be accepted; C. If you have ever been enrolled or recognized in any other reservation you cannot enroll in Pechanga. The membership enrollment will be opened the first month of each year by the Band's Enrollment Committee. (Emphasis is in the original.) (Pechanga Band 1978)

The Constitution and By-Laws established the Band's Enrollment Book, which included all of those who satisfied the criteria for membership specified in Article II. The Enrollment Book recorded the names of 307 individuals as members, along with their lineal descent (Pechanga Band 1979).

The Enrollment Committee, comprised of elected officials from the Band's membership, were required to adhere to strict guidelines in the review of new membership applications, the form for which was approved by a vote of the general membership in 1980 (Karshmer n.d.; Pechanga Band 1996a and 1996b). The guidelines included requirements that the committee have ten members but that at least six had to be present for a quorum, that committee members were not to be under the influence of alcohol or drugs, that committee members were to take an oath of "confidence and secrecy" regarding application documents and discussions at all of their meetings, that all documents be kept in a bank vault, that unresolved disagreements within the committee go before the general membership, and that the committee adhere to all requirements set forth on the application forms to be approved by the general membership. The guidelines included a copy of Article II of the Constitution and By-Laws and confirmed that the Band's annual open enrollment period would be January 1 through January 31 (see Pechanga Band 1996b).

In October 1980, after a year of disruptive behavior through which they had stalled tribal elections, a small group led by Russell "Butch" Murphy announced at a general membership meeting that they were breaking away from the tribe and forming their own tribe. The group did so and held their own elections in January 1981: fifty-nine individuals voted four people onto a council. This council went to the BIA and requested recognition as the official Pechanga Band and approval of their election results. The BIA approved both requests until the Pechanga Band held its elections under its ratified Constitution on April 25, 1981, with 149 individuals voting. The BIA then withdrew its recognition of the "splinter group" and recognized the validity of the April elections as conducted by the official Pechanga Band (Karshmer n.d.).

According to the legal brief submitted by the Pechanga Band to the assistant secretary of the BIA that contested the recognition of the splinter group (who had appealed the BIA's withdrawal of their recognition), the Pechanga Band decided in the midst of this conflict to have a sixteen-month open enrollment period—from January 1979 to July 1981—to receive membership applications from as many as possible (Karshmer n.d.). At the end of this period, a total of 456 individuals were enrolled in the Band. Forty-five individuals were informed by letter that they needed to supply additional information to establish their lineal descent; twenty individuals were informed by letter that they did not satisfy the Band's membership criteria (mostly involving individuals who had been adopted). In the end, only twenty people remained with the splinter group (ibid.).

In 1989, the Enrollment Committee disenrolled six descendants of Apis on the grounds that they were adopted and not lineal descendants. Controversy surrounded this action because of the provisions of Article II that allowed membership for those who had been adopted.

In 1995, the Pechanga Band began modest gaming operations. Evidently, at that time, an influx of membership applications were received, particularly from adults (it has been the norm that the majority of applications came from existing members for their newborns and children under five years of age). At a special meeting of the general membership on February 25, 1996, the Band approved by a majority vote the request from the Enrollment Committee that a moratorium be placed on all new adults and their children applicants (only those applications that had been received through January 31, 1996, were to be processed). This moratorium was meant to provide the committee with some breathing room for working through the applications (see Pechanga Band 1996a and 1996b). However, it has remained in effect because it has been repeatedly approved by the general membership.

In 2002, the Enrollment Committee included eleven members. The chair of the committee breached confidentiality in revealing information about membership applications to noncommittee members and was replaced. The new chair, a descendant of Paulina Hunter, along with other committee members, initiated an internal review of the Enrollment Committee's work dating back to the 1996 moratorium. In their review, they found a number of applications that should have been processed and approved but that had been put in after the establishment of the moratorium and had been left unprocessed. Because the Enrollment Committee had violated the provisions of the Band's Constitution and By-Laws and guidelines by these actions, the new chair of the Enrollment Committee contacted the committee's independent attorney, John Cohen, a staff attorney with California Indian Legal Services, and asked for advice on how to handle the matter. The committee also made a formal request to the Band's council for an internal audit, which Cohen was to conduct as independent counsel, and which was to focus on the committee's actions in handling and processing all membership applications dating back to the 1996 moratorium.

In reaction to these two requests, the committee's attorney was quickly replaced by counsel from the Band's legal department — John Macarro (the brother of the chair, Mark Macarro). The Band's council never took action on the request for the internal audit and instead removed eight of the eleven members from the Enrollment Committee, including the new chair, and locked them out of their offices. The three individuals who remained on the committee began initiating disenrollments a few months later, including the disenrollments of descendants of Pablo Apis and Paulina Hunter. Concurrent with their efforts, a group calling itself the Concerned Pechanga People (CPP) began a campaign to support the disenrollments on the grounds that the families were not really Pechanga.[28]

Pablo Apis

The first families who received disenrollment letters from the Enrollment Committee were 133 descendants of Manuela Miranda, the granddaughter of Pablo Apis. Apis was a well-known and well-regarded headman or chief. In 1845, he received a land grant from the last Mexican governor of California, Pio Pico, to 2,283 acres of land. The land served as a village site for the Pechanga people in Temecula Valley. The Apis home was the place where the unratified treaty of 1852 was negotiated between the Pechanga Band and U.S. federal agents.

Miranda was orphaned when her mother, Juana Apis, passed away. She then lived with her older sister, Custoria Magee, and her grandmother, Casilda Apis (Pablo's wife), at the village. After the tribe was forcibly evicted from the village in 1875, Miranda married Jose Miranda and moved to the San Jacinto/Hemet area. She was a learned midwife who birthed generations of Native children in the area. She raised some of these children as her own.

Owing to the issues around Miranda's residency, the three members of the Enrollment Committee raised questions about the credibility of her affiliation with the tribe as well as the accuracy of records indicating that she was "one-half Pechanga." They maintained that the 133 of her descendants never should have been enrolled. Their letters to the 133 in 2003 explained that if Apis-Miranda's descendants could not supply adequate proof of Miranda's status as an "original Pechanga Temecula" person and of their lineal descent from her, they would be disenrolled.

In response, the family produced extensive documentation about Miranda, including her lineal descent from Pablo Apis, his status as a reputed headman, and local and BIA records that stated that Miranda was born in 1863 as "one-half Pechanga." They also supplied records that showed that she had enrolled her children—by birth and by adoption—in a local Indian school and that she was identified as a Pechanga person until she died in 1956.

Apparently, the documentation did not satisfy the three members of the Enrollment Committee nor the Band's elected officials, who accused the 133 of falsifying federal and local records. Concurrently, Chair Mark Macarro claimed in several interviews with news media that Pablo Apis might have been a member of another Band of the Luiseño, but he was "just not

Pechanga" (quoted in DeArmond 2004b; see O'Leary 2004b). This claim was made even as the Band's official website — http://www.pechanga-nsn .gov — at the time specifically mentioned Pablo Apis as a historical leader of the Pechanga Band (the page remained up even after the disenrollments occurred).

At the reservation, questions about the legitimacy of Apis's and Miranda's identities were fueled by members of the CPP. Through flyers distributed anonymously to Band members, the CPP claimed that neither Apis nor Miranda had legitimate status as Pechanga people, that they never should have been enrolled in the first place, and that their descendants should be removed immediately from the Band's Enrollment Book to protect the "integrity" of the Band's membership (DeArmond 2004b; O'Leary 2004b).

In January 2004, in response to the Enrollment Committee's letters and the vicious efforts of the CPP, eleven individuals on behalf of the 133 Apis-Miranda descendants filed for a restraining order to prevent the committee from taking action to disenroll them (*Salinas et al. v. Lamere et al.* 2004).[29] They did so in state court under the provisions of PL 280 of 1953, which extended criminal and civil jurisdiction over reservations to specified states including California. The Band's attorney filed a motion challenging the state's jurisdiction. The state judge agreed and the case was removed to federal court.

Robert J. Timlin, the District Court Judge, said that he did not have jurisdiction over the case on the grounds of *Martinez* and dismissed the suit. He questioned the plaintiff's filing against the individuals of the committee — which was a body of the tribe's government — in an effort to skirt the *Martinez* ruling that tribes have sovereign immunity from civil action under the ICRA except in habeas corpus proceedings. The plaintiffs resubmitted their complaint to state court, arguing that PL 280 gave the state jurisdiction over the matters addressed in the case. In February 2004, Superior Court Judge Charles D. Field disagreed but also oddly invited the plaintiffs to return once the committee had formalized its decision if they felt that their due process had been violated.

In interviews with the media following the decision, Macarro insisted that the plaintiffs' arguments were "without legal merit" and were "aimed at undermining tribal sovereignty on a national scale": "We are defending our self-determining right to govern ourselves by our own laws, customs and traditions" (quoted in O'Leary 2004a). No specific explanation or rationale of how the membership criteria or actions of the committee reflected Pechanga "laws, customs and traditions" was offered to either the court or in interviews with the press. Instead, Macarro maintained that these were "internal" matters not to be discussed in public: "This is a private tribal matter. Out of respect for our customs and traditions, we will not comment" (quoted in DeArmond 2005).

Concurrently, the plaintiffs rejected the suggestion that their actions were assaulting Pechanga or tribal sovereignty, locally or nationally. Without a fair and independent tribal court to hear their complaints, and given their charge that the Band's elected officials and the Enrollment Committee were acting in violation of the Band's Constitution and By-Laws, they expressed frustration that they had no other recourse to challenge the tribe's actions than to pursue the matter in court. They insisted that the committee had repeatedly changed its arguments in questioning the validity of Apis's and Miranda's identities, had offered inconsistent requests for documentation that they ignored when submitted, and were being unduly influenced by a small group of malicious tribal members — the CPP — who were out to control tribal affairs and resources (DeArmond and O'Leary 2004a).

In March 2004, the Enrollment Committee voted again to remove the 133 individuals from the tribal rolls; the individuals were so removed. The letters notifying the 133 of the decision said that they had "failed to show proof of lineal descent from original Pechanga people" (cited in Buchanan 2004b). The 133 resubmitted their complaint to the state's Superior Court (*Salinas et al. v. Lamere et al.* 2004). In July 2004, the Pechanga Council held closed hearings in accordance with its Constitution and By-Laws to listen to the arguments of the 133. Following the hearing, the council did not override or request the committee to reconsider its decision.

Later that month, Judge Field asserted jurisdiction over the case on the grounds of PL 280. He said, "To refer issues of this nature to a tribal council, all of whom have a personal stake in the outcome, few if any of whom have legal training, and where the council is under no compunction to follow established due process rights, appears to fall into the category referred to above as a 'lack of an adequate forum'" (*Salinas et al. v. Lamere et al.* 2004). The Pechanga Band appealed. In August 2004, the suit was dismissed by the Fourth District State Court of Appeals. Citing *Martinez*, the court argued that membership was a matter of tribal sovereignty and that jurisdiction over civil complaints about membership had not been assumed in federal law or transferred to California by PL 280.

> In short, we are persuaded that Congress did not intend that the courts of this state should have the power to intervene — or interfere — in purely tribal matters. . . . Whether the potential for corruption in the system created by the influx of gambling wealth to some tribes would justify a change is not for us to decide. . . . If plaintiffs are unable to persuade the tribal council of the merits of their claims, so be it. The courts of this state have no power to intervene. (*Lamere et al. v. Superior Court of Riverside and Salinas et al.* 2005)

Predictably, then, the court reinscribed the fusion of the tribe's legal legitimacy with its protection of its cultural authenticity, even in spite of its criticisms of the tribe's "corruption" and lament over its lack of power to mediate the dispute. These comments notwithstanding, Macarro responded by asserting that "tribal governments have sole jurisdiction and authority to establish and enforce procedures to determine their own tribal citizenship"; he continued, saying that determining the validity of its membership rolls was "central to Pechanga's identity as a distinct sovereign government" (quoted in Newman 2005b).

In March 2005, the 133 filed a second lawsuit against 30 individuals within the tribe's government and the CPP, seeking $38 million in damages for lost per capita shares. They accused the Enrollment Committee of working in collusion with the council and attorneys to oust them so that they could increase their own shares and "consolidate political power and control key jobs and leadership roles" for themselves (quoted in O'Leary 2004d). As with the previous complaints, however, the suit was dismissed. The court maintained that PL 280 did not grant state courts jurisdiction in civil suits and that *Martinez* was clear on the jurisdiction of tribes over membership. In May 2006, the U.S. Supreme Court declined to review the case.

Meanwhile, in 2005, Anthony Miranda, a relative of the disenrolled and a descendant of Apis, circulated a petition calling on the tribe to cease disenrollments. It went before a general membership meeting and was passed overwhelmingly by a voting majority. Under the provisions of the Band's Constitution and By-Laws, this process and vote had the force of making it tribal law. However, it was ignored by the Band's elected officials.

Paulina Hunter

In May 2005, the Enrollment Committee informed Paulina Hunter's ninety descendants that they needed to supply adequate documentation proving lineal descent to an "original Pechanga Temecula" person or face disenrollment. Hunter was born sometime in the 1830s or 1840s. As one of the few survivors of the Temecula massacre of 1846 she had been issued a deed by President McKinley to about twenty acres of land. That land had become Hunter Drive and was located at the base of the Pechanga Reservation where some of her descendants live.

In 2004, the tribe had hired John Johnson as a consultant on genealogical issues. Johnson was the curator of anthropology at the Santa Barbara Museum of Natural History and an expert on "California Indian archaeology, archival records, cultures and history" (Kabbany 2006b; Cooper 2007). He was charged to investigate the tribe's Enrollment Book of 1979 and specifically the status of those individuals that the committee had questions about. He produced an exhaustive report on his findings.

About Hunter's lineage, Johnson concluded that he was "90 percent" confident that Hunter was an "original Pechanga" but later asserted that he was "100 percent" confident that she was Pechanga:

> The reason he said he cannot be 100 percent sure [in the report] is because when studying the lineage of Luiseno Indians—who include the Pala, Pauma, Rincon, La Jolla, Soboba and Pechanga bands—there are three "primary" mission record books missing that detail births, marriages and deaths from 1835–1852. These books were established when the mission was founded. The name "Luiseno" derives from their having lived at or near the Spanish mission San Luis Rey, established in 1798 and located in northern San Diego County near Oceanside. Hunter was born sometime during the 1830s or 1840s, and lived on the reservation in Temecula . . . That is the tie her descendants point to show they are Pechanga descendants. Determining exactly who Paulina Hunter's parents are is not cut and dry without those primary record books, Johnson said. With that, he made his determinations using other various bap-

tismal and marriage records, California census books, Pechanga Indian census records, genealogical evidence and other sources, he said. He determined that Paulina Hunter was an original Pechanga Indian based in part on the fact that the man most likely to be her father, Mateo Quasi-cac, was the only person listed from "Pechanga" in census books from that time. Moreover, he said, Hunter was listed on tribal rolls in the late 19th century and was the recipient of Pechanga Reservation allotment No. 62. "Paulina Hunter would not have been given an allotment if she was not of the Temecula Indians," Johnson said. "So, why was she given an allotment?" What's more, anyone currently enrolled in the Pechanga Band whose ancestors were born between 1835 and 1852 would have the same trouble proving their heritage using primary resource books, he said. "They are all in the same boat as Paulina Hunter," Johnson said. "She is not unique." Johnson said he wrote a lengthy report to the tribe detailing his results in 2004, and sent a letter to them reiterating his findings a few months before the Enrollment Committee's August ruling. (Kabbany 2006a)

In spite of Johnson's conclusions, the Enrollment Committee rejected his findings and proceeded to disenroll the Hunter family in August 2006. Johnson called the disenrollment "unfortunate and not based on solid evidence": "[The Committee] ignored whatever I did in their decision-making. . . . It's too bad economics and politics have been injected into (tribal lineage rulings)" (quoted in Kabbany 2006a). An anonymous Hunter family member concurred: "Because records show Paulina Hunter's mother was baptized at the San Luis Rey Mission, Enrollment Committee members are taking it to mean she was from there. But everyone traveled to that mission to be baptized during that century. . . . These people are targeting certain families. . . . They are just throwing out all the facts. It's all about financial gain. It's all about more money" (ibid.).

Lawrence Madariaga, another descendant of Hunter's, likewise commented on the decision and its consequences for him and his wife, Sophia:

Lawrence Madariaga, 89, is the oldest male living on the reservation. In a written statement, he recounts the endless days he volunteered his time to work to build the reservation irrigation system. "Just three months (after I was honored by the tribe at a Christmas party) for my lifelong service to the tribe and the reservation, I was disenrolled," Madariaga stated. "I have been stripped of all my rights and privileges. . . . Since the disenrollment, I have been told the same reservation clinic that I have worked so hard to build will no longer care for me or provide me with medical service." Medical insurance for his wife, Sophia, 86, has also been revoked. "My wife and I have been together for over 69 years; we are at a loss as to what to do," he said. Several members of the Hunter family continue to live on the reservation. It is unclear whether they will be asked to leave. That decision may involve the Bureau of Indian Affairs. (Kabbany 2006a)

"I have been stripped of all my tribal rights and privileges," the 89-year-old tribal elder said in a statement. . . . "I require extensive medical care, because of my advanced age, including a shot which costs $1,500 every month. Since the disenrollment, I have been told that the clinic, the same reservation clinic that I worked so hard to build, will no longer care for me or provide me with medical service," he said in a statement. . . . "To make matters worse, the tribe discontinued my medical insurance as well. My wife, Sophia, who is 86 years old, and I have been together for over 69 years. And we are at a loss as to what to do." . . . "I was disenrolled even though I could trace my family history back to the Temecula village where my ancestors were from," he said in his statement. "This is documented as far back as the early 1700s." (O'Leary 2006)

Refusing to comment publicly about Johnson's report or the committee's decision, Macarro issued the following statement: "This is a very complex intertribal matter involving Pechanga history and genealogy. . . . Questions about citizenship, therefore, are resolved by the Pechanga Enrollment Committee, the government body with the proper authority and ability to determine if a person meets criteria for Pechanga citizenship. The insinuation that these actions are motivated by politics or profits is reprehensible. The fact is that disenrollments occurred long before Pechanga ever opened its gaming facility" (ibid.).

Macarro's dismissiveness of the criticisms and the real-life effects of disenrollment became particularly acidic in the context of the lives and experiences of individuals like the Madariagas. The seeming indifference garnered so much public criticism that an NBC News affiliate in Los Angeles took notice and followed up by interviewing the Madariaga family for a special report entitled "Without a Tribe" (which aired on February 20, 2007). The

Pechanga Council responded by putting together a statement that aired beforehand. In it, Macarro spoke eloquently and sincerely: "Tonight KNBC is airing a story about tribal membership. As tribal leaders we take seriously our responsibility for guaranteeing fairness. After thorough investigations and hearings it was determined that certain individuals were not legitimate members of the tribe. Our citizenship decisions were upheld by the California and the U.S. Supreme Courts. For more information we invite you to visit our website to learn more about Pechanga's history and culture. Thank you" (C. Williams 2007). Macarro's reassurances fell on unsympathetic ears. Colleen Williams, the NBC News anchor, not only blasted Macarro and the tribe for misrepresenting the legal matters involved in the case but highlighted the effects of disenrollment on people's lives as being anything but "fair."

> That commercial you just saw was paid for by the Pechanga Tribal Corporation in direct response to the story you're about to see. We believe the commercial contains misleading information. It's our understanding that the U.S. and California supreme courts denied review of the Pechanga case. So neither court heard the merits of any case involving Pechanga membership. And the individuals specifically discussed in our report have not been involved in any state or federal court proceedings. This all revolves around an internal battle being waged on Indian reservations across the country. Thousands of Indians are being kicked out of tribes. Critics say it's more about greed than anything else. The tribes say it's about preserving their lineage. (ibid.)

Williams then interviewed some of the Madariaga family. The family is seen sitting together in the elders' home juxtaposed with images of Williams driving around the reservation with Lawrence Madariaga while he commented on the work he had done for the tribe, including playing a key role in bringing water and a sewage system to the reservation, designing and building the reservation's health clinic, and writing the tribe's Charter (see Cooper 2007).

LAWRENCE MADARIAGA: I'm a Luiseño Indian.
WILLIAMS: For decades the Madariaga family called this home—the Pechanga reservation in Temecula. Eighty-nine-year-old Lawrence and his wife Sophia built their house after he came back from serving

in World War II. They raised four children, eight grandchildren, and twelve great grandchildren. . . .

DELLA FREEMAN: I grew up here my whole life. This is my home. This is who I am. This is the only thing I know. Everything I've ever wanted to do in my life is for my people here.

WILLIAMS: This is the ancestral home of the Luiseño Indian Tribe, and the Madariagas say they can trace their family roots here, back more than one hundred years. [Addressing Madariaga] Okay, what is this that we're coming up on?

LAWRENCE MADARIAGA: The clinic, that's my design.

WILLIAMS: Lawrence and Sophie say early life on the reservation was hard, and the tribe lived in poverty. Today, though, because of Indian gaming—specifically, the Pechanga resort and casino in Temecula—those days of poverty are gone. The tribe as a whole, shares in the profit, meaning each and every adult member of the tribe receives a monthly check worth thousands of dollars.

UNIDENTIFIED MAN: We used to get $20,000 a month.

WILLIAMS: A monthly allowance of $20,000?

UNIDENTIFIED MAN: About that.

WILLIAMS: The Madariaga family says last August that monthly allowance abruptly stopped. The family was cut off. The term they use is disenrolled. It means Lawrence Madariaga, his wife, and all their children and their children's children were kicked out of the tribe.

RONNETT HERNANDEZ: They shun you totally, that's what disenrollment means, you're outcasts.

WILLIAMS: They say the children in the family were even kicked out of the reservation school.

AKEVA MCKEVER: My daughter, who was five, and my son, who was eight, they escorted them out and told us that we are never allowed to come back here.

WILLIAMS: While the disenrollment is still emotionally painful for this family, financially it has left them scrambling to make ends meet. The Madariaga family alone had ninety adult members, each receiving that monthly allowance of $20,000.

[Addressing Hernandez] Twenty-four to twenty-five million dollars a year? Does that mean the money that's left, the other families get a bigger piece of the pie?

HERNANDEZ: Yes, but our issue here again is our heritage, our heritage. We always knew who we were; my father always taught us who we were.

WILLIAMS [Addressing Madariaga] So this is all yours in here?

LAWRENCE MADARIAGA: All the family. Yes.

WILLIAMS: The Madariagas are the second family recently disenrolled at Pechanga—bringing the total number at this one reservation to over 220 adults. [Addressing Lawrence Madariaga] What relation are you to Paulina Hunter?

MADARIAGA: Her great-grandson.

WILLIAMS: The Madariagas trace their family roots back to a woman by the name of Paulina Hunter. In fact, Hunter Lane is one of the first streets you notice as you drive onto the Pechanga reservation. There's no doubt this twenty acres in the middle of the Pechanga Reservation was deeded to Paulina. They have the paperwork to prove it, from the 1890s, signed by President McKinley. But now tribal leaders question whether Paulina Hunter was in fact a Temecula Indian. In a letter dated May 3, 2005, the Pechanga Enrollment Committee asked the family to provide documentation to show their family's "chain of lineal descent" to prove tribal membership. That same Enrollment Committee even hired a renowned anthropologist to trace the family's history, but they may have been surprised by what he found. (C. Williams 2007)

Williams then interviewed Johnson about his report to the tribe. He confirmed that based on his forty years of experience as a genealogist in California, he was "100 percent" sure that Hunter was "definitely" a Pechanga Indian. Williams then interviewed Macarro, who had only agreed to the on-camera interview the day before the report was to be aired.

MACARRO: When the tribe had nothing, people did not want to be a part of the tribe. When it appeared the tribe might have something, soon, then it seemed like a whole bunch of people came out.

WILLIAMS: Mark Macarro is the tribal chairman for the Pechanga tribe.

MACARRO: This has never been about money. This is about the integrity of tribal citizenship here at Pechanga. If there was a cornfield instead of a casino, these same challenges would have taken the same path to the same conclusion.

WILLIAMS: Macarro admits the tribal Enrollment Committee hired Dr. Johnson as an independent expert but chose not to go with his findings. [Addressing Macarro] Let me tell you what he told us.

MACARRO: Okay.

WILLIAMS: "Paulina Hunter, she is definitely a Pechanga Indian, 100 percent, for sure."

MACARRO: As it was reported to me, there was a percentage figure of estimation, and it was 90 percent. And it was regarded as nonconclusive. And let me further state again that courts have affirmed that not anthropologists but tribes themselves have the responsibility to maintain the integrity. Only tribes know their own history. (ibid.)

Macarro's insistence that the disenrollments were about preserving the "integrity" of the tribe's culture and identity was inflected through his insistence on the absolutes of tribal sovereignty and self-government. He thereby infused the legal status and rights of the Pechanga Band with the cultural authority of knowing and being able to represent Pechanga traditions and identity that circularly affirmed tribal sovereignty and self-government. In doing so, he sealed up the cultural "integrity," knowledge, and jurisdiction against what he presents as opportunistic frauds who falsely claim to know and represent Pechanga culture and identity because they merely want a share of gaming money. He thus conflated the allegedly false claims to membership by new applicants following tribal wealth with the historical families the tribe was actually disenrolling.

Families Dismembered, Tribe Rejoined

The disenrollments of the descendants of Pablo Apis and Paulina Hunter included 223 individuals. As stated above, in the Enrollment Book of 1979, 307 members of the Band are recorded; by the close of the first extended open enrollment period in July 1981, 456 were enrolled in the Band.

Of the 307 in the Enrollment Book of 1979 (the 1981 membership list is not available), 87 are lineal descendants of the Apis family, and 44 are lineal descendants of the Hunter family. There are no Macarro surnames recorded. Whatever factors contribute to this absence (particularly glaring in the context of the disenrollments), the Band's governmental and legal leadership should have understood better the historical difficulties of documenting lineal descent as well as the cultural relevance of other kinds of practices than documentary in defining tribal kinship and belonging.

When the disenrollments began in 2003, the Pechanga Band Council claimed that the Band's membership was around 1,460. This seems a bit inflated given that only twenty-four years had passed since the Enrollment Book closed and twenty-two since the initial open enrollment period closed. But, taking the 1,460 figure as a starting point, this figure would indicate that the Band's disenrollment of 223 individuals involved about 16 percent of its total membership. When it began in 2003, per capita shares in the Band's gaming profits were in the neighborhood of $10,000 to $12,000 per month. After the disenrollments were completed in 2006, per capita checks skyrocketed to the neighborhood of $40,000 per month.

What makes all of the greed and corruption so troubled and troubling is the way that the Pechanga Band and other tribes throughout the country have rationalized the disenrollments of historically affiliated families on the grounds of exercising their legal rights to sovereignty and self-government. This sovereignty and self-government are asserted through membership as not only legally absolute and unchallengeable but as culturally integral. Emboldened by the terms of the *Martinez* ruling, it is a sovereignty and self-government that is inflected through racialized notions of Native authenticity. It allows tribes to recover and perpetuate stereotypical notions of their cultural mysteries and complexities (which they cannot possibly discuss with outsiders) in order to dismiss both public scrutiny and internal accountability of their actions as anti-Indian and antitribal sovereignty (see Barker 2006).

Chapter 6 more fully takes up the politics and ethical implications of these articulatory practices in relation to U.S. nationalism, patriotism, and religious conservatism. For here, I want to trouble the story of tribal greed and corruption within disenrollment by suggesting that it is managing more than the "capital" of material gain.

Several different kinds of tribal public relations campaigns followed the groundswell of statewide condemnations of tribal disenrollments by gaming tribes; this condemnation seemed to quickly cool the kind of support that the tribes had garnered during the campaign for the Indian Self-Reliance Act. Several wealthy tribes, including most notably the San

Manuel Band of Mission Indians, took on the task of representing in several TV and print media ads that California Indian tribes were committed anew to "self-reliance" and responsible state citizenship—heralding the economic self-sufficiency of gaming tribes, the employment of mostly nonmembers by tribal businesses, the investment of tribal revenue into local and state governments, and the support of tribes without gaming. These ads were occasioned by the pressure of the Schwarzenegger administration on tribes to renegotiate their gaming compacts in order to help offset the state's escalating budget deficit. As during the Proposition 1A campaign, tribes represented themselves as the good-willed, "self-reliant" Indians who were willing to help the state and local governments out of their fiscal crises and to help the state support nongaming tribes. The rhetoric of "self-reliance," however, was taken right out of anti-immigrant campaigns that characterized immigrants, particularly from Mexico, as exploitative drains on the state's limited financial resources. The tribes borrowed from the discursive formula to represent themselves as the real Indians who cared about their neighbors and the state, positioned anew against those who came into the state illegally to take advantage of public services like education and health care or against the outright frauds and fraudulent leeches who sought to share in the tribal gaming pot.

"Self-reliance," then, strategically deflected the challenges to tribal cultural authenticity and legal legitimacy that the public criticisms of the greed and corruption within tribal disenrollment had produced. Tribes were not just a bunch of greedy capitalists out to take advantage of public goodwill or state resources; they were self-sufficient, hard-working, tax-paying citizens who were being targeted by ethnic frauds.

The representational parallelisms between the self-reliant, authentic, and legitimate Native and the illegal, inauthentic fraud provided an effective way for tribes to distance themselves from all things illegal and welfare. But it did so in a particular kind of way that went about recovering a Native authenticity within California against the historic relations of Natives with "immigrant" communities that might otherwise be seen to mark a compromised Native culture and identity. In other words, Native histories of relocation, cultural exchange, social transformation, and intermarriage with the Spanish and Mexicans in California were profoundly complex and often off the proverbial grid of the historical record. Forced relocation, dispossession, and enslavement demanded that several different Native groups, families, and individuals live together on missions and rancheros. Some Spanish and Mexicans — not among the powerful military and upper classes — also found themselves living on and near the missions or working as farmhands. Throughout this time, many Natives passed for Mexicans to find paid work and escape the attention of militias and raids by ranchers for forced laborers (Forbes 1982).

The results of these and other very complicated histories were regular though uneven incidents of intermarriage and cross-identification among Spanish, Mexicans, and Native people. After statehood, however, while those of Spanish descent and Mexicans certainly lost their privileged status as citizens and landholders and were often violently subjugated to the discriminations of a dominating European-American class (Heizer and Almquist 1977; Almaguer 1994), Native peoples were systematically murdered and dispossessed of their lands by public militias and federal agents. Those who survived often lived in isolated areas in the mountains and deserts or passed as Mexicans — impoverished, unemployed, malnourished, and starving (Riffe 2005).

I believe that these complicated histories inform disenrollment practices in California today. Similar to the purging of the descendants of Freedmen and Black Indians by the Seminole Nation (in 2000) and the Cherokee Nation (in 2007) of Oklahoma in the name of making a citizenship of *real* Seminole and Cherokee "by blood" (Sturm 2002), the disenrollments of those with lineage to the missions and rancheros seem to be a purging of those Natives with mixed Spanish-Mexican descent in the name of making "real" California Indians. It certainly pretends an integrity and isolation of tribal culture and identity that is not borne out in the complex social histories that characterized Native communities in what was to become California.

Such actions beg the question of how the purging of Spanish-Mexican connections is not also a positioning against how Mexican, Mexican American, and Chicano identified communities and individuals claim an indigenous history, culture, and identity and therefore a unique set of legal rights to sovereignty and territory within national narrations. As Tomás Almaguer has observed (1994), the Mexican landholding class that assumed control of California from 1821 to 1848 and remained in power for some time afterward was complicit in the enslavement, starvation, rape, and murder of Native peoples (Heizer and Almquist 1977; Forbes 1982). The reclamation of indigenous identity by Mexicans, Mexican Americans, and Chicanos in the post-1960s period of California history has been met with varied but passionate reactions by Native communities. Some have perceived it as a denial of the complicity of Mexicans in Native enslavement, genocide, and dispossession; some have seen it as a New Age exploitation of Native culture and identity; some have resented the presumption of a shared cultural affiliation when the lives and experiences of Mexicans and Natives have been so different; and some have welcomed the political solidarities and remembrance of histories of Spanish-Mexican-Native mixes and cultural exchanges. In other words, the disenrollments of those with Spanish-Mexican lineage seem to take on a very politically charged position in respect to these varied perceptions about the politics of Spanish-Mexican-Native relations and in particular of Mexican-Chicano claims to indigeneity in California (and in conversation with the suppression of these lineages and cultural exchanges in the *Martinez* trial as discussed in chapter 4).

But to complicate matters even further (as if they needed to be), the Pechanga and other gaming tribes in California are purging their memberships to reauthorize their legal status and rights against the vicious public attacks on gaming tribes as being "nouveau Indian" at best and "ethnic frauds" at worst (Kroft 1994; Spilde 1999; Benedict 2001; Barlett and Steele 2002a, 2002b; Darian-Smith 2004; Cramer 2006). In these attacks, tribal legal status and rights are represented as based on laws that are themselves racially biased.[30] The constant questioning of the legal legitimacy of tribes—going back to California statehood—has solicited and even been complicit in tribal claims of cultural "integrity."

The difficult question that remains for tribal governments is what kinds of tribal sovereignty and cultural tradition result from the shoring up of the discourses and ideologies of authenticity from U.S. national narrations. The rhetorical move might work to reauthorize the remaining members and their tribe as legitimate—by being recognized as legitimately Native within those narrations—but it rearticulates a sovereignty, self-government, and cultural tradition that derives from nationalist and racist ideologies and practices enacted in the service of Native domination. This might be the sovereignty, self-government, and cultural tradition recognized as legally legitimate by the United States, but at what cost?

Enroller

enrollment *n.* **1** an enrolling or being enrolled **2** a list of those enrolled **3** the number of those enrolled. . . . **enroll** *v* **1** to record in a list **2** to enlist **3** to accept as or cause to be a member **4** to roll up; wrap up **5** to make a final fair copy of . . . **VI** to enroll oneself or become enrolled; register; enlist; become a member.

dis- **1** discount **2** distance *Abbrev.*

— *Webster's New World Dictionary, Third College Edition*

Enrollment is from the French *enroller*, meaning "to make, to put in."[31] Disenrollment, then, is to *re-enroll* the remaining members as legally legitimate and culturally authentic — an "Indian member" entrenched within the terms and conditions of national narrations and so doing the work of the kinds of racisms, sexisms, homophobias, and religious conservatism that propel those narrations forward.

The question that lingers is about the kinds of sovereignty and self-government that tribes define for themselves and their members by disenrollment. I have two immediate responses to these questions before taking them up more fully in the next chapter.

First, in 2007, John Gomez Jr. (Pechanga Band) formed a nonprofit organization called American Indian Rights and Resources Organization (AIRRO), which includes those who have been disenrolled from around the country. In addition to serving as a place of alliance building and information sharing about human and civil rights laws, organizations, and their web sites, AIRRO's mission is to seek a legislative reform of the Indian Civil Rights Act of 1968 that will allow tribal members to seek substantive redress for civil rights violations by their tribal governments:

> AIRRO recognizes that there is a growing trend within Indian Country where Indians and non-Indians alike are being denied or stripped of basic rights including, but not limited to: right to due process, equal protection under the law, voting and employment rights, and citizenship. AIRRO will serve as a resource for those seeking information or assistance regarding the Indian Civil Rights Act of 1968 and other laws which impact the human rights and civil liberties of Indians and non-Indian individuals. AIRRO will also work to assist individuals in order to protect, promote, and preserve their basic human rights and civil liber-

ties and to effect change which will ensure equal rights and equal protections for all. (http://www.airro.org/main.html, accessed December 15, 2008)

This reform could require tribal governments to establish an independent body to review civil complaints about their actions (obviously that is distinct from its elected representatives and their appointees), or it could envision an oversight or "super" court or legal body like the United Nations that was empowered to review the complaints and render a decision. In either case, AIRRO's objectives make explicit the serious implications of disenrollment practices for the legal provisions of tribal sovereignty and self-government in international and United States law. As tribes respond with impunity to these implications, insisting on noninterference in "internal" tribal matters in the name of protecting the "integrity" of tribal cultures and identities, they not only lose potential political allies in their struggles for sovereignty and self-determination within international relations but they also demonstrate a serious need for there to be a greater degree of accountability to human and civil rights within tribal governments and laws. Not merely on occasion of their violations by disenrollment but because those are the same sets of laws and principles to which tribes so uncompromisingly appeal as providing and ensuring their collective rights to sovereignty and self-determination. Just as a matter of legal credibility within international and national political affairs, tribes cannot appeal to laws as recognizing and protecting their collective rights to self-government, territorial integrity, and cultural autonomy when they themselves refuse to be accountable to them.

My second point is that Native peoples have often dismissed the principles and provisions of civil rights as reflecting the worst kinds of "Western" ideologies of individualism and self-interest (Barker 2006, 2008). Those Natives who appeal to civil rights are often accused of trying to force "Western" values and norms on Native communities, of being complicit with ongoing processes of colonization and imperialism by advocating those ideologies, and of undermining the core traditional beliefs that define Native culture and identity.

The presumed binaries between the Western and the Native within these arguments do a number of different things. They pretend that Native activists have not been focused on Native sovereignty and self-determination all along, even while appealing to human and civil rights principles. They also pretend that issues of individual identity, freedom, equality, belonging, affiliation, kinship, gender, sexuality, health, education, employment, and age are not definitive aspects or concepts within Native cultural histories and values, so this privileges Western, romantic narrations of Native culture and identity.

In other words, the binaries assign a particularly "Western" epistemological genealogy to Native cultural perspectives and knowledge about individual identity, freedom, equality, belonging, affiliation, kinship, gender, sexuality, health, education, employment, and age. And, in so doing, does this not affirm and perpetuate the kinds of racisms, sexisms, homophobia, and religious fundamentalisms that have defined "Western" nationalisms and ongoing histories of colonization and imperialism in the first place?

Rejecting these kinds of binaries allows for other kinds of questions to be asked and considered. These questions might include those about Native epistemologies of culture and identity and social formations as well as those concerning Native understandings and political objectives for sovereignty and self-determination. From there, Native peoples can begin to better address what kinds of legal principles, governance structures, and social ethics they want to be accountable to and how this accountability would work (Alfred 1999).

For instance, what AIRRO is working for is not a complete dissolution of tribal legal status and rights but for a different form and forum of legal accountability within tribal government and law. The objective suggests that if tribes are going to assert collective rights to sovereignty and self-determination under the provisions and principles of international and constitutional law, then they must be accountable to the provisions and principles regarding the human and civil rights of both groups *and* individuals that that law is based on. This will mean some difficult changes in both federal and tribal law and legal practice. It will require that the United States fully acknowledge and protect the human and civil rights of tribes and tribal members without exercising undo interference or administrative controls over tribes, allowing tribes the freedom to redefine their government structures, constitutions, and laws in more culturally relevant ways. But it will also mean that tribes must fully acknowledge and respect their obligations to protect those same human and civil rights provisions and principles of their citizens as expected of all sovereign nations within the international community. In doing so, tribes potentially reclaim their cultural perspectives as relevant in the context of their forms and exercise of governance. Revitalizing their membership along their cultural histories for determining affiliation and belonging will likewise make relevant the international human and civil rights provisions and principles on which their sovereignty and self-determination is based.

Part III TRADITION

tradition c.1380, from O.Fr. *tradicion* (1292), from L. *traditionem* (nom. *traditio*) "delivery, surrender, a handing down," from *traditus*, pp. of *tradere* "deliver, hand over," from *trans-* "over" + *dare* "to give" (see *date* (1)). The word is a doublet of *treason* (q.v.). The notion in the modern sense of the word is of things "handed down" from generation to generation. *Traditional* is recorded from c.1600; in ref. to jazz, from 1950. Slang *trad*, short for *trad(itional jazz)* is recorded from 1956; its general use for "traditional" is recorded from 1963.

Online Etymology Dictionary

6 Of Marriage and Sexuality

I n the midst of a great deal of national attention on movements for and against marriage
equality rights for same-sex couples, the elected
officials of the Cherokee Nation of Oklahoma
and the Navajo Nation passed laws in 2004 and
2005 to define marriage as being between a man
and a woman of the opposite sex and prohibiting
same-sex marriage rights (Fletcher 2006). These
laws mirrored the provisions of the U.S. Defense
of Marriage Act (DOMA) of 1996 and a rash of
state ballot initiatives in November 2004 that did
the same in the name of a national security and social stability that attempted to cover up its hateful prejudice of homosexuality (Dick 2009). Both
the Cherokee and Navajo insisted that their actions
reflected their rights as sovereign nations and the
social values of their unique cultural traditions.
They asserted that their actions were aimed against
"homosexual activists" out to use tribes to legitimate their own political agendas. That both tribes

did so in the name of Christian patriotism avowed the conservatism and bigotry of anti-marriage-equality movements throughout the country (Diamond 1995, 1998; E. Kaplan 2004; Chauncey 2005; Sueyoshi 2006; Goldberg 2007; Hedges 2007).

The Context of the Nation

It all began when the Supreme Court of the State of Hawai'i ruled that the state must have a compelling interest in order to justify prohibiting against same-sex marriage rights (*Baehr v. Lewin* 1993). The decision was rooted in the efforts of many lesbian and gay activists to secure marriage equality for same-sex couples as a civil rights matter. It served to reignite legal action on all sides of the political spectrum seeking to claim marriage as a category of their own. Lesbian and gay activists and their allies saw the *Baehr* decision as a catalyst for other lawsuits as well as for organizing ballot initiatives to extend marriage rights to same-sex couples that would address related issues of inheritance, health care, child custody, and adoption (Leong and Sueyoshi 2006). Opponents sought to pass a constitutional amendment, federal law, and state legislation that would forever reserve marriage rights for heterosexual couples.

These objectives collided in September 1996 when President William J. Clinton signed the DOMA into law. Sponsored by conservatives from both the Republican and Democratic parties,[1] the DOMA establishes that in "determining the meaning" of any federal law, or in rendering an "interpretation of the various administrative bureaus and agencies of the United States," "'marriage' means only a legal union between one man and one woman as husband and wife, and the word 'spouse' refers only to a person of the opposite sex who is a husband or a wife" (Section 3). Further, the DOMA explicitly protects the jurisdiction of states, territories, and tribes over marriage laws by providing that no one "shall be required to give effect to any public act, record, or judicial proceeding of any other State, territory, possession, or tribe respecting a relationship between persons of the same-sex" (Section 2).

In response to the DOMA's ratification, multiple constituencies organized legal actions that would achieve their respective political aims.[2] Lesbian and gay activists sought to confront the constitutionality of the DOMA and establish state legislation to extend marriage rights to same-sex couples.³ These efforts reached a crescendo in February 2004 as lesbian and gay couples stormed city halls to file for marriage licenses (Sueyoshi 2006). Under the leadership of Mayor Gavin Newsom, San Francisco welcomed the storm and quickly became the focus of media attention. It issued licenses to same-sex couples in defiance of not only the DOMA but of California's Proposition 22 of 2000, which had passed by a 61.4 percent majority to ban same-sex marriage.⁴

Amid what he characterized as a nationwide assault on the DOMA by the few against the will of "the American people," President George W. Bush advocated for a constitutional amendment that would settle the matter (Dick 2009). In February 2004, in a speech from the White House, he asserted that there was an urgent need to guard the DOMA and the "overwhelming consensus in our country for protecting the institution of marriage" against "aggressive" "activist judges and local officials." He indicted government officials in San Francisco, Massachusetts, and New Mexico for issuing licenses to same-sex couples in defiance of the DOMA and the "consensus" of "the American people." He reassured that the DOMA guaranteed that no state or city would be forced to "recognize any relationship" defined in another as being legal. He maintained that the suggestion otherwise had produced social "uncertainty" and public anxiety about the future of the country. This anxiety was because of the centrality of marriage in the foundations of civil society and democracy. He vowed to protect marriage by securing a constitutional amendment that "activist courts" could not ignore. In rhetorical turn, Bush linked these assurances to questions of "national concern" and so of the abilities of America to be a "good influence" on the rest of the world. The insinuation was that same-sex marriage and homosexuality posed an imminent threat to national security, social stability, and the nation's aims to spread democracy to the rest of the world.

> After more than two centuries of American jurisprudence, and millennia of human experience, a few judges and local authorities are presuming to change the most fundamental institution of civilization. . . . My administration will vigorously defend [DOMA]. . . . An amendment to the Constitution is never to be undertaken lightly. The amendment process has addressed many serious matters of national concern. And the preservation of marriage rises to this level of national importance. The union of a man and woman is the most enduring human institution,

honoring—honored and encouraged in all cultures and by every religious faith. Ages of experience have taught humanity that the commitment of a husband and wife to love and to serve one another promotes
the welfare of children and the stability of society. Marriage cannot be
severed from its cultural, religious and natural roots without weakening
the good influence of society. Government, by recognizing and protecting marriage, serves the interests of all. (Bush 2004)

Bush's statement and proposed Federal Marriage Amendment (also referred to as the Marriage Protection Amendment) mobilized his political base, credited with defining his administration's agendas. This base
included conservatives mostly within the Republican Party and from
Christian affiliations or organizations like the Alliance Defense Fund, Cau-
cus for America, Christian Coalition of America, Concerned Women for
America, Family Research Council, Focus on the Family, Liberty Council, Moral Majority, National Organization for Marriage, and Redeem the
Vote. In response, several of these organizations issued press releases immediately following Bush's statement. The Christian Coalition went so far
as to announce a "Let's Take America Back" campaign to get the constitutional amendment passed (www.cc.org, posted February 24, 2004). What
was particularly misleading about this was that many of these same organizations had helped set Bush's agenda for the amendment (Diamond 1995,
1998; E. Kaplan 2004; Goldberg 2007; Hedges 2007; Dick 2009).

For example, James Dobson, the director of Focus on the Family, and
his wife, Shirley Dobson, had published extensively in support of a constitutional amendment on marriage. Their writings include *Marriage under
Fire: Arguments against Same-Sex Marriage* (2004), authored by Dobson
and posted on Focus on the Family's web site under educational materials, and *Marriage under Fire: Why We Must Win This Battle* (2007), which
was co-authored by James and Shirley Dobson and published by Tyndale
House.[5] In both forums, the Dobsons implored fellow Christians to take
the threats of same-sex marriage and homosexuality seriously. James Dobson began his education materials with his view of how the "homosexual
marriage" has eroded social stability, sexual identity, and the "traditional
family" in other countries:

We've already seen evidence from the Scandinavian countries that de-
facto homosexual marriage destroys the real McCoy. These two entities

cannot coexist because they represent opposite ends of the universe. A book could be written on the reasons for this collision between matter and antimatter, but I will cite three of them. First, when the State sanctions homosexual relationships and gives them its blessing, the younger generation becomes confused about sexual identity and quickly loses its understanding of lifelong commitments, emotional bonding, sexual purity, the role of children in a family, and from a spiritual perspective, the "sanctity" of marriage. Marriage is reduced to something of a partnership that provides attractive benefits and sexual convenience, but cannot offer the intimacy described in Genesis. Cohabitation and short-term relationships are the inevitable result. Ask the Norwegians, the Swedes, and the people from the Netherlands. That is exactly what is happening there. (Dobson 2004)

Further, Dobson claims that "homosexual marriage" will lead to polygamy, group marriages ("three men or three women"), marriage between family members and blood relations ("daddies and little girls"), and marriages between humans and animals ("donkeys")—all in the name of protecting "gay rights." Finally, Dobson claims that homosexuals are out to destroy "traditional marriage" in order to establish an entirely "different legal structure" opposed to Christian values: "We must all become soberly aware of a deeply disturbing reality: The homosexual agenda is *not* marriage for gays. It is marriage for no one. . . . With the family out of the way, all rights and privileges of marriage will accrue to gay and lesbian partners without the legal entanglements and commitments heretofore associated with it. These are just a few reasons why homosexual marriage is truly revolutionary. Legalizing it will change everything, especially for the institution of the family" (Dobson 2004).

Despite the alarm that organizations like Focus on the Family rang about same-sex marriage rights and issues of sexuality, Bush's Federal Marriage Amendment was defeated by the U.S. Senate in July 2004 (50–48). As an apparent reaction to this defeat, anti-same-sex marriage propositions dominated state ballots in November 2004 and mobilized people to the polls (Dick 2009).[6] Ten states voted to ban same-sex marriage and define marriage as being a legal union between a man and a woman of the opposite sex.

Heralding the election results as an endorsement of his policies, Bush presented himself and his administration as offering much-needed protection of the foundations of civil society and democracy against the evils of homosexuality, moral licentiousness, and social decay. But the real effectiveness of the rhetoric was not so much or only in its characterizations of a particular set of social values as normal or civil (though it did do that to great effect). It was in how those particular social values were rearticulated through U.S. national narrations that mattered (Somerville 2000; Duggan 2004; Puar 2007).

The rearticulation was embedded in Bush's and his administration's successes in deploying the images and complex public reactions to 9/11 to centralize their power in the name of world democracy and homeland security.[7] They had effectively used 9/11 to justify the consolidation of the powers of the president's office and to pass troubling laws including the Patriot Act of October 26, 2001, to conduct "intelligence gathering" and the policing of immigrants with hubris for the Geneva Convention and other human and civil rights laws.[8] In the same way that terrorists were being described as filled with hate for America and Americans and out to destroy the nation's "very way of life," marriage-equality advocates and nonheterosexual people were described as being outside not only accepted social values and norms but outside the nation as unpatriotic deviants colluding—unwittingly or not—with those terrorist forces out to destroy America.

Disturbingly, the "homonationalism" of the Bush administration was not an aberration or mistake from an otherwise norm of the nation's commitments to democracy, freedom, and equality (Somerville 2000; Duggan 2004; Puar 2007). It represented how U.S. nationalism had been defined all along to privilege heterosexuality—in all of its uses to capitalism, patriarchy, and Christianity—and advance sexist and homophobic practices in the name of God and country. The Bush administration merely provided the legitimation and venue for the rearticulation of these ideologies into national policy. These policies, in fact, were the result of a long history of grassroots organizing by conservatives to reestablish what they perceived to be the Christian foundations of the country in government (Diamond 1995, 1998; E. Kaplan 2004; Goldberg 2007; Hedges 2007).

But so, too, were lesbian and gay activists focused on marriage equality as well as an ending to legal discrimination and hateful violence against their communities. The DOMA was passed in the midst of the almost immediate pressure Clinton received when elected into office from lesbian and gay activists and their allies to reform the military's policies regarding homosexuals in the service (his much-compromised "don't ask, don't tell" policy was passed in 1993). Clinton's willingness to open up those conversations solicited heated reactions from military leaders, elected officials, and conservatives from all sides of the political spectrum who feared the "liberal" president would threaten American society and national security by supporting the "gay agenda." Clinton's military policy and support of the DOMA quieted but did not settle these concerns. In fact, they further ignited legal activism by lesbian and gay people as well as by conservatives who sought state legislation and a constitutional amendment to ban same-sex marriage rights.

Into this political fray, the Cherokee Nation and the Navajo Nation passed laws that mimicked the DOMA and state propositions to ban same-sex marriage rights and define marriage as being a union between a man and a woman. The Cherokee National Council pursued its efforts in the context of challenging its own district court's issuance of a marriage license to two women. The Navajo Council went further to restrict against "plural marriages" and "marriages between blood relatives." The overwhelming number of elected officials and attorneys for both of the tribes explained that their actions were motivated by concerns about the nation's need to protect "family values" against the "gay agenda." Invoking what had become code words for American patriotism, the tribes situated themselves as joining forces with "the American people" to protect America against the threats that homosexuality and same-sex marriage posed for national security and social stability.

While many Natives and particularly those who identify as lesbian and gay or "third gender" or "two spirit" (Jacobs, Thomas, and Long 1997) were not particularly surprised by the Cherokee and Navajo actions—having had to live all along with the realities of sexism and homophobia in their communities (Roscoe 1989; Jacobs, Thomas, and Long 1997; Gilley 2006; Denetdale 2008)—many were taken aback. Some, including Cherokee and Navajo people, felt that the laws were nontraditional, hateful, and divisive. Others were concerned that their tribal governments would follow suit. But many non-Native lesbian and gay people and civil rights activists were likewise shocked and concerned by the tribes' actions. They had not expected the Cherokee and Navajo to act in ways that they perceived as sexist and homophobic, particularly given what they understood to be the traditions of the tribes regarding marriage and sexuality. Those same assumptions led many conservatives to be especially relieved.

The numerous reactions to the Cherokee and Navajo laws were due to the incredible proliferation of stereotypes and misrepresentations of Native traditions about marriage and sexuality within many different forums — including scholarship, creative work, and activism (Roscoe 1989; Jacobs, Thomas, and Long 1997). Generally, the narratives go that Natives have been radically accepting and even have had great spiritual reverence for same-sex-oriented people and those of "third gendered" or "two spirit" identities (Jacobs, Thomas, and Long 1997); that those traditions offer viable alternatives for understanding gender and sexuality away from the binary and hierarchical terms of "Western culture" and its "compulsory heterosexuality" (Rich 1980); and, that lesbian, gay, bisexual, and transgendered (LGBT) people were and are viable members of Native communities who often hold public office and spiritual leadership roles. These representations have been put to work in many different contexts to challenge "compulsory heterosexual" norms, avow the humanity of nonheterosexual people, and assert nonheterosexual human and civil rights — often against the acrimony of sexist and homophobic discrimination and hate-crime violence.

But perhaps because of the political efficacy of this representational work — and the natural coalitions it suggests between Natives and lesbian and gay people — the resulting misunderstandings about Native traditions have solicited and even contributed to certain expectations about how Native peoples would engage national debates and state propositions banning same-sex marriage. Many expected tribal governments to offer meaningful support and even alliance for same-sex marriage rights on the grounds that their traditions would naturally lead them to support same-sex couples' efforts to overturn the DOMA and establish marriage equality. Many assumed tribal governments already possessed such kinds of legislation. Having done so, the narrations went, tribal governments were sure to win many others over to the "gay agenda." So, the Cherokee and Navajo Councils' affirmation of the DOMA confounded deeply held assumptions about Native traditions, more so since the tribes took such action in the name of affirming their traditional values as being similar to those held by Christians and conservatives (Denetdale 2008).

These expectations are entrenched within the theoretical paradigms of social evolution and cultural assimilation. These paradigms have produced problematic notions of Native culture and identity that fix standards for measuring perceived changes within the terms of a whole cascade of binaries and hierarchies that assume authenticity (and inauthenticity). The belief is that if Native cultures and identities can be fixed in a specific time and place, they can be measured for degrees of deviation and loss from that place to another. This logic makes a flawed assumption, however, that Native culture and identity—or any other for that matter—*can be* frozen in time as if they were then whole and pure to be measured against another time.

The problems with this approach are explicit in studies of the relationship between Native traditions and Christianity. Native traditions are fixed in an authentic, historic past. Christianity is fixed as a force behind colonialism and imperialism, culminating in federal programs of assimilation that aimed at wiping out Native traditions in the name of salvation and civilization. To the degree that the cultural expressions of a given Native group or individual are perceived to be Christian, they are said to have been colonized or assimilated. Colonized, assimilated Indians are the first but estranged cousins of the Vanishing Indian—evidence of the successes of federal efforts and the tragic losses of the culturally authentic.

Theories about social formation provide a much more nuanced and provocative approach for thinking about Native cultures and identities. Under any given historical and social set of conditions, cultures and identities are negotiated within the specific relations of power that define those formations (Foucault 1972; Grossberg 1996). In thinking about the relationship between Native traditions and Christianity, social formation suggests that Native cultures and identities are *always* in negotiation, transformation, change, and exchange and so never possess a moment of "authenticity."

In horrible moments of colonization or forced assimilation, Native peoples actively negotiated what their cultural traditions meant in order to give their traditions meaning. Native peoples were never merely victims, sell-outs, or warriors against the forces of colonialism or Christianity—as those narrations assign them to be. They are agents in defining, claiming, asserting, and rearticulating their cultural identities under various social conditions in which Christian ideologies played a part. Sometimes it meant rejecting Christianity as a force of colonialism and imperialism, sometimes it meant incorporating particular aspects of Christianity as a strategy of cultural preservation or simply as an aspect of cultural exchange, and sometimes it meant inviting Christianity as a new, different form of self-definition.

In any of these and still other negations and identifications, social formation allows for a much more generous perspective on how Native peoples have invited and deflected Christian doctrines, institutions, and identities than merely situating them as *either* authentically traditional *or* colonized and assimilated. These binaries and value judgments produce troubled accounts of Native Christian identities (Treat 1996) and Native peoples' relationships to the Christian Right (A. Smith 2008) that come disturbingly close to political apologia.[9] This is because of the ways that those accounts presume the irreconcilability of Native traditions and Christianity as they are defined within social evolutionary and assimilationist narratives.

The question, then, in understanding the Cherokee and Navajo Councils' mimicking of the DOMA and state propositions banning same-sex marriage rights and defining marriage as being between a man and a woman is not about the binaries of assimilation. Rather, it is about how the legal actions and representations of Cherokee and Navajo "tradition" negotiate the terms of U.S. "homonationalism" (Puar 2007). What implications does that negotiation have for Native notions and exercises of sovereignty and self-determination? What Native "nation" results from the "tradition" of anti-same-sex marriage rights? Are there any other epistemologies about marriage and sexuality being articulated by Native peoples, and what kind of social formations do they anticipate?

Marriage Acts at Cherokee

Along with nine other states in November 2004, Oklahoma voted to reserve marriage rights for heterosexual couples. Concurrently, its legislature passed a resolution urging the U.S. Congress to reconsider and pass the Federal Marriage Amendment that had been defeated by the Senate in July 2004.

In a unique compact with the Cherokee Nation, marriages registered with the Cherokee Nation District Court are recognized by the State of

Oklahoma (Romano 2004). In May 2004, when two Cherokee women applied for a marriage certificate with the court, it appeared to the conservative base of Oklahoma and then nationwide that same-sex couples "could conceivably circumvent state law to establish a legal union not approved by the state" (Romano 2004) in the name of tribal sovereignty (Kannady 2004/2005). By ignoring the provisions of the DOMA, which protected states from just such a situation, the mere suggestion that same-sex couples could use tribes to further their own political agendas ignited concerns about the scope of tribal sovereignty and self-government. The Cherokee National Council responded by affirming not only the concerns but a sovereignty and tradition that was decidedly of a Christian and conservative America.

Dawn McKinley and Kathy Reynolds are citizens of the Cherokee Nation and committed life partners. In 2003, Reynolds was hospitalized for emergency care; McKinley was not only denied access but was "kicked out" of Reynolds's room by hospital staff because they did not recognize her as a legal relative. Meanwhile, they consulted with Reynolds's blood relatives on the course of her treatment. Reynolds commented later that "it didn't seem right that the person closest to [her] should be left out" (Associated Press 2004d).[10]

Shortly afterward, David Cornsilk, a citizen of the Cherokee Nation and a human rights activist and cultural historian, advised McKinley and Reynolds that under Cherokee traditional law marriage was considered "genderless" (see www.cornsilks.com; Editorial, 365Gay.com 2004). Cornsilk maintained that Cherokee law used terms translated into English as "provider" and "cooker" and not as "husband" and "wife" (Rock 2004). He contended that the gender neutrality of the terms indicated a value for multiple gender identifications and sexual orientations, complementing the tribe's matrilineal customs. Cornsilk advised McKinley and Reynolds that "there was no reason they should not be allowed to marry" and have their union legally recognized by the Cherokee Nation (Editorial, 365Gay.com 2004).[11]

On May 13, 2004, McKinley and Reynolds applied for a marriage certificate at the Cherokee Nation District Court in Tahlequah, Oklahoma. McKinley remembers that the clerk told her that she "might have a hard time finding a minister" but that she had "no problem" issuing one to them (Hamilton 2005). In fact, McKinley and Reynolds had already secured a minister willing to perform the ceremony who was certified by the Nation. So, on May 18, they were married in Tulsa's Mohawk Park (ibid.).

Following the ceremony, McKinley and Reynolds attempted to register the certificate. The clerk explained that on May 14 Darrell R. Matlock, the chief justice of the Cherokee Nation Judicial Appeals Tribunal (JAT), ordered a moratorium on the issuance or filing of any marriage certificates to same-sex couples. On May 19, McKinley and Reynolds tried again to register their certificate and were again turned away (Hamilton 2005). Later, McKinley commented on the flood of media coverage that followed: "A lot of people misunderstood this and thought it was an activist movement.... It wasn't" (Associated Press 2004d). "We just wanted recognition of our relationship.... We were very naïve. We thought we'd get married under Cherokee law and that would be the end of it" (Romano 2004).

A month later, on June 11, 2004, Todd Hembree, the legal counsel for the Cherokee National Council, filed a letter with the district court objecting to the court's issuance of a marriage certificate to a same-sex couple. The court set a hearing for June 18. But on June 16, Hembree filed a Petition for a Declaratory Judgment with the JAT (*In the Matter Reynolds and McKinley*, JAT-04–15). He wanted the court to declare McKinley's and Reynolds's certificate invalid though the petition did not name McKinley and Reynolds as defendants. However, because of the implications of the petition, McKinley and Reynolds became de facto defendants and were called to court. But they had been unable to secure representation from any one of the thirty-five attorneys on the list of those permitted to argue before Cherokee court. According to McKinley, "One day I went down the whole list and couldn't find anyone willing to take the case. One guy laughed and hung up on me" (Romano 2004). They believed that the refusals were because of the attorneys' concerns about losing lucrative tribal and corporate clients in the conservative political climate of Oklahoma.

Finally, Cornsilk contacted the National Center for Lesbian Rights (NCLR), a nonprofit advocacy group in San Francisco, on their behalf. The NCLR agreed to take the case; Lena Ayoub, a staff attorney, was assigned to represent them. Also on June 16, Hembree filed an application for a temporary injunction seeking to prevent McKinley and Reynolds from registering their certificate with the district court (*Petition for Declaratory Judgment*, JAT-04–15). Two days later, the court granted Hembree's motion.

Hembree's actions reflect how deeply concerned Cherokee officials were with public perception. Throughout the country, people were paying attention to the case because it suggested that if McKinley and Reynolds succeeded in filing their certificate, Cherokee and non-Cherokee same-sex couples would have a way of circumventing state law to become legally married through tribes. Never once did Hembree or tribal officials explain that just such a scenario was prohibited by the DOMA. Instead, they corroborated the fears by reassuring everyone who asked that the marriage between McKinley and Reynolds violated Cherokee traditions and laws and that the Nation was committed to stopping it. This contention was reinforced in several interviews granted by Hembree:

> When you read [Cherokee] statute in its entirety, there is no doubt that it was meant to be a marriage between a husband and a wife.... As I said it is my firm belief that it's not gender neutral, its gender specific and I do not want the laws of the Cherokee Nation and my tribe to be made a mockery of. (KOTV 2004)

> I took action because I feel strongly that our laws have to stand for something. . . . The Cherokee statute is not gender-neutral. It is meant to be between [a] man and a woman. In my view, they are trying to circumvent Oklahoma law. (Romano 2004)

> I have no personal animosity towards the McKinleys. . . . I just don't want the validity of Cherokee law to be in question or made a mockery of . . . Indian tribes and reservations don't live in a vacuum. The same social mores that affect the dominant society are present in Cherokee society. (Associated Press 2004d)

> The lawyer . . . also asserts that the majority of the people in the Cherokee Nation support traditional marriage. He notes that in the 14 Oklahoma counties where Cherokees live, voters supported the state constitutional amendment to ban same-sex marriage. (Martin 2005)

Hembree clearly asserted a cultural authority in Cherokee traditions that was meant to discredit as inauthentic the perspectives about marriage and sexuality claimed by McKinley, Reynolds, Cornsilk, and their allies. The contrast produced entirely irreconcilable claims on Cherokee traditions and law that were as much about claims of the power to know, represent, and govern what was to be considered Cherokee as they were about the terms of marriage and sexuality being debated.

On June 14, 2004, the Cherokee National Council voted unanimously (15–0) to pass a proposal to ban same-sex marriages and define marriage as being between a man and a woman. Linda Hughes O'Leary, a council member, was its sponsor. Another council member, Don Gavin, stated, while complaining about the lack of time to review the proposal, that he supported it "as a Baptist deacon" (Previch 2004). Another council member quoted anonymously stated, "This is rural Oklahoma and our citizens' views reflect the rest of the state. Cherokees are opposed to this marriage taking place" (Romano 2004).

The vote was directed at a nervous anti-same-sex marriage movement. It was meant to reassure its multiple constituencies that the Cherokee Nation would not allow "homosexual activists" to use tribal law to undermine the DOMA. It thereby reconstructed Cherokee traditions as fundamentally Christian and conservative in a context where this would be readily interpreted to mean an affirmation of Bush's and the Christian Right's position on the dangers of same-sex marriage and homosexuality to national security and social stability.

On July 12 McKinley and Reynolds filed a Motion to Quash and a Motion to Dismiss Hembree's petition on the grounds that he lacked standing to file his complaint. Under the Cherokee Constitution and By-Laws, to file such a petition he would have had to prove that he had experienced the requisite "individuated harm" by the couple's actions. McKinley and Reynolds argued that he had not done so. And on August 12, they filed a Motion for Summary Judgment on the same grounds. On August 20, Hembree countered with a Response to the Motion to Dismiss. He argued that he had brought the petition to ensure proper interpretation of Cherokee law as an attorney for the council charged with its protection.

On December 10 the Cherokee Nation's District Court overruled the three motions filed by McKinley and Reynolds. One week later, McKinley and Reynolds appealed the court's judgment to the JAT. Six months later, on June 3, 2005, the JAT ordered McKinley and Reynolds to file a procedural motion explaining their appeal by July 8. They complied. They argued again that Hembree had no standing to file the petition and that observing that was "necessary to protect people's right to conduct their lives in privacy and peace, without being hauled into court by third parties who have no relationship to them and no direct interest in the matter being litigated." They argued that he could not file such a claim of "individuated harm" "merely because he believes" their marriage "to be invalid and would like to obtain this Court's opinion on that question" (*McKinley and Reynolds' Motion to Dismiss*, JAT, July 8, 2005, 2; see Kannady 2004/2005).

Hembree's public response was heated: "The entire Cherokee Nation will suffer if the justices dismiss the case. Ours will be the only tribe in the U.S. to recognize same-sex marriages, which is clearly a violation of our own statute. . . . My interest in this case is to be sure the law is followed. I don't have anything against the couple personally; however, I do believe in following the letter of the law" (quoted in Snell 2005b). Again, Hembree represented the issues through the polarized terms of a Christian conservatism that aligned the Cherokee Nation with the perspectives and interests of a nationwide movement against marriage equality for same-sex couples. But his *repeated* and *repetitive* remarks were not merely authoritative, conservative, and homophobic. They were these things within the terms of a Christian Right's conservatism—with all of its implications for signifying a particular kind of nationalism and patriotism—while insisting on them as reflecting the true cultural traditions of the Cherokee Nation. And it is a repetitiveness that marks an anxiety of affect. The determined challenge by Hembree and the council members of the authenticity of the perspectives of other Cherokee citizens about Cherokee tradition, law, marriage, and sexuality marks the fact of cultural difference within the Nation. This difference calls attention to the political motivations and interests of interpreting traditions into law. As the elected officials and legal counsel of the Nation insist that they are merely *applying* traditional laws and not *interpreting* them—as a direct distinction from "homosexual activists" that seek laws to reflect their special interest—the differences of interpretation challenge their privileged positions in institutionalizing their views within the laws of the Nation.

But not everyone was in line. On August 3, 2005, to the dismay and alarm of Hembree and the majority of the Nation's officials, the JAT found that under Cherokee law "the Petitioner, Todd Hembree, . . . failed to show that he will suffer individualized harm and that he, therefore lacks standing to maintain this action" (*Order Granting Motion to Dismiss*, Cherokee Nation

Supreme Court, JAT-04–14). In a press release issued by the NCLR about the decision, Ayoub stated that "permitting same-sex couples to marry does not individually harm or affect other people" (NCLR 2005).[12]

McKinley and Reynolds were relieved to hear about the dismissal: "We are so happy that the Court dismissed the case. Our relationship is precious to us and we're grateful for the support we've received from throughout the world" (ibid.). "We're excited, we're happy. We're determining what our next step is going to be" (Associated Press 2005b).

Hembree responded as well by deferring to the JAT's authority: "This is a decision by the highest court in our land. There's now no legal prohibition to having their marriage officially recognized" (Associated Press 2005b). But two days later, on August 5, he and the Council filed a Petition for Declaratory Judgment seeking to block the registration of McKinley's and Reynolds's marriage certificate. In explaining their motives, O'Leary stated that the JAT "ruled that Todd [Hembree] had no standing in the case. We are the legislators for the Cherokee Nation. We make the laws, and we do have standing" (Snell 2005b). "We don't want gay marriages in the Cherokee Nation. It's that simple" (Editorial, 365Gay.com 2005). Hembree concurred:

> Cherokees have a strong traditional sense of marriage. . . . Throughout our history, there's never been a tribal recognition of same-sex marriage. . . . It's unfortunate that we're having to deal with it. . . . But the Cherokee Nation needs to know that their laws stand for something and no perceived loophole is going to make a mockery of those statutes. (Hamilton 2005)

> If we aren't the appropriate people to bring it up then who is? My clients took an oath to always promote the heritage, culture and language of the Cherokee Nation, and same-sex marriage has never been a part of the Cherokee culture. . . . They have misinterpreted the statute. The statute itself says that marriage will be between husband and wife. Both terms have a very distinct, legal meaning and are gender-specific. (Associated Press 2006)

On August 16, 2005, the Cherokee Nation District Court ordered McKinley and Reynolds not to attempt to file their marriage certificate until resolution of the petition. The court also granted them until September 8 to file a response. McKinley and Reynolds did so and argued that the petitioners could not base their legal standing solely on their status as council members. Under Cherokee law, the petitioners were obligated to "demonstrate individualized harm, based on the deprivation of an established legal right" and that in not being able to do so "their action should be dismissed" (*Respondents' Motion to Dismiss Petitioners' Amended Petition for Declaratory Judgment*, JAT-05-11, September 8, 2005, 5).[13]

On January 4, 2006, the JAT issued their decision, finding that the petitioners had no legal standing to make their claim (Hales 2006): "Members of the Tribal Council, like private Cherokee citizens, must demonstrate a specific particularized harm. In the present case, the Council members fail to demonstrate the requisite harm" (Tanner 2006). Reynolds responded:

> Dawn and I are private people, and we simply wish to live our lives in peace and quiet, just as other married couples are permitted to do.... We are grateful to the Court for applying the law fairly and for protecting our privacy and our rights as equal citizens of the Cherokee Nation. (Editorial, *Tulsa World* 2006)

> Since the tribe has become so Westernized and adopted Christian religions and European ways, they strayed away from traditional Cherokee values.... Cherokees are very private where they respect each other and respect how they live.... We really thought our tribe would be accepting of us. That hasn't proven to be the case. (Tanner 2006)

McKinley and Reynolds decided not to file their certificate or pursue any additional legal action in the Cherokee Nation's courts. They have since refused to make any additional public comments about their experiences.

Marriage Acts in Navajo

Navajoland, the largest reservation in the United States, borders the states of Arizona, Colorado, New Mexico, and Utah. Arizona, Colorado, and Utah voted to ban same-sex marriage and adopt the DOMA as state law. New Mexico has done neither—two bills that would have done so were defeated in February 2008.

On April 22, 2005, the Navajo Nation Council passed the Diné Marriage Act (DMA) by a 67–0 vote with two abstentions (Dempsey 2005b). The intent of the act, sponsored by Larry Anderson Sr., a council delegate, was "to promote strong families and strong family values" (Dempsey 2005a). It amended Title IX of the Navajo Nation Code to "recognize valid marriages contracted outside of the Navajo Nation, with the exception of plural marriages, marriages between blood relatives, and marriages between persons of the same-sex" (Dempsey 2005b).

In principle and provision, the DMA reproduced the DOMA and in doing so ignited serious debates among Navajo citizens about their relationship to U.S. nationalism and social values (Denetdale 2008). Within these debates, very diverse ideas were expressed about the way the DMA invited the Christian conservative attitudes and provisions of federal law into the Navajo Nation, with concerns about how this did and did not affirm Navajo sovereignty and tradition. Many Navajo were concerned not merely with the "letter of the law" but with how the DMA would function within Navajo social and spiritual relationships.

In response to the concerns, Anderson asserted repeatedly in public that the DMA was based on Navajo cultural traditions and that it explicitly affirmed Navajo sovereignty: "In the Navajo way, you don't have same-sex marriages. . . . The Navajo Nation is considered a sovereign government. We have our own laws and way of life" (Dempsey 2005a). Anderson claimed that the Navajo should be able to ban same-sex marriage as part of the "same freedom" that the United States enjoyed in passing the DOMA (Dempsey 2005a).

The overwhelming number of council delegates agreed. They embraced the values of Christian conservatism as tradition (Pavlik 1997) and defined a sovereignty that functioned within those values as tradition (Denetdale 2008). Repeatedly to the press, they adopted the terms of sexist, homophobic, and anti-same-sex marriage discourses to express their sense of urgency to "defend the foundations of [their] society" against homosexuality and marriage rights for same-sex couples:

> Katherine Benally supported the legislation, citing "God's will. . . . This is how we want it, this is what we want," she said. Edward Jim agreed. "We get up and pray every morning," Jim said. "We believe in a god who despises same-sex unions." By supporting same-sex unions, Lorenzo Curley said, the Navajo Nation will be swept away by outside doctrine. "This legislation will only further our stance," Curley said. "We're here to defend the foundations of our society." (Dempsey 2005a)

But not everyone agreed. Deflecting national debates as a non-Navajo issue, Ervin Keeswood Sr., one of the two council delegates to abstain from voting on the DMA, remarked to the press that, "I'd like to know, Mr. Anderson, what's the driving force behind this? Is there now today a long line of Navajos who want same-sex unions? . . . It's really a property-rights issue on the outside. If there are such issues in Navajo country, then I can understand this" (Dempsey 2005b). Otherwise, Keeswood said, "The legislation . . . promotes negativity and 'something called discrimination'" (ibid.).

Many Navajo agreed: "Traditionalists opposed the legislation, citing a traditional story when *Nadleeh*, a Navajo word for one who has both male and female spirits, did the work of women successfully" (Dempsey 2005b). "Other critics of the legislation had said its sponsor, Delegate Larry Anderson of Fort Defiance, was attempting to rewrite cultural history to parallel conservative Christian backlash against gay rights across the United States" (Dempsey 2005c).

Joe Shirley Jr., the president of the Navajo Nation, vetoed the DMA on May 1, 2005. He explained his decision in a couple of different ways. First, he distanced same-sex marriage debates in the United States from the Navajo Nation by characterizing the debates as a national obsession with "gay rights" and homophobia. He saw the DMA as not only a Navajo version of the DOMA (and a bad one at that) but as part of a broader cultural transformation within Navajoland toward the Christian Right. Shirley rejected this move as he asserted a very different set of principles and so priorities for the Nation as traditional: "Same-sex marriage is a non-issue on Navajoland. . . . So why waste time and resources on it? We have more important issues to address" (Dempsey 2005c). "The legislation veiled a discriminatory aspect in the guise of family values, which goes against the Navajo teaching of non-discrimination and doing no psychological or physical harm" (Norell 2005a). Shirley thereby represented the DMA as failing to address the serious social problems confronting the Navajo Nation (Dempsey 2005c) but also explained that if the Navajo people made an initiative to ban same-sex marriage he would support it: "To do otherwise is to allow Navajo government to unnecessarily intrude and interfere into private, personal lives" (ibid.).

Anderson responded to Shirley's veto by accusing Shirley of ulterior political motives that were weakening the sovereignty and social values of the Navajo Nation (Norell 2005c): "The president's action to reject this worthwhile legislation appears to manipulate and to gain popular acceptance and preparation for his re-election campaign slogan for the upcoming Navajo Nation primary and general election" (Editorial, Indianz .com 2005). "As the Navajo Nation promotes stable family units and preserves and strengthens family values, we are a step closer to addressing crime, child abuse, drug abuse and other social, environmental and health care issues" (Norell 2005c).

Anderson then called for council delegates to override Shirley's veto. This call mobilized many Navajo people who identified as traditionalists to form the Diné Council for Cultural Preservation (DCCP). The DCCP organized several demonstrations and a petition in support of Shirley's veto. Their petition stated that the DMA "violated Diné law and the sanctity of life by invoking intolerance and legal discrimination" (Norell 2005c). "Passage of the Diné Marriage Act of 2005 will undermine the effort of ensuring healthy families by invoking blatant discrimination toward 'different' members of the family structure" (Dempsey 2005d). The DCCP reclaimed Navajo tradition away from the council and criticized the kinds of sexism and homophobia on which they believed the DMA was based in the name of a United States with Christian and conservative values.

On the day Anderson pleaded with fellow council delegates to override the veto, the DCCP organized a rally outside the building. "Among those rallying for gay rights were Navajo elders who defended the choices of their grandchildren" (Norell 2005c).

> Charles Cambridge, Navajo from Huerfano, N.M. who holds a doctoral degree, said, "This is the dumbest thing that I have seen the tribal council do. I will provide expert testimony in any legal action against this anti-Navajo cultural legislation." Percy Anderson, Navajo from Manuelito, N.M., was among the writers of the online petition opposing the legislation. "The response has been tremendous. . . . My dear aunt, who is a retired elementary school teacher, called me and volunteered to obtain signatures from Navajo elders. She is quite involved at the community level and is an active mobilizer." Another Navajo opposing the ban, Sherrick Roanhorse, said . . ."How is a discriminatory and unjust act going to solve and fix breakdowns in our Navajo way of life? [Larry Anderson] told us, for gay Navajo couples, 'That's their choice to make. But, they must understand that there are laws and policies within the

Navajo Nation government system that prohibits them to practice that here. Is he saying we are not welcome home? . . . He says he is traditional, but his extreme actions and beliefs contradict our Navajo belief system of humbleness, tolerance, and living a life in harmony with all that surround us. . . . We may need more checks to balance our council's overreaching power." (ibid.)

The DCCP garnered wide support among Navajo who perceived the DMA as a dangerous affirmation of non-Navajo cultural perspectives and social values. Affirming these claims, Shirley observed that he had not received a single communication from any Navajo person opposing the veto: "To the contrary, the Office of President and Vice President received an unprecedented number of unsolicited e-mails and telephone calls in support of the president's veto, of the reasons he stated for vetoing the legislation, and thanking him for the veto" (Norell 2005b).

In reaction, many council delegates reiterated their backing of the DMA on traditional grounds. Karen Francis explained:

"The legislation that was passed by the council has nothing to do with lifestyle, only with marriage. . . . While there is a role for people who possess both male and female characteristics/spirits in Diné philosophy, that role is not marrying another person of the same-sex. Most medicine men agree that there is no marriage between male and male, or female and female. The council is bringing the fundamental laws of the Diné into the Navajo Nation Code through the passage of this legislation. . . . The approval of the Diné Marriage Act, for example, strengthens the Diné Fundamental Law by implementing the principles of relationships — the male and female order of our society, which includes Mother Earth [female] and Father Sky [male]. These relationships extend into the perpetuation of the Diné foundation, the Diné people and culture."
. . . Responding to criticism from Navajo gays, Francis said the council delegates do not make their decisions in isolation. She said council delegates return to their chapters and ask Navajos how they should vote. They also consult with experts, including medicine men and traditional practitioners. . . . Defending the marriage act as a means of upholding the sanctity of marriage, Francis said the council validated Navajo common law by defining the ideology of marriage. "The Navajo Council, in its actions to approve the Diné Marriage Act, took the next logical step

in clarifying, not interpreting, Navajo common law — as should be done to other areas of Navajo law, as prescribed by the Diné Fundamental Laws adopted by the council in November 2002." (Norell 2005b)

Francis's remarks characterized how she and other council delegates were claiming the power of understanding and representing Navajo tradition against Shirley and those involved in the DCCP. She represented herself and other delegates as merely *applying* Navajo tradition and not as politically *interpreting* it to suit their own political views and selfish aims. This aimed at diffusing the accusations that the council was overly influenced by non-Navajo cultural values and political agendas — and particularly the Christian Right's — in passing a law that had nothing to do with Navajo people and their lives.

Of course, the tension throughout these debates was that Christian and conservative viewpoints had long since impacted Navajo culture and identity in uneven ways but in ways that had significantly changed their cultural histories regarding not only marriage and sexuality but their government and legal practices (Pavlik 1997; Denetdale 2006, 2008). As for the Cherokee leadership, the challenge for the council was in representing these histories in such a way that recovered their cultural authenticity and silenced — even shamed — their critics as inauthentic. They did so in part by claiming that they had been manipulated by "outside," "gay" influences and agendas. But this effort was thwarted because the DCCP, Shirley, and other Navajo were able to represent the council's actions as being anything but organic. Drawing out the parallels between the DMA and DOMA, they were able to show how the council's interpretations of Navajo tradition were modeled directly on national and fundamentally homophobic movements against same-sex marriage rights. This, in turn, threw everyone's claims to "tradition" into the light of political intention.

For the council and their conservative base, the rearticulation of same-sex marriage rights and homosexuality into the discourses of national movements betrayed an anxiety over the "threat" of the cultural perspectives of the DCCP, Shirley, and others about Navajo traditions regarding marriage and sexuality. The council and its supporters knew that the cultural fluencies of their opponents not only challenged their credibility but required a very different set of laws and policies than the DMA. This in turn challenged their positions of power within the Nation but also posed a different set of challenges for the Navajo in relation to the Christian conservative agendas dominating national politics. The DMA was, after all, both explicitly and implicitly intended to quiet the concerns motivating those agendas and the renewed scrutiny of tribal traditions and legal rights.

Of course, nothing is ever so simple. Many LGBT Navajo affirmed the more conservative perspectives associated with the Christian Right even as they advocated for a culturally traditional inclusion of their sexual orientations and partnerships within the Nation. For instance, Sherrick Roanhorse, a citizen of the Navajo Nation and an active member of the Log Cabin Republicans, wrote in response to the DMA:[14]

> This act is one that divides the Navajo people and promotes discrimination against gay Navajo people. This is wrong. Traditionally, Navajo people are tolerant and do not promote divisions among their people. Respecting all kinship is the foundation of our people, the family.... Nadleeh is a term to describe a two-spirit person. Some say a true two-spirit is a hermaphrodite and try to justify discrimination against those who may not be hermaphrodites: gay people. Today, Nadleeh has evolved into a broader term that includes all gay people. Nadleeh are essential to the Navajo way of life. They exist in our history, creation stories, songs, and ceremonies.... I have no real idea why the council chose to seek the passage of the resolution, Diné Marriage Act of 2005. Some delegates mentioned the promotion of family values and a better foundation for the Navajo youth. I am a young Navajo and I do not need the government to bestow their views on me. It is not the role of the council to promote personal beliefs of elected representatives of the Navajo people. If the council wants to promote harmony, they should not take actions to divide us and promote discrimination.... The Navajo people have other needs, such as more funding and support for Navajo jail facilities, scholarships, and roads. ... As you know, Log Cabin Republicans of New Mexico strongly opposed so-called "defense of marriage" legislation in the last session of the New Mexico Legislature because of its discriminatory nature, and we stand with our allies in the Navajo Nation in opposing this legislation, as well. (quoted in Norell 2005a)

Roanhorse's argument offered no serious critique of conservative conceptualizations of marriage, family, or sexuality. Instead, it advocated against discrimination and for a harmony in line with such platforms. Claiming marriage rights for same-sex couples in this way merely reaffirmed conservative perspectives and agendas—it did not pose any demands for conservatives to reconsider the viability of other sexual identities or social relationships. In other words, the "pro-marriage" perspective of Native lesbian and gay constituencies—as within marriage equality movements nationwide (Leong and Sueyoshi 2006)—did nothing to really challenge the cultural perspectives and social values about marriage and sexuality defining conservative ones.[15]

Meanwhile, the DCCP organized a rally on June 1, 2005, in support of Shirley's veto. DCCP representatives opened the rally by stating, "Let it be made clear that we do not have an issue with procreation, but with how the issue of marriage has become a disguise to promote the beginning of legalized discrimination toward a segment of our society. . . . We ask you, the Navajo Nation Council, to be cognizant of the oppression that has been dealt with on all Native peoples for hundreds of years and to not pick up the tools of the oppressors" (Dempsey 2005d). Louva Hartwell remarked, "I don't like the message [the DMA] sends to my daughter, that gay people are second-class citizens" (ibid.). Vivian Arviso elaborated, "It's a non-Navajo issue being brought in from white America and being made a Navajo issue. . . . We need to have healthy families. The problem is really, if we don't support young people, if we don't give them a sense of well-being, then we create this dysfunction. The legislation is blaming gay people for lack of family values among men and women" (ibid.). Carrie House stated, "Navajo oral traditions of the Nadleeh were and are about Nadleeh being revered, held in high esteem, are balancing factors in culture, language, arts, society, economy, and most important, maintaining good family ties and values. . . . To say gay people are ruining lives is false. . . . When did Christian values become traditional for Navajo culture?" (ibid.). The debates over the DMA polarized around the cultural authenticity of Christian conservatism and Navajo tradition. The competing claims of power and knowledge about what was going to be defined as authentically Navajo affirmed the notion of there being a tradition that was authentic against one that was not. In doing so, the terms of debate were accepted from national narrations, wherein Native cultures are forced into the binaries of authenticity and inauthenticity.

But if traditions are understood, instead, as constructed within specific processes of social formation, then everyone negotiates the terms of social relations and conditions with others through his or her own interpretations of what those traditions are and how they are important. In other words, the represented divides between Christian conservatives and cultural traditionalists were constructed as such in order to accomplish the political work of challenging one another's standing and rights to represent and govern what was and is Navajo.

Two days after the DCCP rally, on June 3, 2005, the Navajo Nation Council voted 62–14 with twelve abstaining to override Shirley's veto and so make the DMA law. Kenneth Maryboy, a delegate, explained the override: "In the traditional Navajo ways, gay marriage is a big no-no. . . . It all boils down to the circle of life. We were put on the earth to produce offspring. . . . My supporters told me to stay firmly against it, especially the ministers who join people in marriage" (Associated Press 2005a). Anderson likewise commented that

> this law does not intrude and interfere with private and personal lives. If we accept the president's assertion, then the Navajo Nation ought to (repeal) the entire Title Nine of the Navajo Nation Code and other laws, for that matter. However, the president's assertion is incorrect . . . As the Navajo Nation promotes stable family units . . . (it) preserve(s) and strengthen(s) values. We are a step closer to addressing crimes, child abuses, drug abuses and other social, environmental and health care issues. The president failed to visualize the positive impacts of this legislation on the Navajo Nation. . . . Many mothers, fathers, and grandmothers and grandfathers, aunts and uncles . . . are saddened with disbelief that the president vetoed this legislation with no substantive position. . . . States cannot dictate what social practices are acceptable on the Navajo Nation. . . . Our clan system and marriage ceremony, which this (Navajo) Nation relied on for centuries upon centuries, should not be thrown aside because of disagreements on social practices among states outside the Navajo Nation. (quoted in Maniaci 2005)

The DCCP issued a statement thanking Shirley for his strong stand against discrimination and the council delegates who voted against the override: "Once again, with this override, we see the continued power struggle that is hurting our governmental system. The outrage of this result will only add to the growing cries for aggressive governmental reform in the next coming years" (Diné Coalition for Cultural Preservation 2005).

Treason

treason c.1225, from Anglo-Fr. *treson*, from O.Fr. *traison* (11c.; Fr. *trahison*), from L. *traditionem* (nom. *traditio*) "a handing over, delivery, surrender" (see **tradition**). O.Fr. form influenced by the verb *trair* "betray." In old English law, *high treason* is violation by a subject of his allegiance to his sovereign or to the state; distinguished from *petit treason*, treason against a subject, such as murder of a master by his servant.

—*Online Etymology Dictionary*

During 2004 and 2005, the councils and attorneys of the Cherokee and Navajo Nations legislated against same-sex marriage rights and asserted definitions of marriage and sexuality that affirmed the discourses and ideologies of U.S. nationalism then articulated from Christian and conservative viewpoints. And they did so unapologetically—asserting those definitions and the social values as embodying their own culturally authentic traditions. Native lesbian and gay couples and their allies were dismissed as inauthentically traditional, immediate threats to tribal sovereignty in the interests of achieving their own selfish political agendas (Jacobi 2006).[16]

In the terms of U.S. national narrations, the Nations' characterizations of Native lesbian, gay, and "third gender," "two spirit" people and their allies as culturally inauthentic served to sever them from the legal status and rights of tribal governance and law making. These articulatory practices formed a "Nation" that fit easily within the ideologies and practices of U.S. nationalism and its articulations of sexism, homophobia, and religious fundamentalism (Somerville 2000; Duggan 2004; Puar 2007). While that "Nation" may not pose a viable political, legal, or social threat to national security or social order, it opens up the ethical implications of what kinds of sovereignty and self-determination Native peoples define for themselves and so seek to exercise within and in relation to one another. Will this Nation's sovereignty and self-determination replicate the relations of domination and dispossession defined for Native peoples within the United States? Will it perpetuate the current social realities of inequality, disparity, and exploitation defined for Natives within U.S. nationalism and patriotism? Will it redeploy sexist and homophobic ideologies to justify discriminatory practices and violence toward "third gender," "two-spirit" people? Will it convert Native governance and cultures into the intolerance and violence of religious conservatism and homophobia? And what of the constitutive role of racism and ethnocentrism within these processes? For here, I will offer three observations (which can really be considered one).

First, I have been much involved now for several years in working with Native colleagues and community members in the San Francisco bay area to facilitate tribal consultations toward the redevelopment of our universities' repatriation and curation policies on all matters implicated by the Native American Graves Protection and Repatriation Act of 1990. I have been taken aback continually by what I have experienced as a huge disconnect between the conversations about tradition that take place among Native peoples when it concerns their ancestors and the conversations that occur among Native peoples about tradition when it concerns issues of marriage and sexuality. The generous, heartfelt commitments that many Native people express toward their ancestors — and the emotionally and spiritually difficult, labored efforts they make on behalf of their repatriation home — is often articulated through discrete but related traditions and teachings about their ethical responsibilities to one another and the generations that have come before them and will come in the future. Told through genealogical and oral history practices, these convictions are often infused with profound and passionate claims of relationship that defy archaeological and anthropological theories, are inherently discriminating but generous and inclusive, and are at the heart of fierce legal battles over "cultural affiliation." I have not been able to make sense of the keen relevance of Native epistemologies regarding relationship and responsibility when it concerns the repatriation and curation of ancestors and those when it concerns lesbian and gay couples and "third gender," "two spirit" people. The only sense of it that I can make is that it has something to do with the politics of power and knowledge in mediating current social and interpersonal relationships. It seems that Native peoples are much more fierce about issues of social justice and generous in claiming relationships with their ancestors than they are with one another now (see Gilley 2006).

Second, Taiaiake Alfred (1999) has argued that Native peoples must confront the terms and conditions of their legal status and rights under nation-state law (see also Alfred 2005). Rejecting "self-government" as a notion that diminishes the legal authority and customary laws of Native peoples for a federal one that is merely about "self-administration," Alfred asks whether or not "sovereignty" is the appropriate objective for Native peoples if they are genuinely seeking to decolonize their governments, laws, and cultures from their nation-states and achieve any kind of viable degree of self-determination based on their own cultural traditions (see also Coffey and Tsosie 2001). As discussed in the introduction, the lingering issue within Alfred's compelling argument is the serious need within Native communities to talk through in honest and honorable ways with one another exactly what notions of "tradition" they have and seek to have reflected in their governance. In other words, it is not self-evident that a necessarily radical or oppositional form of Native governance will result if based on Native cultural traditions—at least not as those traditions are being articulated by many tribal officials and members through the kinds of racist, sexist, homophobic, and religiously fundamentalist discourses and ideologies that are dominant in U.S. national narrations.

Third, at the etymological heart of "tradition" is "treason." As so many Native peoples from all sides of the national debates about marriage and sexuality have asked, what ever happened to our traditions to live and let live? To let people be? To be respectful of one another? It seems the "treason" within "tradition" is in the pretense that those "other" genealogies, oral histories, and ethical principles of relationship and responsibility are irrelevant to the kinds of nations too often now being asserted as Native.

7 Origins

Through four acts of articulation—recognition, membership, disenrollment, and tradition—I have examined how discourses and ideologies of Native culture and identity are articulated to those of Native legal status and rights and to what consequences within the current formation of Native-U.S. relations and Native social and interpersonal relationships. In part I, I argued that federal criteria and agendas overdetermined the collective status and rights of Native peoples in the United States as racialized "Indian tribes." This happened because Native peoples were coerced to *recognize themselves* to be under federal plenary power and then to mediate their relations with one another through the terms of that subjugation. In part II, I argued that federal and tribal membership policies are a politic of social and interpersonal relationship (un)making. Thereby, Native peoples rearticulate in complex and difficult ways the racist, sexist, and homophobic ideologies of "Indian members" toward achieving their own political ends. In part III, I examined the discursive work of traditions in mediating Native assertions of their legal status and rights to sovereignty and self-determination in ways that have participated in the racism, sexism, and homophobia of certain kinds of religious conservatisms and American patriotisms. This has (unwittingly) contributed to multiple distortions of the histories of colonialism and imperialism in national narrations, the current structures of social disparity and inequality within Native communities, and the complexities of racism, sexism, and homophobia within Native configurations of their own nationhoods and citizenships. The articulation of Native culture and identity to legal status and rights, then, has immediate ethical implications for the course of federal laws and policies regarding Native peoples as well as for the kinds of sovereignties and social relationships Native peoples (seek to) make with one another.

Nowhere are these implications more evident than for those who have been the most disenfranchised and dispossessed by the articulations of culture and identity to legal status and rights by Native peoples. Despite the fact that many have refused to speak publicly about their struggles (out of concern for the privacy of their families and friends, out of sheer political exhaustion, or out of respect for the ongoing struggles of their governments for sovereignty and self-determination in a nation-state that has a deplorable history of respecting neither), I have attempted to understand these issues from the diverse historical and social contexts of their experiences and perspectives. As Michel Foucault argues in *Discipline and Punish* (1979), it is from the positions of those who actively *resist* their subjugation that power is best understood. The unrecognized, the *un-* and *dis-* enrolled, and those treated as undesirable or dangerous—like mixed-race, queer people, and women (not necessarily mutually exclusive)—have paid the highest price for how Native legal status and rights are defined and asserted by Native peoples. And the consequences are real. They go to the health and well-being of whole families and individuals who are expunged or silenced in the name of the righteousness and justice of Native sovereignty and self-determination.

But the truth is that not all have invited the subjectivities defined for them—or the agencies assigned to them—within U.S. national narrations. Without wanting to romanticize the resistance, it is important to say that the fissures within the narrations produced by Native antagonisms toward the positions of domination they are ascribed—under the guise of their being empowered as recognized, enrolled, and traditional—mark the possibilities for rearticulating Native sovereignty, self-determination, and tradition in ways that do not reaffirm U.S. nationalisms and the ideologies of racism, sexism, homophobia, and religious conservatisms that co-produce them. It is from within those possibilities that the political efficacy of strategies for decolonization and self-determination rest—in what Ernesto Laclau and Chantal Mouffe (1985) and Stuart Hall (in Grossberg 1996) define as the potentially revolutionary shift (never complete) within articulatory practices from hegemonic and essentialist relations of oppression to those characterized by the antagonisms of a radical democratic politics.

Before thinking through what that politics demands of Native peoples, I would like to spend a brief moment considering the persistent and altogether contradictory motivations that inform Native peoples' pursuits for the authentic. These pursuits define the "heart and soul" of Native political projects for decolonization and self-determination and must be better understood if they are going to offer any kind of antagonism toward a radical democratic politics within Native communities (Laclau and Mouffe 1985).

Contradictions

One of the most empowering things for me about Native epistemologies is that within the many unique beliefs and practices that define them is the related acceptance of contradictions between them. This acceptance means that the Delaware, Cherokee, Santa Clara Pueblo, Pechanga Band, Navajo, Native Hawaiian, and Alaska Native people have their own unique cultural teachings and customs regarding genealogy, belonging, responsibility, gender, and sexuality. While related in some particulars, the disagreements between them are not seen as needing to be fixed or made to fit neatly together in some master or metanarrative or "world history" in order for them to be considered meaningful and truthful by Native peoples.

Following this principle, I would like to suggest two contradictory things about the significance of Native peoples' pursuit for the culturally authentic: (1) The pursuit for the authentic (original) is constructed within U.S. national narrations to further Native domination; and (2) there is relevance and importance in Native traditions and teachings (origin points) for providing other viable understandings of society, relationships, and social responsibilities.

Some Musings on the Pursuit for the Authentic

Genealogy is gray, meticulous, and patiently documentary. It operates on a field of entangled and confused parchments, on documents that have been scratched over and recopied many times. . . . Why does Nietzsche challenge the pursuit of the origin, at least on those occasions when he is truly a genealogist? First, because it is an attempt to capture the exact essence of things, their purest possibilities, and their carefully protected identities, because this search assumes the existence of immobile forms that precede the external world of accident and succession. The search is directed to "that which was already there," the image of a primordial truth fully adequate to its nature, and it necessitates the removal of every mask to ultimately disclose an original identity. However, if the genealogist refuses to extend his faith in metaphysics, if he listens to history, he finds that there is "something altogether different" behind things: not a timeless and essential secret, but the secret that they have no essence or that their essence was fabricated in a piecemeal fashion from alien forms. Examining the history of reason, he learns that it was born in an altogether "reasonable" fashion—from chance, devotion to truth and the precision of scientific methods arose from the passion of scholars, their reciprocal hatred, their fanatical and unending discussions, and their spirit of competition—the personal conflicts that slowly forged the weapons of reason. Further, genealogical analysis shows that the concept of liberty is an "invention of the ruling classes" and not fundamental to man's nature or at the root of his attachment to being and truth. What is found at the historical beginning of things is not the inviolable identity of their origin; it is the dissension of other things. It is disparity.

—MICHEL FOUCAULT, "Nietzsche, Genealogy, History"

Within U.S. politics, Native assertions of a strong political subjectivity as recognized, enrolled, and traditional is a powerful strategy for responding to the disempowered subjectivities assigned to them within national narrations. This is because those narrations rely on subjectivities of their own to do the work of making Native peoples known and governable (Foucault

1972; Ong 1995). Asserting a resolute subjectivity—especially one that claims to be the truth against the fraud—is an effective tactic of empowerment. But it is one fraught with troubles.

Resisting in the truth of one's legal status and rights as recognized, enrolled, and traditional can rely on the same notions of Native culture and identity as those (in)forming the discourses and ideologies of a U.S. nationalism rested on Native domination. It unsettles nothing. For in claiming a subjectivity that is legitimate against the bastard, the authentic against the fake, the truth against the fraud makes use of the same binaries to resist subjugation as are used in producing relations of domination. A reversed hierarchy is still a hierarchy. There is, then, no revolution—only inversion. So exactly what does this mean? Does it mean that we are all fated to repeat the sins of our oppressors? That there is no opposition? That resistance is truly futile?

It means something else.

Appeals to metaphysical truths and essential identities—as foundations for legal status and rights, as evidence of cultural authenticity—represent the pursuit for origin, for "capturing the exact essence of things, their purest possibilities, their carefully protected identities" in a truth that was there before contamination, for an original, "that which was already ... adequate to its nature" (Foucault 1977, 142). It is a pursuit that is entirely understandable. Given histories of colonization and imperialism and the social realities of racism, sexism, homophobia, and religious fundamentalism that co-constitute them, the pursuit for origin is a desire for a truth beyond political discord, social conflict, and the demoralizing experiences of hatred, brutality, and imprisonment. But it is also a pursuit that is problematic, and even cruel. Because the pursuit for origin(al) is a promise for an escape from history and politics that can never be. It denies the historical realities of accident, succession, alienation, passion, personal conflict, dissension, and disparity (ibid.) in a promise for an impossible ahistorical, extra-political existence and experience. It pretends the possibility of knowledge and authenticity before history and change affected them—narrating knowledge and culture as if they can be pure or contaminated, sacred or profane, found or lost. The pursuit itself keeps the promise of truth present, all in the effort to deflect the historical conditionality of the "piecemeal," the social contexts of the "masked," and the constructedness of "reason" (ibid.).

The truth is that the pursuit of native or aboriginal authenticity binds Native peoples to this logic:

> **native.** L born: see NATURE. **1** inborn or innate rather than acquired **2** belonging to a locality or country by birth, production, or growth: indigenous . . . **3** related to one as, or in connection with, the place of one's birth or origin . . . nativity L *nativus*, NATIVE 1 birth, esp. with reference to place, time, or accompanying conditions . . . the Nativity 1 the birth of Jesus . . .[1]

> **aboriginal** . . . **aborigine** 1858, mistaken singular of *aborigines* (1547, the correct singular is *aboriginal*), from L. *Aborigines* 'the first inhabitants' (especially of Latium), possibly a tribal name, or from *ab origine*, lit. 'from the beginning.' Extended 1789 to natives of other countries which Europeans have colonized. Australian slang shortening *Abo* attested from 1922.[2]

For Native peoples, the pursuit of origin is an irony of altogether biblical proportions. After all, to desire a prehistory—an *aboriginal*—is to desire the very metaphysical essence of the Native. This Native is located entirely by and within the narrations of Christian theology and "Western" science.[3] Therefore, it is impossible to reconcile the Native to Christianity or science because they construct an authentic Native that is contrary to all things Christian and scientific.

In other words, the Christian and the scientist—as individual, as knowledge, as theoretical and methodological perspective—cannot be a Native within the narrations of Christianity and science. To the extent that those narrations are a part of the configuration and perpetuation of U.S. nationalism they are made necessary again to U.S. colonial and imperial projects aimed at Native domination. This is evident in powerful ways by the fact that the narrations make this Native not only the *only* authentic Native but the sole condition on which all legal status and rights as Native to sovereignty and self-determination are based. It is ironical still because these presumably "very different" narratives of human origin and social history—Christianity and science—are actually (telling) the exact same story (Dumont 2008).

Despite current political debates between "creationists" and "evolutionists," this sameness is evidenced in how Natives have mobilized the narrative paradigms of Christianity and science to tell their histories and epistemologies. How they once lived in a kind of paradise, free from the sins of the West, until being forced to Fall into Western culture by the evils of colonialism — their once Pure Cultures and Identities having been forever lost or contaminated by the social forces of Christianity and Civilization, with the concerted aim now to return, recapture, and emulate those original cultures. So that, while seeming to claim an *alternative* origin that is *authentically* Native — one that is all the while critical of the historical and political consequences of Christianity and science — the pursuit for the origin/aboriginal works to reinforce the narratives of Christianity and science. Because the true, authentic Native is only possible within the very narratives that it promises to transcend.

The political challenge that this knowledge system presents to Native peoples is in having to find an origin before Christianity and science that is only meaningful within the histories of Christianity and science. But if Native peoples are to secure the recognition and protection of their legal status and rights as defined therein, they must be able to demonstrate their *aboriginality* — as pursuit, as essence, as a truth that transcends.

To put this in a slightly different way, the discursive work of Native legal status and rights in U.S. politics has made Native rights contingent on a particular kind of Native: a Native in or of an authentic culture and identity. And it is *that* Native that has been made opposite and opposed to all things Christian and scientific: authentic only if absent of Christianity and science, recognizable only if possessing identities and truths beyond colonial and imperial history and politics. These conditionalities actually make it possible for those in power within the ideologies and institutional structures of Christianity and science to alleviate themselves of any responsibility for having to know or to recognize Native cultures and identities in any other terms.

As a consequence, the ideologies and institutions of Christianity and science are able to maintain their discursive power and knowledge over Native narrations and self-definitions by demanding the absence of the historical and political within them. This makes it impossible for Native peoples to narrate the historical and social complexities of cultural exchange, change, and transformation — to claim cultures and identities that are conflicted, messy, uneven, modern, technological, mixed. Because in those narrations and claims, Natives lose all rights to sovereignty and self-determination as inauthentically Native. And so in numerous ways that are painful and pained, too many Native peoples have chosen to purge from their midst those individuals (those with mixed blood, feminists, et cetera) and those cultural histories (of other genders and sexualities) that do not fit the tale of their cultural authenticity and legal legitimacy as Natives within.

Some Musings on Native Epistemologies

In "Descent into Race," Carol Goldberg-Ambrose asks, "What is wrong with treating Indian classifications as racial classifications, even when they are tribally based? Why not require 'race-neutral' criteria for tribal membership and affiliation, focusing on cultural involvement or performance?" (2002a, 1388–89). She answers that the U.S. government's imposition of blood quantum criteria on tribes

> should not delegitimize tribal control over membership criteria that refer to descent, given that descent is a tribal concern tracing to the culture's most sacred narratives. . . . One cannot simultaneously recognize tribes as governments with national and international standing as indigenous peoples, and reject as racialized the very measures needed to provide for their survival and well-being. The better approach is for courts to accept that legislating for the welfare of Indian nations entails benefiting groups defined largely by kinship and descent. . . . [The] rejection of descent-based criteria feeds the tendency of non-Indian courts to racialize tribal membership and to impose cultural performance requirements that misunderstand the nature of tribal belonging while undermining both individual Indians' identity and tribal interests. (1393–94)

Goldberg-Ambrose's argument poses an interesting conundrum for understanding Native epistemologies of kinship and lineal descent. Do those epistemologies necessarily equate kinship and descent with race's blood degree, as they are equated within European and American philosophies and sciences? Hasn't one of the main arguments within Native studies been that Native teachings about kinship and lineality are understood in much different kinds of ways — such as in the inclusion of not only humans but humans in relationship to other beings and places? How and why did race's blood become shorthand within tribes for kinship and descent?

Eva Marie Garroutte (2003) gets at these issues by responding to what she sees as the "scornful treatment" of Native statements as "racist," "essentialist," "intellectually deficient," and "politically rabid" when they address the importance of genealogical descent (120). She argues that "even a cursory examination reveals that sacred stories about the importance of kinship, defined in terms of genealogical descent, abound in tribal oral traditions" (121). Her argument suggests that instead of assuming that the intellectual *routes* of such ideas go back solely through their racialized constructs within European or American knowledge systems, it might be more productive and useful to examine their *roots* in Native epistemologies (Gilroy 1995).

One of my premises is that Native cultures and identities are not merely or only what they are defined to be within U.S. national narrations—narrations that have their own political aims at Native dispossession and disenfranchisement and work to discipline and otherwise coerce Native peoples to think of their legal and political options and cultural selves in those terms. While rearticulated through the "historical grooves" of all of their previous articulations as such (Hall, in Grossberg 1996, 143), Native cultures and identities are meaningful and relevant in the social contexts of their rearticulations—made to mean particular things toward particular kinds of social formations. So Native peoples have full agency—and so full ethical responsibility—for how they choose to define and represent their cultures and identities.

There are many stories throughout this book about Native governments, communities, and individuals who oppose the articulations of Native culture and identity within U.S. national narrations. Their antagonistic rearticulations of what it means to be Native are remembering Native epistemologies as providing much more demanding and generous understandings of affiliation, belonging, and kinship than those within the discourses and ideologies of U.S. nationalism. One of the most radical aspects of this is within the insistence of the legal validity of Native claims for traditional territorial reacquisition (de-occupation) as a fundamental aspect of the decolonization and self-determination of Native peoples (LaDuke 1999; Kauanui 2008). It is exactly to those kinds of reformations that the United States so actively resists—against Native cultures and identities being understood as current, meaningful, and relevant to the legal claims of Native peoples within the contexts of international and federal law. After all, if the only authentic Natives are prehistorical and precolonial, then Native rights to self-government and territorial integrity are *pro forma* at best.

On the Decolonization of Relationship

The interdependency of humankind, the relevance for relationship, the sacredness of creation is returning as a fact of life. It is ancient, ancient wisdom.

—REBECCA ADAMSON, "First Nations Survival and the Future of the Earth"

We believe that we're hooked together, the way that we are intertwined, the way that we live with one another, all of this one being.

—OREN LYONS, "A Democracy Based on Peace"

Human beings are not separate from the rest of the natural world but were created to live in an integral relationship with it; that's what we have to offer. Understanding these indigenous principles provides understanding of love. . . . All creation and compassion for each other comes from this understanding.

—TOM GOLDTOOTH, "Protecting the Web of Life"

Of all the traditional ceremonies extant and actively practiced . . . ceremonies derived from or related to these holy places have the highest retention rate because of their extraordinary planetary importance. . . . Their underlying theme is one of gratitude expressed by human beings on behalf of all forms of life. They act to complete and renew the entire and complete cycle of life, ultimately including the whole cosmos present in its specific realizations, so that in the last analysis one might describe ceremonials as the cosmos becoming thankfully aware of itself.

—VINE DELORIA, JR., *Spirit and Reason*

In her introduction to the edited volume *Original Instructions: Indigenous Teachings for a Sustainable Future*, Melissa Nelson writes, "For many of us, the process of re-indigenization means we have to decolonize our minds, hearts, bodies, and spirits and revitalize healthy cultural traditions. We also have to create new traditions, new ways to thrive in this complex world during these intense times" (2008, 14). Nelson argues that Native peoples are survivors of a relentless and violent historical holocaust and live today with the "historical trauma" (16) of their experiences of government policies aimed at their genocide, dispossession, assimilation, termination, and economic exploitation and, I would include, the hateful racist representa-

tions and determined ignorant stereotypes of Natives that fuel those policies and that have been used to rationalize their consequences.

> Such extreme experiences . . . [have] created a systemic problem of
> psychological disempowerment and trauma for American Indians. So-
> cially unacknowledged and individually untreated, these traumas are in-
> herited intergenerationally. . . . This trauma manifests as internalized
> oppression. . . . Internalized oppression is a result of the socioeconomic
> and psychospiritual domination of oppressive political systems that
> seek to colonize and control culturally diverse peoples (their knowledge
> and practices), usually for economic labor and religious conversion. The
> political structures of oppression—racism, poverty, violence, accul-
> turation, stress—become so dominant in the minds of the oppressed
> peoples that they begin to believe these dominant narratives and inter-
> nalize this oppression. As the well-known South African social justice
> activist Steven Biko stated, "the most potent weapon in the hands of the
> oppressor is the mind of the oppressed." (15–16)

Native intellectual, creative, and political work for sovereignty and
self-determination has taken on the real need for the decolonization of Native governments and laws, territorial rights, natural resource management,
repatriation, human genetics, whaling rights, sports, food/nutrition, language, storytelling, enrollment, and the need for returning to formal treaty
relations between the United States and Native nations (Barker 2005a;
Wilson and Yellow Bird 2005). But the discursive and ideological troubles
that I have explored in this book suggest that these projects must still fully
interrogate and reform the troubled notions of Native culture and identity through which Native status and rights are articulated. I believe that
the political and social efficacy of decolonization projects—from land reacquisition to storytelling—rests *principally* and *principledly* on the radical
reformation of Native social and interpersonal relations. Healthy, vibrant
Native nations and communities—and meaningfully rich traditional teachings and practices—cannot result from social and interpersonal relations
based on disrespect, indifference, discrimination, hate, and violence.

Of course, this is easier said than done. What this will require is that the
recognized, the landed, the enrolled, men, "full bloods," heterosexuals, fun-
damentalists, and conservatives within Native communities *must become
partners* with the unrecognized, landless, disenrolled, women, "mixed-

race," queer, and nonconservative activists within Native communities in order to address the historical trauma, social inequalities, and interpersonal violence that characterize too many Native social relations. This will mean that those privileged by current configurations of rights and entitlements within U.S. national narrations must acknowledge that privilege and stop acting like it results from some organic, metaphysical truth about who they are or is an inevitable outcome of the way things should be. Privilege is legally and socially constructed. It can be undone.

Likewise, Native people must stop acting like *their* understandings and perspectives about Native cultures and identities are more authentic than others. Cultures are meaningful in the context of social and interpersonal relationships and so are inherently historical and political. Nothing will change between Native peoples until they acknowledge the social conditions of their cultural understandings and knowledge-making practices (interpretations) and are honest about their political agendas in asserting them. In that, there is great social responsibility and great potential for revolution. No longer will Natives expect themselves or one another to mimic an unknowable, unattainable past. No longer will they feel nostalgia for what they cannot attain. They will take serious and lasting responsibility for the ever-changing historical and political complexities of their cultural beliefs, practices, and customs and so be able to empower one another to do the same. They will, as Melissa Nelson writes, remember and reinvent traditions as a means of healing and revitalization. They will, as David Cornsilk says, just allow one another to be. That kind of deep respect for one another is the fundamental principle on which project of decolonization and self-determination rest and that have been so profoundly lost in Native acts of the recognizable, enrollable, and traditional "Indian."

Notes

....

Introductions

1 See Brown and Kohn 2008 for a collection of personal stories from Delaware people about their experiences through termination and recognition.

2 I have chosen "Native peoples" for this project to mark a focus on the indigenous peoples of lands now occupied by the United States. It is not a stable referent in the politics examined herein, any more so than "indigenous," "Indian," or "aboriginal" would be. In fact, part of the story told in subsequent chapters will be about how others are forced in and out of the "Native" category in legal struggles for sovereignty and self-determination.

3 For related tales, see Taylor 1998 and Owens 1998.

4 I am indebted to the theorization of the nation and its never-completed representational work at maintaining itself as a totalizing political force by Homi K. Bhabha in his "Introduction: Narrating the Nation" in *Nation and Narration* (1990), and by Benedict Anderson in *Imagined Communities* (1991).

5 This is incredibly ironic given the fact that the colonial nations of North America and Europe demanded that Native peoples transform their governments, legal practices, and religions in order to secure their seats at the proverbial negotiating table. See Silva 2004, 36.

6 For a compelling account of the theoretical problems of case law, see Carrillo 2002.

7 In his seminal essay "Nietzsche, Genealogy, History" (1977), working through Friedrich Nietzsche's *On the Genealogy of Morals: A Polemic* (1887), Michel Foucault asks, "Why does Nietzsche challenge the pursuit of the origin, at least on those occasions when he is truly a genealogist?" (142). He argues that it is because the "pursuit of the origin" is the "attempt to capture the exact essence of things, their purest possibilities, and their carefully protected identities, because this search assumes the existence of immobile forms that precede the external world of accident and succession" (ibid.). Foucault describes this kind of search as aiming toward "a primordial truth fully adequate to its nature," that "necessitates the removal of every mask to ultimately disclose an original identity" (ibid.). He counters this with the work of the genealogist, who "refuses to extend his faith in metaphysics" and "listens to history" where "he finds that there is 'something altogether different' behind things: not a timeless and essential secret, but the secret that they have no essence or that their essence was fabricated in a piecemeal fashion from alien forms" (ibid.). This exposes the history of reason as not a history of essential truth but one of "chance" resulting from a "devotion to truth" (ibid.). That, in fact, the "precision of scientific methods" arose not from reason (objectivity) but "from the passion of scholars, their reciprocal hatred, their fanatical and unending discussions, and their spirit of competition—the personal conflicts that slowly forged the weapons of reason" into claims of scientific objectivity (ibid.). So the results of scientific inquiry are not the discovery of truth but of an irrational "attachment to being and truth": "What is found at the historical beginning of things is not the inviolable identity of their origin; it is the dissension of other things. It is disparity" (ibid.). Such concepts as "liberty," therefore, arise from conflicts between groups and individuals and their emotional, faith-based attachments to *particular* "beings and truths" (see chapter 7).

8 The Alaskan Native Claims Settlement Act of 1971 has been similarly criticized because it literally transcribed Alaskan Natives into "shareholders" of regional corporations set up to manage their lands and moneys (see chapter 1).

9 I will use several different dictionary and etymology sources throughout this book. The different sources are meant to signify primarily the lack of coherence in what words mean because their meanings are about interpretative practices that are historically conditional and socially contextual. I simulate, then, the readability of the significance of words by refusing to allow a single authority for their definition.

10 All of the above definitions come from the *Online Etymology Dictionary*, http://www.etymonline.com.

11 I heard this criticism several times, and loudly, from Native students and community members during my short tenure in the department at the University of California, Davis, from 2001 to 2003. It was a criticism they shared of D-Q University, with which the Native American Studies department shared a historical alliance

and affiliation, and whose demographics had shifted so dramatically during the 1990s that D-Q lost accreditation and BIA funding for not having enough tribal people enrolled.

1 Of the "Indian Tribe"

1 For other narrations of recognition policies and the ideologies on which they rest, see Barker 2003, 2005a, and 2005/2006.

2 It seems germane that the U.S. Constitution was conceived and ratified within New England, where Native people were radically erased from the landscape — physically and imaginatively (J. O'Brien 1997; Den Ouden 2005).

3 This exclusivity was furthered in the Indian Trade and Intercourse Acts of 1790 and 1834, which, in addition to regulating Indian and non-Indian trade, reserved the exclusive right to purchase lands from Indians to the U.S. Congress (R. Miller 2006).

4 Several treaties with tribes, including the first one ratified with the Delaware Tribe of Indians in 1778, promised tribal representation in Congress and tribally controlled states of the union, which, if even partially effected, would have reversed tribal exemption from federal and state taxation.

5 In the *Handbook of Federal Indian Law* (1940), Felix S. Cohen observes that "the fact that Congress has, by legislation, repealed, modified, or disregarded various Indian treaties has been thought by some to show that Indian treaties are of inferior legal validity. The fact is, however, that the power of Congress to enact legislation in conflict with treaties is well established in the field of foreign affairs, as well as in the field of Indian affairs" (34).

6 Many other treaties were negotiated and never ratified, such as all eighteen treaties signed with tribes in California (Heizer 1972).

7 The entire language of the plaintiffs throughout the long history of *Cobell v. Salazar* (1996) has been not only to challenge the BIA's negligent management of its trust responsibilities but the way that such trust has characterized tribes as being uncivilized and dependent. See www.indiantrust.com (Barker 2005/2006).

8 What is so insidious about these narrations are the multiple ways that they have been deployed to make it possible for just about anyone to appropriate Native cultures and identities as their own, sometimes even in the name of American nationalism and patriotism (R. Green 1988, 1990; Vizenor 1994; P. Deloria 1998; Denetdale 2008). But it is also at the ideological heart of anti-mixed race discourses within Native communities that pit the "mixed blood" — made to embody cultural loss and compromise — against Native sovereignty (Owens 1998; Barker 2003).

9 Apparently, at the time, an independent commission was also considered but through the lobbying efforts of recognized tribes, the National Congress of American Indians, and the BIA, it was decided that despite the glaring conflicts of financial interest the BIA should control the process of deciding recognition cases (M. Miller 2004).

10 Miller 2004 traces the origins of these evaluative categories to *Montoya v. U.S.* (1901) in which tribes were defined as "a body of Indians of the same or similar race, united in a community under one leadership or government, and inhabiting a particular though sometimes ill-defined territory." The common law decision informed the "Indian tribe" of the Indian Reorganization Act (1934) and Felix Cohen's *Handbook of Federal Indian Law,* which expanded the definition to include political and ethnological factors that were folded into the BAR criteria (M. Miller 2004, 28).

11 According to the GAO report, of the then 561 recognized tribes, 47 (8 percent) had been recognized since 1960 by Congress (16) and the BIA (31). Of the 31 tribes recognized by the BIA, 14 of the 250 that had applied were extended recognition status through the BAR with 10 decisions before 1978 and 7 outside of the program (2001a, 2–5). According to the BIA, as of April 4, 2008, 562 tribes had federal recognition status (the Mashpee Wampanoag Tribe was acknowledged by the BAR).

12 The BAR modified its criteria and procedures in 1994, 1997, and 2000 only to speed up decisions for some and greatly stall decisions for others (GAO 2001a). Upon his exit as assistant secretary, Carl Artman issued a notice announcing the modifications of "internal" administrative procedures within the BAR to address specific situations perceived to slow the process down, including the emergence of splinter or factional groups within tribes, the lack of response from tribes to the BAR requests for additional information, and requests for expedited processing from "uniquely qualified groups" (Federal Register Notices 73[101], May 23, 2008).

13 The U.S. Census in 2000 recorded 16,005 as Alaska Native and another race and 92,182 as Alaska Native and no other race. It also recorded 119,241 Alaska Natives of mixed and single identifications as living in Alaska, but this includes the roughly 11,000 who also identified as American Indian.

2   In *Cherokee v. Delaware*

1 Cherokee and Delaware conflicts have taken place entirely within the traditional territories of other Native nations, including the Osage and Wichita. This has complicated their respective claims and assertions of rights to self-government and territorial integrity in the fourteen counties of the Cherokee Nation in northeastern Oklahoma to which they were relocated.

2 "Indian Territory" was an ever-shifting set of reserved lands by the United States for tribal relocation and resettlement, generally in that area that would become the states of Kansas (1861), Nebraska (1867), and Oklahoma (1907).

3 The status of the Freedmen within the Cherokee Nation has never been fully resolved (Sturm 2002). The Freedmen and their descendants were extended Cherokee citizenship by the provisions of the Cherokee's 1866 treaty with the United States. In 1983 Ross Swimmer, the principal chief at the time, initiated legislation that required possession of the Certificate of Degree of Indian Blood (CDIBs are discussed further in chapter 3) in order to vote in Cherokee elections. This had

the effect of disenfranchising the Freedmen's descendants because their rolls (the Freedmen Rolls), which were kept separate from the main rolls (Dawes Rolls), did not record "Indian blood" and so they could not register with the BIA for a CDIB. Several unsuccessful federal and tribal suits followed for discrimination against the Freedmen at Cherokee voting polls. In September 2004, Lucy Allen filed a lawsuit on behalf of the Freedmen's descendants in the Cherokee Nation Supreme Court against the National Council for barring Freedmen citizenship (*Allen v. Cherokee Nation Tribal Council* 2004). In March 2006, the court ruled that the Freedmen's descendants were allowed to register because their ancestors were recorded as citizens on the official rolls of the Nation and the Cherokee Constitution of 1975 did not restrict membership by blood quantum. In June 2006, the Council voted to exclude the Freedmen and their descendants from the rolls and called for a special election to amend the Constitution accordingly. In March 2007, the Nation voted 77 percent in favor of expelling the Freedmen. Appeals are pending within the Nation and legislation has been proposed through Congress to withdraw recognition status and funding from the Cherokee Nation if it does not honor the terms of the 1866 treaty regarding the Freedmen. It is impossible to disentangle the swirling discursive mess caused by the Council's claims about who is and is not legitimately Cherokee by lineality or by law on the instance of the Freedmen from those of the Delaware. They attempt to maneuver political conflicts not only within the Cherokee Nation but between the Cherokee and the United States over the terms of Cherokee jurisdiction (complicated further by the same-sex marriage debates that were concurrent with Allen's lawsuit and the special election, discussed further in chapter 6).

4 All of the "Five Civilized Tribes" had similar if not same provisions in their "reconstruction treaties" (see Debo 1940; Treaty with the Choctaw and Chickasaw 1866, Treaty with the Creeks 1866, and Treaty with the Seminoles 1866 available in Kappler 1975).

5 Many scholars have observed the political importance and implications of the change from "treaties" to "agreements." See, for instance, Prucha 1994 and Anaya 1996.

6 The General Allotment Act was repealed by the Indian Reorganization Act of 1934 (Deloria and Lytle 1984).

7 Other tribal lands were likewise exempted. "That the provisions of this act shall not extend to the territory occupied by the Cherokees, Creeks, Choctaws, Chickasaws, Seminoles, and Osage, Miamies and Peorias, and Sacs and Foxes, in the Indian Territory, nor to any of the reservations of the Seneca Nation of New York Indians in the State of New York, nor to that strip of territory in the State of Nebraska adjoining the Sioux Nation on the south added by executive order" (Section 8, General Allotment Act 1887).

8 The decision had implications not only for other tribes that had been relocated into the Cherokee Nation (including the Loyal Shawnee and Euchee), but also for the Freedmen and their descendants who had been granted Cherokee citizenship

in the Cherokee-U.S. treaty of 1866. The assertion by these other constituencies of this decision in claiming their citizenship status and revenue sharing has inadvertently undermined Delaware legal claims to independence.

9 The Cherokee were exempt from the General Allotment Act of 1887 under the terms of their treaty with the United States in 1835. Further, in 1871, the U.S. Senate suspended treaty making with tribes. Hence, the 1902 negotiations for allotment with the Cherokee resulted in an "agreement" and not a treaty to allot (Bledsoe 1909).

10 The National Council was likewise working to prevent the Loyal Shawnee, Euchee, and Freedmen and their descendants from making similar claims to citizenship status and rights in the Nation.

11 The 1890 and 1904 rulings have been used successfully by the Cherokee Freedmen in their efforts to secure and protect their treaty rights as "native Cherokee" within Cherokee courts and also within courts in the United States. Therein, the Freedmen have asserted that they, like the Delaware, were extended the status and rights of "native Cherokee" under the terms of Cherokee treaties (*Allen v. Cherokee Nation*, Cherokee Supreme Court, March 7, 2006). In other forums, Delaware efforts to separate from the Cherokee, and specifically to overturn the 1890 and 1904 decisions, have been harshly criticized by the Freedmen and their allies as ignoring the legal facts and undermining Freedman rights (see John Cornsilk's web site, www.cornsilks.com, for frequent blog postings on the questions of Delaware status and rights).

12 As the Supreme Court would decide in 1905, "We will construe a treaty with the Indians as 'that unlettered people' understood it, and 'as justice and reason demand, in all cases where power is exerted by the strong over those to whom they owe care and protection" (*United States v. Winans*, 198 U.S. 371, 380–81).

13 The BIA forbids dual tribal membership within its funding to tribes, which must demonstrate that they have a unique membership as funding is based on population (see chapter 3).

14 They would also change for the Loyal Shawnee and Euchee but not in respect to the Freedmen and their descendants, who were quickly segregated within the Nation and slowly disenfranchised from their rights as citizens under the 1866 treaty (Sturm 2002).

15 For many Delaware people, the money was understood to be a liquidation of tribal assets following termination in 1979, ironically the year the funds were distributed.

16 My grandparents—Herbert Barker Sr. and Marie Barker—and particularly my grandmother helped the tribe's documentary efforts (Brown and Kohn 2008, 237–38).

17 The evidence for this argument was based solely on U.S. government documents and court decisions, because nothing in Delaware-Cherokee relations since 1867 indicated that the Delaware Tribe had willingly or knowingly given up anything of the kind. In fact, intertribal relations had been characterized by Delaware attempts initially to rescind the agreement and relocate elsewhere in the Territory

and then when forced to settle in Cherokee borders to resist and oppose their legal incorporation as Cherokee citizens by refusing to vote or hold office in the Nation.

18 There were many Cherokee citizens who did not support the lawsuit and were critical of Smith and the Council's actions and interpretations of the issues. See, for example, John Cornsilk's (Cherokee) web site, John C.'s Place at www.corn silks.com. Cornsilk notes that Smith's election to office was only supported by 20 percent of registered Cherokee citizens who live in Oklahoma. Smith has won largely because of nonresident Cherokee votes. This lack of support by local Cherokee seems owing to several of Smith's policies, including those about the Delaware Tribe and Cherokee Freedom. A lack often represented by the public edits made to Smith's entry on Wikipedia.com (accessed January 2009).

3 Of the "Indian Member"

1 In the *Handbook of Federal Indian Law* (1940), Felix S. Cohen delineates some of the restrictions of these rights through tribal treaties and federal statutes to show that not all tribal members have access to the same set of rights regarding tribal property and resources and that those rights are filtered through the rights of the tribe. These can include restrictions of access and share to tribal resources to those who were granted membership status because they "married in" (such as discussed in chapter 4).

2 As addressed by Sue-Ellen Jacobs, Wesley Thomas, and Sabine Long in their edited volume *Two Spirit People: Native American Gender Identity, Sexuality, and Spirituality* (1997), "third gender" and "two spirit" are conflicted terms within Native communities for those who do not identify themselves and their sexual identities according to heterosexual norms. I will, therefore, use these terms with quotes to maintain their conflictedness.

3 Ironically, colonial-settler officials and traders often sought Native women as wives in order to have access to their knowledge and labor — necessary to their very physical survival in unfamiliar regions — and to garner alliance with powerful Native families (Van Kirk 1983).

4 Applying to Indian Territory, the Curtis Act of 1898 included provisions that abolished tribal courts and extended federal jurisdiction over tribes except in cases of false claims to membership as related to landholdings in tribal territories; that stated that individually owned lands in tribal territories by United States citizens had to be sold back to the tribes who wanted to include them in the allotment process within two years; that charged the Dawes Commission with the responsibility of administering allotment once the census rolls and land surveys were concluded; and authorized the Secretary of the Interior to lease lands for no more than fifteen years for mineral extraction and to provide revenue shares to tribal members.

The Burke Act of 1906 provided that citizenship was not to be granted to tribal members who took allotments until the end of the twenty-five-year trust period or who had "adopted the habits of civilized life." It also charged the Secretary of the Interior with determining the competency of tribal members to manage the demands of private property ownership and to determine the legal heirs of allottees who died. It provided that tribal members determined to be competent and granted a fee patent were to be made citizens.

The Omnibus Act of 1910 provided that the Secretary of the Interior could end the trust period on trust patents at any time before the twenty-five-year period if the tribal member was deemed to be competent. It also allowed the Secretary of the Interior to lease tribal lands, allotted or not, as well as to sell tribal natural resources.

5   The census rolls are sometimes referred to as the Dawes Rolls after the act's sponsor, Henry L. Dawes, a retired senator from Massachusetts.

6   In the *Handbook of Federal Indian Law* (1940), Cohen reports that determinations of competency were not permanent. An individual could be deemed competent to manage one property but inherit another and have to go through competency review again (168).

7   The specific size of the allotments assigned to individuals followed a complicated formula tied to the estimated value and location of the lands in question (see McDonnell 1991).

8   The *Cobell* (1996) civil suit against the BIA's management of Indian Individual Money accounts tied to the sale and leasing of the trust lands has exposed the BIA's corrupt malfeasance in administrating Indian lands and assets.

9   As will be discussed more fully in chapters 4 and 5, one of the things that is so disturbing and ironic about all of this is that the historical conditions informing the production of the rolls (including grave political duress for tribes and federal malfeasance) and the subsequent requirement of securing government and church documentation for validation of lineal descent (agencies with principal roles in the colonization process) must be treated by the United States and tribes as acceptable or irrelevant in protecting the legal legitimacy of the rolls and so the cultural authenticity of a tribal identity that can be recognized and affirmed by rights. In other words, federal and tribal officials must treat the rolls and censuses as "conclusive evidence" and not as historically and politically produced in order to protect and continue to invest the legally legitimate and culturally authentic tribal member with status and rights in tribal governance and property (see P. Deloria 2004).

10   Interestingly, since the United States was extending citizenship to persons born into tribes perceived as sovereigns but not "foreign nations" (a distinction made under the Supreme Court's ruling in *Worcester v. Georgia* 1831, discussed in chapter 1), dual citizenship was not considered to be at issue. United States citizenship and tribal membership could coexist because the United States had established that tribes were not "foreign" but "domestic" polities under the authority of Congress.

11   As Felix Cohen observes (1940), not all tribal property and rights are equal. This is

because of the tribes' diverse histories of territorial rights as well as to differences in treaty provisions for things like hunting, fishing, or logging.

12 The IRA did not apply to Oklahoma or Alaska, later extended by the Oklahoma Indian Welfare Act and the Alaska Indian Welfare Act of 1936.

13 By the 1980s many of these programs and funds had been extended to all tribes irrespective of their IRA status under the auspices of affirming tribal self-determination.

14 Taiaiake Alfred (1999) writes that Deloria and Lytle's analysis of the IRA makes an important distinction between tribal governments who are merely *self-administrating* (under the IRA or not) and those who manifest their cultural traditions in the forms of governance that they practice.

4 In *Martinez v. Santa Clara* (and Vice Versa)

1 Federal statute provides for tribal jurisdiction over tribal members and Native nonmembers on reservations but not over non-Natives on reservations.

2 On the grounds of recognizing the viability of tribal cultures, the ICRA did not include the guarantee that the United States would not establish a national religion, the separation of church and state, the guarantee of a republican form of government, the right to a jury trial in civil cases, and the right of the poor to legal representation in criminal cases.

3 The Santa Clara Pueblo are referred to as being culturally a part of the "eastern" or Rio Grande Pueblo (of New Mexico) and they speak the Tewa dialect of the Tanoan language group (also including Tiwa, Towa, and Piro [Dozier 1970]).

4 The Ordinance was reaffirmed by a council resolution in 1944.

5 For instance, the literature in law and philosophy is as extant as the debates about the decision in relationship to sovereignty. Angela R. Riley (2007) has observed the way that the decision has been used adversely in generalizations about all tribes and their attitudes and treatment of tribal women and their children. These generalizations render tribes "illiberal"—that is, as not embodying or accountable to the liberal democratic principles guiding the United States—and so undeserving or at least rendering questionable their rights to self-government as a reflection of United States values for cultural pluralism. In other words, *Martinez* is read as putting individual civil rights and liberties at odds with pluralism's accommodation and even affirmation of tribal rights to self-government and cultural autonomy. The conundrum within these theoretical approaches is how to resolve the conflict. Riley argues against any further intrusions by the federal government into tribal decision-making powers owing to the already invasive history of colonization. But Eric Reitman (2006) insists that the jurisdictional powers of federal review of habeas corpus complaints provided by the ICRA ought to be extended to cover a broader range of the civil rights guaranteed to Indians living under tribal jurisdiction in order to ensure equality rights for tribal members. Meanwhile, Bethany R. Berger (2006) argues that the court's decision in *Martinez*

should not be framed at all by liberal theories but should look rather to republican and communitarian ideas, which reject the notion that individuals are separate from the community, "embracing instead the importance of the community in creating and providing the site for sovereign actualization of the individual" (824). Tribes then, she says, must be understood as communities "for whom the condition to function effectively is a fundamental good not only for tribes but their individual members" (825). In this regard, she finds the Supreme Court's decision in *Martinez* affirms tribal rights and independent peoplehood.

6   See Valencia-Weber (2004) for another review of the kinds of literature surrounding the Martinez case.

7   There is a perception within much of the literature that Santa Clara women were overwhelmingly marrying "whites" and that it was specifically these white men and their children who were being discriminated against. However, during the trial and in the literature cited here, there is more mention of the fact that Santa Clara women were marrying men enrolled with other tribes more than marrying white men. Since specific data on intermarriage rates are unavailable for the Santa Clara Pueblo, however, it is not possible to be more exact than to offer general observations—either about the total number of Santa Clara men and women marrying out or about the trends in whom they were choosing to marry.

8   For an excellent analysis of the work of discourses of tradition and custom in tribal court contexts, see Justin B. Richland's *Arguing with Tradition: The Language of Law in Hopi Tribal Court* (2008). Richland draws out the important ways that Hopi people bring their understandings of tradition, knowledge, and authority to bear on the legal procedures that guide the operation of their court proceedings, particularly in the context of intratribal disputes over property claims.

9   Many have observed that Ortiz was criticized and even ostracized by many Pueblo people for seeming to reveal to outsiders what they considered to be private or secret religious beliefs. Ortiz insisted that he had not revealed as much as he corrected published accounts. Further, Elsie Clews Parsons complained that Pueblo people often delighted in giving her misinformation in order to protect their religious beliefs from outside interrogation (see Johnson 1997).

10   Of course, the works of Harrington, Parsons, and Ellis are far too exhaustive to name here. See Harrington (1916), Parsons (1939), and Ellis (1951, 1967).

11   Throughout the treatied areas, this trend continued. In California, 27 percent of land grant claims were rejected; in New Mexico, some 76 percent were rejected (Klein 1996).

12   Generally, within tribal communities "progressives" were those who supported the goals of the policy efforts of the United States and "conservatives" were those who adhered to traditional leadership and perspectives (see Perdue 1981).

13   According to the U.S. Census of 2000, the tribe had a reported membership of 980.

14   Resnik observes that it was also in line with federal common law, which had historically tied children's rights to their fathers (1999).

15 Tim Vollman (2004) reflects on some of the interesting social exchanges during the trial between the witnesses and the judge, which left him feeling that the judge was personally sympathetic to the women but felt obligated to uphold the Ordinance as an embodiment of the tribe's rights to self-government.

16 Vollman (2004) remembers that both sides attempted to secure Alfonso Ortiz as a witness but he refused to testify.

17 While Myles identifies their division as the Winter People, Julia and Audrey identified it as the Summer People. This is no doubt an error of transcription rather than one of understanding.

18 Apparently also at the same time, Myles said that many women at the Pueblo had formed a committee to get the matter of the membership of their children addressed by the council. During Julia Martinez's testimony, these efforts become a little clearer, indicating that they were focusing first on meeting with tribal leadership and then in lobbying local officials and BIA agents.

19 All quotes are taken from trial testimony, Transcript of Proceedings, *Martinez & Martinez v. Romney, Santa Clara Pueblo, & Tafoya*, in the District Court for the District of New Mexico (1975). All errors in the original transcription are preserved.

20 If there were about forty women who had married out, and about eighty mixed marriages in all, it would mean a fairly even distribution of out marriages between men and women.

21 Though never explained during testimony, it sounds like Singer was putting the documentation together for the BIA application for CDIBs. Once the Martinez family had the necessary documentation in place from the committee establishing that their children possessed at least one-quarter Santa Clara blood, the children were issued CDIBs. Ironically, after the *Martinez* decision the issuance of the CDIBs would require tribal enrollment and not merely a blood quantum.

22 The U.S. Census of 2000 showed that close to eleven thousand people were reported to live on the reservation.

23 Valencia-Weber (2004) reports that the tribe still reported having a committee that is examining the issues.

24 According to Julia Martinez's grandson, Fred Myles Martinez, in an open forum discussion at the University of New Mexico, Albuquerque, in October 2010, Julia and Audrey Martinez secured permission from the Santa Clara governor and council to take the complaint to the New Mexico district court.

25 When the Martinez lawsuit was initially filed, the defense motioned to dismiss the case on the grounds that the District Court lacked jurisdiction to decide on "intratribal controversies affecting matters of tribal self-government and sovereignty." The District Court rejected the motion. It found that jurisdiction had been conferred by the ICRA and that the tribe, therefore, was not immune from lawsuit for violations of civil rights so guaranteed. The case proceeded to trial.

26 See, for instance, *Poodry et al. v. Tonawanda Band of Seneca Indians et al.* (1996), in which a writ for habeas corpus review was filed by members who had been banished from the tribe's reservation and disenrolled on grounds of treason.

27   One of the few written responses to the case by a Santa Clara Pueblo person is by
     Rina Swentzell (2004). Swentzell was married to a nonmember and had children
     with him. She had an M.A. in Architecture and a PH.D. in American Studies from
     UNM, where she taught in the area of culture and architecture at the School of
     Architecture and Planning. In her two-page statement, she writes, "I was 39 years
     old when the Supreme Court ruled on the *Santa Clara v. Martinez* case. Even then,
     I wanted the courts to rule in favor of the tribe—to rule for sovereignty" (97).
     She goes on to refer to the work of Ortiz in *Tewa World* (1969) and the inher-
     ent respect for the complementarity and reciprocity between men and women in
     Pueblo worldviews. But she concludes that the only way for the Supreme Court
     to respect this world was for it to affirm tribal sovereignty over women's rights.

28   According to Elmer R. Rusco (1990), there are very few tribes today with funda-
     mentally gendered provisions for membership or voting:

> Four tribal constitutions discriminate by gender in establishing membership
> in the tribe. The constitution of the Cachil Dehe Band of Wintun Indians pro-
> vides that: [i]f a female member marries a non-Indian, she will automatically
> lose her membership and will be required to leave the Community within
> ninety days after written notice has been served upon her by the Business
> Committee; Provided, That this provision shall not apply in the case of any
> marriages consummated prior to the approval of this Constitution and By-
> Laws. The governing document of the Hopi Tribe of Arizona provides that
> members shall be those on a tribal roll taken in 1937, those born of mothers and
> fathers who were on this roll, and "[a]ll children born after December 31, 1937,
> whose mother is a member of the Hopi Tribe, and whose father is a member
> of some other tribe." The constitution of the Kiahlagee Tribal Town provides
> that "[a]ll adult offspring of a marriage between a male member of the Kiah-
> lagee Tribal Town or Tribe may become members of the Town by applying for
> admission, when accepted and approved by a majority vote of the members
> present at any regular Kiahlagee Tribal Town membership meeting." One of
> the categories of possible membership in Laguna Pueblo, as stated in its con-
> stitution, is, "All persons of one-half or more Laguna Indian blood born after
> approval of this revised Constitution (1) whose mother is a member of the
> Pueblo of Laguna; or (2) whose father is a member of the Pueblo of Laguna,
> provided the child is born in wedlock." Two constitutions discriminate by gen-
> der in setting minimum ages for voting in tribal elections. The Crow Tribe's
> constitution states that "[a]ny duly enrolled member of the Crow Tribe, except
> as herein provided, shall be entitled to engage in the deliberations and voting
> of the council, provided the females are 18 years old and the males 21 years."
> A resolution of the Quapaw Tribe adopted in 1956, which functions as its con-
> stitution, states that it is the desire of the individual male members, 21 years
> of age and over, and female members, 18 years of age and over, to establish a
> responsible administrative body to represent, speak and act for the individual
> members of the Quapaw Tribe on matters affecting the properties and general

business of the Tribe. Presumably this language specifies the voting rules for the Tribe. (269)

5 In Disenrollment

1 Within federal law and treaties, tribes reserved the right to exclude nonmembers from reserved lands excepting federal agents carrying out the duties of their offices (Wilkins 2004, 236–37).

2 Within their tribal constitution, the San Pasqual Band of Mission Indians assigns the BIA with the responsibility of determining its membership. After a year of intertribal conflicts that had rendered the elected council ineffective in conducting government or business affairs, they decided to formally disenroll sixty of its members. But in December 2008, the BIA denied the tribe's proposal (Soto 2008).

3 David E. Wilkins (2004) describes the varied historical contexts in which tribal banishment and disenrollment practices occurred. He concludes that tribes reserved such practices for severe cases almost always involving a punishment for crimes such as murder, rape, and incest but always with the proviso that the individual could be reinstated if he or she met certain conditions (245). In other words, acts of banishment or disenrollment that were considered permanent were extremely rare.

4 It is an attack that carries over to unrecognized tribes in claims that they do not meet the demands of racial authenticity (Cramer 2006, 315).

5 The Native California population from the pre-invasion era has been estimated from 175,000 to 1.5 million (Forbes 1982).

6 In 1856, the state issued a bounty of $0.25 per scalp. In 1860, the state increased the bounty to $5.00 per scalp (see Forbes 1982; Trafzer and Hyer 1999).

7 The records of the ICC are available at the National Archives, Record Group 279, http://www.archives.gov.

8 See also E. Green 1923; United States Congress 1966; Heizer 1972, 1978, 1979, 1993; Beals 1974; Dyer 1975; Phillips 1981; Garner 1982; Costo and Costo 1987, 1995; Hurtado 1988; Pincetl 1999; Bouvier 2001; Field 2003; Laverty 2003; Secrest 2003; Riffe 2005.

9 For instance, San Diego and Imperial counties of California have more reservations than any other county in the United States but the twenty reservations are very small, with total landholdings of just over 124,000 acres (according to the California Native American Liaison Branch for District 11).

10 These conflicts have evolved into questions about whether tribes can operate gaming facilities off-reservation. Richard Pombo, a Republican from the Eleventh District of Northern California and Chair of the House Resources Committee, submitted a bill that would greatly limit off-reservation gaming by preventing tribes from moving across state lines and requiring tribes to secure state and local approval. Pombo has accepted thousands of dollars in campaign money from gaming tribes. While some tribes support the measure in efforts to curtail any

urban tribal casino development, many oppose and seek amendments to the IGRA that would better regulate BIA consultation with tribes on casino proposals, including the National Indian Gaming Association (Daly 2005).

11 In *Seminole Tribe of Florida v. Buttersworth* (1981), the Fifth Circuit Court of Appeals granted an injunction preventing the county sheriff from interfering with high-stakes bingo games conducted by the Seminole on Seminole lands. The county argued that the games awarded prizes that exceeded amounts allowed under state law and that Florida had jurisdiction over reservation lands under Public Law 280 (see Cattelino 2008).

12 The Cabazon Band of Mission Indians and the Morongo Band of Mission Indians, both located in Riverside County, California, operated bingo games on their reservations. The Cabazon also operated card games. Since the facilities were open to the public, both Riverside County and the state of California sought to apply their laws governing the operations of gaming. The Cabazon and Morongo filed for declaratory relief in federal District Court, holding that neither the county nor the state had any authority to enforce its gambling laws on reservations. The Court of Appeals affirmed (*California v. Cabazon Band of Mission Indians* 1987).

13 The IGRA defined three types of gaming: Class I includes all traditional social gaming, like the Seneca's peach pit game; Class II includes bingo, pull tabs, punch boards, tip jars, and card games; Class III includes everything else, like horse and dog racing, casino gambling, and slot machines.

14 The NIGC is composed of a chairperson and two commissioners, each of whom serves on a full-time basis for a three-year term. The chairperson is appointed by the president and must be confirmed by the Senate. The secretary of the interior appoints the two commissioners. Under the IGRA, at least two of the three must be enrolled members of a federally recognized Indian tribe, and no more than two members may be of the same political party. The NIGC maintains its headquarters in Washington, with five offices in Portland, Oregon; Sacramento, California; Phoenix, Arizona; St. Paul, Minnesota; and Tulsa, Oklahoma. At the time this book went to press, Tracie L. Stevens (Tulalip Tribes of Washington) serves as chairperson and Steffani A. Cochran (Chickasaw Nation of Oklahoma) and Daniel Little (a former manager of government affairs for the Mashantucket Pequot Tribal Nation) serve as commissioners. See http://www.nigc.gov.

15 National Indian Gaming Commission, Growth in Gaming Revenues, 2007.

16 For a glimpse at the seriousness of the outrage, see McLean and Elkind (2003) and Eichenwald (2005), both of which include an analysis of media coverage on public reactions to the energy crisis.

17 Schwarzenegger's antitribal gaming stance also garnered contributions from Las Vegas with the family-owned Palms Resort raising $1 million for his efforts (Thompson 2004).

18 In 1999 and 2000, Las Vegas casinos, labor unions, horse-racing tracks, card clubs, and the Walt Disney Company funded the anti-Prop 5 and 1A campaigns (Goldberg and Champagne 2002, 51).

19 In July 1999, the National Gambling Impact Study Commission reported that tribal gaming revenues had nearly doubled from 1995 to 1999, from $5.5 to $9.8 billion. Of the 561 tribes with recognition status, only 193 (34 percent) participated in gaming and only 27 (5 percent) generated more than $100 million annually. Those 27 tribes accounted for about two-thirds of all tribal gaming revenue: $6.4 billion of the $9.8 billion total (General Accounting Office 2001a, 9). In a review of the National Indian Gaming Commission Accountability Act of 2005 ordered by the U.S. Senate Committee on Indian Affairs, the Congressional Budget Office issued a cost assessment that claimed that over the 2000–2004 period, tribal revenue from gaming increased an average of 14 percent per year to about $19 billion in 2004. According to the latest Casino City Indian Gaming Industry Report, annual tribal gaming revenue had reached $26.4 billion in 2009, with another $3.2 billion earned from non-gaming revenue at gaming facilities.

20 See Barlett and Steele 2002a and 2002b. See also the press releases on the "backlash" against tribes from the Pechanga Band of Luiseño Indians, the California Indian Nations Gaming Association, the National Indian Gaming Association, the National Congress of American Indians, and the Center for the Integration and Improvement of Journalism (some of which are archived by the Native American Studies Department at the University of California, Riverside).

21 Stand Up for Californians had a web site (standup.quiknet.com/about.html) that is no longer active. All quotes were taken from there on November 25, 2002.

22 For an exceptional analysis of the politics of gaming and anti-Indian movements in another state context, see Jessica R. Cattelino's *High Stakes: Florida Seminole Gaming and Sovereignty* (2008). Cattelino analyzes the co-production of tribal sovereignty, economics, and culture in the context of Florida Seminole gaming and its facilitation of cultural revitalization efforts.

23 As Carole Goldberg and Duane Champagne (2002) discuss, Robert B. Porter argues that tribes cannot sustain their unique sovereign, government status while seeking power in state politics. In other words, Porter believes that tribal sovereignty and state citizenship are incompatible. Gaming, then, becomes a means to dissolving the integrity of tribal sovereignty. Goldberg and Champagne disagree and argue that in California, the relationship has been much more complex and multidirectional (57).

24 The CSAC (n.d.) fact sheet, from which this list was quoted, contains the following note: "Data compiled from the 2002 Field Directory of the California Indian Community, Department of Housing and Community Development. 96 Tribes noted population out of 108 listed in the Report. Those Tribes that left this item blank or noted 0 in population were not included in the total number of Tribes."

25 The U.S. Census of 2004 reported the American Indian/Alaskan Nation population at 4.1 million, or 1.5 percent of the total population. The BIA estimated tribal enrollment to be about 1,978,099 in 2005. In California, the census total for American Indian/Alaskan Native population was 687,400. Less than 10 percent of that population belong to California tribes.

26 For instance, in December 2008, the Robinson Rancheria of Pomo Indians Council initiated the disenrollment of anywhere from 50 to 74 of its total 347 enrolled
members (Larson 2008).

27 Mark Macarro, the chairperson of the tribe, in addition to having a significant
role in the Prop 5 and 1A campaigns, has chaired the California Nations Indian
Gaming Association (CNIGA), a nonprofit organization of forty federally recognized tribes that "is dedicated to the purpose of protecting Indian gaming on
federally-recognized Indian lands. It acts as a planning and coordinating agency
for legislative, policy, legal and communications efforts on behalf of its members
and serves as an industry forum for information and resources" (CNIGA 2008).

28 For news coverage of the disenrollments, see Nguyen 2004; Buchanan 2004a,
2004b, 2004c, 2004d; DeArmond 2004a, 2004b, 2005; DeArmond and O'Leary
2004a, 2004b; O'Leary 2004a, 2004b, 2004c, 2004d, 2006; Sahagun 2004a, 2004b;
De Atley 2005; Newman 2005a, 2005b; Cooper 2007.

29 The eleven included Michael Salinas, Juanita Sanchez, Andrew Candelaria, Bobbi
Candelaria, John A. Gomez Jr., William Salinas, John A. Gomez Sr., Marie Batolo-
mei, Louis Alfred Herrera Jr., Nellie Lara, and Theresa Spears.

30 See statements on sovereignty and tribal gaming by the Citizens for Equal Rights
Alliance at www.citizensalliance.org. See also Benedict 2001; Barlett and Steele
2002a, 2002b; Riffe 2005; Barker 2005/2006.

31 *Online Etymology Dictionary*, http://www.etymonline.com.

6 Of Marriage and Sexuality

1 The DOMA was sponsored by Bob Barr (R-Ga.), Steve Largent (R-Okla.), Jim
Sensenbrenner (R-Wisc.), Sue Myrick (R-N.C.), Ed Bryant (R-Tenn.), Bill Emer-
son (R-Mo.), Harold Volkmer (D-Mo.), and Ike Skelton (D-Mo.).

2 The U.S. Constitution's supremacy clause would mean that the DOMA's definition
of marriage and spouse would ultimately trump any state, territorial, or tribal definitions except that the DOMA also provides states, territories, and tribes with the
jurisdiction to decide whether to recognize marriage rights established elsewhere.

3 The legal activism seemed to explode in 2004. On March 3, Multnomah County,
Oregon, became the second county in the country where same-sex marriages were
legally performed, igniting a still unresolved legal order on April 20 by Frank Bear-
den, an Oregon circuit court judge, that the state must "accept and register" marriages of same-sex couples to ensure identical rights for same-sex couples under
the state constitution (Editorial, *New York Times* 2004; Siegal 2004; Kershaw
2005). On March 5, the Wisconsin State Assembly and the Kansas House approved state constitution amendments to ban same-sex marriage or civil unions
(Foust 2004; Hibbitts 2004). On March 11, California's Supreme Court ordered
San Francisco to stop performing same-sex marriages. Officials complied but the
city attorney sued on the grounds that prohibiting same-sex marriages was unconstitutional on a state level. On March 16, commissioners from Rhea County,

Tennessee, asked the state to allow county officials to ban same-sex marriages and civil unions by being able to charge them with "crimes against nature" but the request was withdrawn after public protest. On May 17, Massachusetts became the first state to legalize same-sex marriages (Gardner 2004). On August 13, California's Supreme Court ruled by a 5–2 vote to nullify 4,037 marriage licenses issued to same-sex partners. The court reasoned that Gavin Newsom, the mayor of San Francisco, had overstepped his authority and violated the state constitution's prohibition against same-sex marriage (see National Conference of State Legislatures 2007).

4 California's Proposition 22 of 2000 was struck down by California's Supreme Court in May 2008, effectively granting same-sex couples the right to marry. This right was overturned by Proposition 8 in November 2008 and was upheld by the California Supreme Court. An appeal is still pending at the time this book was written.

5 Numerous books on the dangers of same-sex marriage and homosexuality were published within the historical moment of 2004, a review of which is beyond the scope of this chapter. Most focus on the legal activism of LGBT people for marriage equality and the dire consequences this will have for the nation. See, for instance, Kennedy and Newcombe 2004, Sears and Osten 2003, Stanton and Maier 2004, and Staver 2004.

6 Since the states within the United States govern marriage, each has its own statute. At the time of this writing, same-sex marriages are performed in Massachusetts (2004), Connecticut (2008), Iowa (2009), Vermont (2009), and New Hampshire (2010), as well as the District of Columbia (2010). Same-sex unions without marriage are legally recognized in Hawaii (1997), California (1999), Maine (2004), New Jersey (2007), Washington (2007), Maryland (2008), Oregon (2008), Colorado (2009), Nevada (2009), and Wisconsin (2009). In New Mexico, New York, and Rhode Island, there are no bans in place on same-sex marriage, but there is no legal recognition of same-sex unions.

7 September 11 was also mobilized within Native discourses to represent Native patriotism. For instance, as Jennifer Denetdale (a Navajo) writes, "After September 11, Diné and American nationalism merged in ways that have conflated American and Navajo values so that Navajos' historical experiences of injustice and oppression under American nationalism are erased" (2008, 289).

8 The Patriot Act was amended on March 2, 2006, in response to the criticisms that it directly subverts human and civil rights but to no real avail in its implementation.

9 James Treat's edited volume *Native and Christian: Indigenous Voices on Religious Identities in the U.S. and Canada* (1996) provides articles and stories of Native peoples attempting to reconcile their Native and Christian identities; Andrea Smith's *Native Americans and the Christian Right: The Gendered Politics of Unlikely Alliances* (2008) insists on the need for alliances between Natives and the Chris-

tian Right for effecting progressive social change. Both Treat and Smith anticipate readers who are unsympathetic to the idea of Native Christians.

10 "Once granted access, McKinley said she was so afraid of being kicked out again that she didn't leave Reynolds' hospital bedside for seven days. During that time, her brother died in a motorcycle accident" (Associated Press 2004d).

11 Cornsilk, McKinley, and Joe Shirley Jr., the Navajo Nation president, provided an interview about the issues on the Democracy Now web site in May 2005 (Democracy Now 2005).

12 The NCLR press release solicited a statement from Richard LaFortune, the campaign director for 2SPR (2 Spirit Press Room), a Native queer media project based in Minneapolis, Minnesota: "This decision speaks to the primacy of native sovereignty and traditions that demonstrate acceptance and dignity of all human beings and our spiritual traditions" (NCLR 2005).

Coverage of the JAT's decision extended into multiple kinds of news forums: Native (Indianz.com); legal (The Legal Reader), political (Reason Online: Hit and Run: Free Minds and Free Markets); LGBT rights (PlanetOut, MySoCalledGayLife, Advocate.com), religious (Ontario Consultants on Religious Tolerance, ReligiousTolerance.org), and conservative (AFA, Marriage Digest).

13 In a legal brief filed with the JAT, Brian Gilley (PH.D., Anthropology, University of Vermont), who is of Cherokee descent, concurred by reclaiming Cherokee "traditions." "There is overwhelming evidence for the historic and cultural presence of multiple gender roles and same-sex marriage relations among most if not all of Native North Americans, including the Cherokee, and that they historically shared in the institution of marriage" (quoted in Hales 2006).

14 The Log Cabin Republicans are gays and lesbians who seek to work within the Republican Party for sexual equality: "Log Cabin's mission derives from our firm belief in the Principals of limited government, individual liberty, individual responsibility, free markets and a strong national defense. We emphasize that these Principals and the moral values on which they stand are consistent with the pursuit of equal treatment under the law for gay and lesbian Americans" (Log Cabin Republicans 2006).

15 Many LGBT people who identify as progressives have been critical of the LGBT movement for marriage equality because of its affirmation of political and social conservatism (see Leong and Sueyoshi 2006).

16 As discussed in the introduction, civil rights are often pitted against the concerns and interests of tribal sovereignty (see also Barker 2006, 2008).

7 Origins

1 *Webster's New World Dictionary, Third College Edition.*

2 *Online Etymology Dictionary*, http://www.etymonline.com.

3 "Western science" is of course an impossible term. Here, I am thinking of the work

of Bruno Latour (1987) and Donna Haraway (1989). Both provide a sociology of scientific knowledge as a practice deeply entrenched within the ideologies and subjectivities of colonialism, racism, and sexism. Both disrupt notions of scientific "objectivity" and "reason" as defined within post-Enlightenment philosophies that abstracted them from the contexts of historical and social formations.

Adams, Jim. 2000. "Anti-Indian Groups Fail at Ballot
    Box." *Indian Country Today*, April 1. http://www
    .indiancountry.com.
———. 2001. "Gover Says 'Bring It On' to Yet Another
    BIA Probe." *Indian Country Today*, August 1. http://
    www.indiancountry.com.
———. 2002a. "Anti-Pequot Politicians Will Appeal
    Recognition." *Indian Country Today*, September 13.
    http://www.indiancountry.com.
———. 2002b. "Senate Crushes Dodd's Call for Tribal
    Recognition Freeze." *Indian Country Today*, Septem-
    ber 30. http://www.indiancountry.com.
Adamson, Rebecca. 2008. "First Nations Survival and the
    Future of the Earth." *Original Instructions: Indigenous
    Teachings for a Sustainable Future*, ed. Melissa Nelson,
    27–35. Rochester, N.Y.: Bear and Company.
Adcock, Clifton. 2009. "Delaware Tribe on the Brink of
    Federal Recognition." *Tulsa World*, June 9. http://www
    .tulsaworld.com.
Albers, Patricia, and Beatrice Medicine, eds. 1983. *The
    Hidden Half: Studies of Plains Indian Women*. Lanham,
    Md.: University Press of America.

Alfred, Taiaiake. 1999. *Peace, Power, Righteousness: An Indigenous Manifesto*. Toronto: Oxford University Press.

———. 2005. "Sovereignty." *Sovereignty Matters: Locations of Contestation and Possibility in Indigenous Struggles for Self-Determination*, ed. Joanne Barker, 33–50. Contemporary Indigenous Issues Series 6. Lincoln: University of Nebraska Press.

Allen, Paula Gunn. 1986. *The Sacred Hoop: Recovering the Feminine in American Indian Traditions*. Boston: Beacon Press.

Almaguer, Tomás. 1994. *Racial Fault Lines: The Historical Origins of White Supremacy in California*. Berkeley: University of California Press.

Althusser, Louis. 1971. *Lenin and Philosophy and Other Essays*. New York: Monthly Review Press.

———. 1990. *Philosophy and the Spontaneous Philosophy of the Scientists and Other Essays*. New York: Verso.

Amnesty International. 2004. "Stolen Sisters: Discrimination and Violence against Indigenous Women in Canada: A Summary of Amnesty International's Concerns." http://www.amnestyusa.org.

———. 2007. "Maze of Injustice: The Failure to Protect Indigenous Women from Sexual Violence in the United States." http://www.amnestyusa.org.

Anaya, S. James. 1996. *Indigenous Peoples in International Law*. New York: Oxford University Press.

Anderson, Benedict. 1991. *Imagined Communities: Reflection on the Origin and Spread of Nationalism*. Revised and expanded edn. New York: Verso.

Arendt, Hannah. 1948. *The Origins of Totalitarianism*. (2004; repr., New York: Schocken).

Associated Press. 2004a. "Ex-Wilson Aide to Negotiate Tribal Gambling Compacts." *Reno Gazette-Journal*, January 7. http://www.rgj.com.

———. 2004b. "Dispute over Gambling Money in SoCal Tribe Outside Federal Jurisdiction." *Reno Gazette-Journal*, February 3. http://www.rgj.com.

———. 2004c. "Gay Couples Marry in New Mexico." *CNN News*, February 20. http://www.cnn.com.

———. 2004d. "Married Cherokee Lesbian Couple Battle for Recognition." *Advocate.com*, May 19. http://www.advocate.com.

———. 2005a. "Native Nations Divided on Gay Marriage." 365gay.com, June 4. http://www.365gay.com.

———. 2005b. "Cherokee Nation Court Dismisses Lawsuit against Same-Sex Marriage." The News on 6, August 3. http://www.kotv.com.

———. 2006. "Cherokee Court Mulls Same-Sex Marriage Case." *Joplin Globe*, January 9. http://www.joplinglobe.com.

Atheism.com. n.d. "Gay Rights and Gay Marriage: Chronology of Events." *Atheism.com*, n.d. http://www.atheism.com.

Barker, Joanne. 1995. "Indian Made: Sovereignty, Federal Allotment Policy, and the

Work of Identification." Qualifying essay, History of Consciousness Department, University of California, Santa Cruz.

———. 2000. "'Indian-Made': Sovereignty and the Work of Identification." PH.D. diss., University of California, Santa Cruz.

———. 2002. "Looking for Warrior Woman (Beyond Pocahontas)." *this bridge we call home: radical visions for transformation*, ed. AnaLouise Keating and Gloria Anzaldúa, 314–25. New York: Routledge.

———. 2003. "Indian™ U.S.A." *Wicazō Śa Review* 18, no. 1: 25–79.

———. 2004. "The Human Genome Diversity Project: 'Peoples,' 'Populations,' and the Cultural Politics of Identification." *Cultural Studies* 18, no. 4: 578–613.

———. 2005a. "For Whom Sovereignty Matters." *Sovereignty Matters: Locations of Contestation and Possibility in Indigenous Struggles for Self-Determination*, ed. Joanne Barker, 1–32. Contemporary Indigenous Issues Series 6. Lincoln: University of Nebraska Press.

———, ed. 2005b. *Sovereignty Matters: Locations of Contestation and Possibility in Indigenous Struggles for Self-Determination*. Lincoln: University of Nebraska Press.

———. 2005/2006. "Recognition." Special joint issue of *Indigenous Nations Journal* and *American Studies* 46, nos. 3/4: 117–45.

———. 2006. "Gender, Sovereignty, and the Discourse of Rights in Native Women's Activism." *Meridians: Feminism, Race, Transnationalism* 7, no. 1: 127–61.

———. 2008. "Gender, Sovereignty, and the Discourse of Rights in Native Women's Activism." *American Quarterly* 60, no. 2: 259–66.

Barker, Joanne, and Clayton Dumont. 2006. "Contested Conversations: Presentations, Expectations, and Responsibility at the National Museum of the American Indian." *American Indian Culture and Research Journal* 30, no. 2: 111–39.

Barker, Joanne, and Teresia Teaiwa. 1994. "Native InFormation." *Inscriptions*, ed. María Ochoa and Teresia Teaiwa, 16–41. Santa Cruz: Center for Cultural Studies, University of California.

Barlett, Donald L., and James B. Steele. 2002a. "Special Report on Indian Casinos: Wheel of Misfortune: Casinos Were Supposed to Make Indian Tribes Self-Sufficient. So Why Are the White Backers of Indian Gambling Raking in Millions While Many Tribes Continue to Struggle in Poverty?" *Time Magazine*, December 16.

———. 2002b. "Playing the Political Slots: How Indian Casino Interests Have Learned the Art of Buying Influence in Washington." *Time Magazine*, December 23.

Bartfield, Chet. 2004a. "Rincon Beset by Suits, Infighting; In Latest Setback, Challenge to New Compacts Hits Snag." *Union Tribune*, July 8. http://www.signonsandiego.com.

———. 2004b. "Governor Delights Diners in Old Town: Schwarzenegger Pushes Gaming Initiatives Defeat." *Union Tribune*, October 15. http://www.signonsandiego.com.

Beals, Ralph Leon. 1974. *Indian Land Use and Occupancy in California*. New York: Garland.

Beinart, Peter. 2002. "Lost Tribes: Native Americans and Government Anthropologists Feud over Indian Identity." *American Indians and U.S. Politics: A Companion Reader*, ed. John M. Meyer, 143–54. Westport, Conn.: Praeger.

Benedict, Jeff. 2001. *Without Reservation: How a Controversial Indian Tribe Rose to Power and Built the World's Largest Casino*. New York: Harper Perennial.

Berger, Bethany Ruth. 1997. "After Pocahontas: Indian Women and the Law, 1830–1934." *American Indian Law Review* 21, no. 1: 1–62.

———. 2004. "Indian Policy and the Imagined Indian Women." *Kansas Journal of Law and Public Policy* 14, no. 1: 103–14.

———. 2006. "Indian Law at a Crossroads: Liberalism and Republicanism in Federal Indian Law." *Connecticut Law Review* 38:813–31.

Berkhofer, Robert F., Jr. 1979. *The White Man's Indian: Images of the American Indian from Columbus to the Present*. New York: Vintage.

Berthelsen, Christian. 2003. "Bustamante Told Not to Use Loophole: Judge Bars Transfer of Campaign Finance Funds." *San Francisco Chronicle*, September 23. http://www.sfgate.com.

Bhabha, Homi K. 1990. "Introduction: Narrating the Nation." *Nation and Narration*, ed. Homi K. Bhabha, 1–8. New York: Routledge.

Bieder, Robert E. 1986. *Science Encounters the Indian, 1820–1880: The Early Years of American Ethnology*. Norman: University of Oklahoma Press.

Biolsi, Thomas. 2001. *"Deadliest Enemies": Law and the Making of Race Relations on and off the Rosebud Reservation*. Berkeley: University of California Press.

Blackfeet Reservation Development Fund. 2006. Indian Trust: *Cobell v. Salazar*. http://www.indiantrust.com. Washington: Native American Rights Fund.

Bledsoe, Samuel Thomas. 1909. *Indian Land Laws: Being a Treatise on the Law of Acquiring Title to, and the Alienation of, Allotted Indian Lands. Also a Compilation of Treaties, Agreements and Statutes Applicable Thereto*. Kansas City, Mo.: Pipes-Reed Company (1979; repr., as *Indian Land Laws*, New York: Arno).

Blinkhorn, Martin. 1980. "Spain: The 'Spanish Problem' and the Imperial Myth." *Journal of Contemporary History* 15, no. 1: 5–25.

Bouvier, Virginia Marie. 2001. *Women and the Conquest of California, 1542–1840: Codes of Silence*. Tucson: University of Arizona Press.

Brah, Avtar. 1996. *Cartographies of Diaspora: Contesting Identities*. New York: Routledge.

Brayer, Herbert O. 1939. *Pueblo Indian Land Grants of the Rio Abajo, New Mexico*. University of New Mexico Bulletin 334, no. 1. Albuquerque: University of New Mexico Press.

Briggs, Susan E., Charles L. Briggs, and John R. Van Ness, eds. 1987. *Land, Water and Culture, Perspectives on Hispanic Land Grants*. Albuquerque: University of New Mexico Press.

Broder, John M. 2004a. "More Slot Machines for Tribes; $1 Billion for California."
    New York Times, June 22.

————. 2004b. "As Schwarzenegger Tries to Slow It, Gaming Grows." *New York
    Times*, October 10.

Brown, James W. and Rita T. Kohn, eds. 2008. *Long Journey Home: Oral Histories of
    Contemporary Delaware Indians*. Bloomington: Indiana University Press.

Brown, Rusty Creed. 2006. "Recognition, but at What Cost?" *Indianz.com*, Octo-
    ber 11. http://www.indianz.com.

Bruyneel, Kevin. 2007. *The Third Space of Sovereignty: The Postcolonial Politics of U.S.-
    Indigenous Relations*. Minneapolis: University of Minnesota Press.

Buchanan, Michael. 2004a. "Judge Kicks Dispute Back to Tribe." *North County
    Times*, February 17. http://www.nctimes.com.

————. 2004b. "Pechanga Committee Ejects Members." *North County Times*,
    March 20. http://www.nctimes.com.

————. 2004c. "Pechanga Members Challenge Tribe's Right to Oust Them." *North
    County Times*, April 19. http://www.nctimes.com.

————. 2004d. "Tribal Law Rules in Pechanga Enrollment Dispute, Attorneys
    Claim." *North County Times*, May 17. http://www.nctimes.com.

Bumiller, Elisabeth, and Sheryl Gay Stolberg. 2004. "The 2003 Campaign." *New York
    Times*, August 7.

Burton, Jeffrey. 1995. *Indian Territory and the United States, 1866–1906*. Norman: Uni-
    versity of Oklahoma Press.

Bush, George W. 2004. "President Calls for Constitutional Amendment Protecting
    Marriage," transcript, 24 February. http://georgewbush-whitehouse.archives.gov/.

California Nations Indian Gaming Association. n.d. "Overview." http://www.cniga
    .com.

California State Association of Counties (CSAC). n.d. "CSAC Fact Sheet on Indian
    Gaming in California (As of 11/5/2003)." http://www.csac.counties.org.

Carlson, Leonard A. 1980. *Indians, Bureaucrats and the Land: The Dawes Act and the
    Decline of Indian Farming*. Santa Barbara, Calif.: Greenwood.

Carrillo, Jo, ed. 1998. *Readings in American Indian Law: Recalling the Rhythm of Sur-
    vival*. Philadelphia: Temple University Press.

————. 2002. "Getting to Survivance: An Essay about the Role of Mythologies in
    Law." *The Political and Legal Anthropology Review* 25, no. 1: 37–47.

Carroll, Ahnawake. 2002/2003. "Cherokee Nation Tribal Profile." *Tribal Law Journal*
    3, no. 1. http://tlj.unm.edu/.

Cattelino, Jessica R. 2008. *High Stakes: Florida Seminole Gaming and Sovereignty*.
    Durham: Duke University Press.

Champagne, Duane. 2005. "From Sovereignty to Minority: As American as Apple
    Pie." *Wicazŏ Śa Review* 20, no. 2: 21–36.

Chauncey, George. 2005. *Why Marriage? The History Shaping Today's Debate over Gay
    Marriage*. Cambridge: Basic Books.

Chávez, Lydia. 1998. *The Color Bind: California's Battle to End Affirmative Action.* Berkeley: University of California Press.

Cherokee Nation of Oklahoma. 2002. "Cherokee Nation to Appeal Federal Court Ruling," news release, December 27, http://www.cherokee.org.

———. 2006. "Special Election Results," news release, March 3, http://www.cherokee.org.

Christofferson, Carla. 1991. "Tribal Courts' Failure to Protect Native American Women: A Reevaluation of the Indian Civil Rights Act." *Yale Law Journal* 101, no. 1: 169–85.

Clifford, James. 1988. "Identity in Mashpee." *The Predicament of Culture: Twentieth-Century Ethnography, Literature, and Art,* 277–346. Cambridge: Harvard University Press.

Clinton, William J. 2000. Executive Order 13175, "Consultation and Coordination with Indian Tribal Governments." *Federal Register* 65, no. 218 (9 November): 67249–52.

Coffey, Wallace, and Rebecca Tsosie. 2001. "Rethinking the Tribal Sovereignty Doctrine: Cultural Sovereignty and the Collective Future of Indian Nations." *Stanford Law and Policy Review* 12 (Spring): 191.

Cohen, Andrew. 2004. "Married in Massachusetts." CBS *News: Court Watch*, February 4. http://www.cbsnews.com.

Cohen, Felix S. 1940. *Handbook of Federal Indian Law.* Buffalo, N.Y.: William S. Hein.

Coile, Zachary, and Paul Feist. 2003. "Tribe Plans $2 Million Campaign Donation; Bustamante Called a Good Friend." *San Francisco Chronicle*, September 3. http://www.sfgate.com.

Collier, John. 1934. *Memorandum, Hearings on H.R. 7902 before the House Committee on Indian Affairs.* 73rd Congress, Second Session. U.S. Department of the Interior, Washington, D.C.

Collins, Robert Keith. 2006. "Katimih o Sa Chata Kiyou? (Why Am I Not Choctaw?): Race in the Lived Experiences of Two Black Choctaw Mixed Bloods." *Crossing Waters, Crossing Worlds*, ed. Sharon P. Holland and Tiya Miles, 260–72. Durham: Duke University Press.

Cook, Curtis, and Juan D. Lindau, eds. 2000. *Aboriginal Rights and Self-Government: The Canadian and Mexican Experience in North American Perspective.* Montreal: McGill-Queen's University Press.

Cook-Lynn, Elizabeth. 1996. *Why I Can't Read Wallace Stegner and Other Essays: A Tribal Voice.* Madison: University of Wisconsin Press.

Cooper, Marc. 2007. "Tribal Flush: Pechanga People 'Disenrolled' En Masse." *LA Weekly*, January 7. http://www.laweekly.com.

Cornell, Stephen. 2008. "The Political Economy of American Indian Gaming." *Annual Review of Law and Social Science* 4 (December): 63–82.

Costo, Rupert, and Jeannette Henry Costo, eds. 1987. *The Missions of California: A Legacy of Genocide.* San Francisco: Indian Historian Press.

———. 1995. *Natives of the Golden State: The California Indians*. San Francisco: Indian Historian Press.

Cramer, Renée Ann. 2005. *Cash, Color, and Colonialism: The Politics of Tribal Acknowledgment*. Norman: University of Oklahoma Press.

———. 2006. "The Common Sense of Anti-Indian Racism: Reactions to Mashantucket Pequot Success in Gaming and Acknowledgment." *Law and Social Inquiry* 31, no. 2: 313–41.

Crenshaw, Kimberlé Williams. 1995. "Mapping the Margins: Intersectionality, Identity Politics, and Violence against Women of Color." *Critical Race Theory: The Key Writings That Have Formed the Movement*, ed. Kimberlé Williams Crenshaw, Neil Gotanda, Gary Peller, and Kendall Thomas, 357–83. New York: New Press.

Crenshaw, Kimberlé Williams, Neil Gotanda, Gary Peller, and Kendall Thomas, eds. 1995. *Critical Race Theory: The Key Writings That Have Formed the Movement*. New York: New Press.

Curtis, Edward S. 1976. *Edward Sheriff Curtis: Visions of a Vanishing Race*. Text by Florence Curtis Graybill and Victor Boesen; photographs prepared by Jean-Anthony du Lac. New York: Crowell.

———. 1977. *The North American Indian. Selections. The Vanishing Race: Selections from Edward S. Curtis's "The North American Indian."* Edited by M. Gidley. New York: Taplinger.

Daly, Matthew. 2005. "Off-Reservation Gambling Bill Splits Tribes." *San Francisco Chronicle*, November 9. http://www.sfgate.com.

Darian-Smith, Eve. 2004. *New Capitalists: Law, Politics, and Identity Surrounding Casino Gaming on Native American Land*. Belmont, Calif.: Thomson/Wadsworth.

Daughters of the Republic of Texas Library. n.d. "Our Association." Daughters of the Republic Library. http://www.drtl.org/drtinc, accessed July 2006.

Davis, Angela Y. 1983. *Women, Race, and Class*. New York: Vintage.

———. 2003. *Are Prisons Obsolete?* St. Paul, Minn.: Seven Stories.

———. 2005. *Abolition Democracy: Beyond Empire, Prisons, and Torture*. St. Paul, Minn.: Seven Stories.

De Atley, Richard K. 2005. "Tribal Ouster Case Gets Hearing. At Issue in the Lawsuit is Court Jurisdiction vs. the Band's Sovereignty, Says a Judge." *Riverside Press Enterprise*, July 6. http://www.pe.com.

DeArmond, Michelle. 2004a. "Ex-Wilson Aide to Head Tribal Talks." *Riverside Press Enterprise*, January 8. http://www.pe.com.

———. 2004b. "Members of Tribe Face Disenrollment." *Riverside Press Enterprise*, February 3. http://www.pe.com.

———. 2005. "Former Pechanga Members Sue Again." *Riverside Press Enterprise*, March 26. http://www.pe.com.

DeArmond, Michelle, and Tim O'Leary. 2004a. "Pechanga Members Facing Ejection Take Dispute to Courts." *Riverside Press Enterprise*, February 1. http://www.pe.com.

―――. 2004b. "Judge Avoids Tribal Dispute: He Refuses to Stop an Attempt by Pechanga Leaders to Oust a 130-Member Family." *Riverside Press Enterprise*, February 18. http://www.pe.com.

Debo, Angie. 1940. *And Still the Waters Run: The Betrayal of the Five Civilized Tribes.* Princeton: Princeton University Press.

Deer, Ada. 1996. Final Decision to Retract 1979 Decision of the Deputy Commissioner of Indian Affairs Regarding the Delaware Tribe of Indians. *Federal Register*, September 23.

Deer, Sarah. 2004. "Federal Indian Law and Violent Crime: Native Women and Children at the Mercy of the State." *Social Justice* 31, no. 4: 17–31.

Deloria, Philip J. 1998. *Playing Indian.* New Haven: Yale University Press.

―――. 2004. *Indians in Unexpected Places.* Lawrence: University of Kansas Press.

Deloria, Vine, Jr. 1969. *Custer Died for Your Sins: An Indian Manifesto.* Norman: University of Oklahoma Press.

―――. 1973. *God Is Red: A Native View of Religion.* New York: Dell.

―――. 1974. *Behind the Trail of Broken Treaties: An Indian Declaration of Independence.* Austin: University of Texas Press.

―――. 1979. "Self-Determination and the Concept of Sovereignty." *Economic Development in American Indian Reservations*, ed. Roxanne Dunbar Ortiz, 118–24. Albuquerque: University of New Mexico Press.

―――. 1995. *Red Earth/White Lies: Native Americans and the Myth of Scientific Fact.* New York: Scribner.

―――. 1999. *Spirit and Reason: The Vine Deloria, Jr., Reader.* Edited by Barbara Deloria, Kristen Foehner, and Sam Scinta. Golden, Colo.: Fulcrum.

Deloria, Vine, Jr., and Clifford Lytle. 1984. *The Nations Within: The Past and Future of American Indian Sovereignty.* New York: Pantheon.

Democracy Now. 2005. "Gay Marriage in America," May 31, accessed December 2008, http://www.democracynow.org.

Dempsey, Pamela. 2005a. "Diné Council Could Ban Gay Marriage." *Gallup Independent*, April 16. http://www.gallupindependent.com.

―――. 2005b. "Navajo Nation Officially Bans Same-Sex Marriage." *Gallup Independent*, April 23. http://www.gallupindependent.com.

―――. 2005c. "Navajo President Vetoes Bill Banning Same-Sex Unions." *Gallup Independent*, May 2. http://www.gallupindependent.com.

―――. 2005d. "Marriage Act Opponents Speak Out: Claim Navajo Nation Government Is Trying to Legalize Discrimination." *Gallup Independent*, June 2. http://www.gallupindependent.com.

Den Ouden, Amy E. 2005. *Beyond Conquest: Native Peoples and the Struggle for History in New England.* Lincoln: University of Nebraska Press.

Denetdale, Jennifer Nez. 2006. "Chairmen, Presidents, and Princesses: The Navajo Nation, Gender, and the Politics of Tradition." *Wicazō Ša Review* 21, no. 1: 9–28.

————. 2007. *Reclaiming Diné History: The Legacies of Navajo Chief Manuelito and Juanita*. Tucson: University of Arizona Press.

————. 2008. "Carving Navajo National Boundaries: Patriotism, Tradition, and the Diné Marriage Act of 2005." *American Quarterly* 60, no. 2: 289–94.

Diamond, Sara. 1995. *Roads to Dominion: Right-Wing Movements and Political Power in the United States*. New York: Guilford.

————. 1998. *Not by Politics Alone: The Enduring Influence of the Christian Right*. New York: Guilford.

Diaz, Vicente M., and J. Kēhaulani Kauanui, eds. 2001. "Native Pacific Cultural Studies on the Edge." Special issue, *The Contemporary Pacific* 13, no. 2.

Dick, Kirby, director. 2009. *Outrage*. Home Box Office Documentaries.

Diné Coalition for Cultural Preservation. 2005. "Official Response to the Council's Override," accessed December 2007, http://www.nativeout.com.

Dippie, Brain W. 1982. *The Vanishing American: White Attitudes and United States Indian Policy*. Middletown, Conn.: Wesleyan University Press.

Dobson, James. 2004. *Marriage under Fire: Arguments against Same-Sex Marriage*. http://www.focusonthefamily.com.

Dobson, James, and Shirley Dobson. 2007. *Marriage under Fire: Why We Must Win This Battle*. Carol Stream, Ill.: Tyndale House.

Dombrowski, Kirk. 2001. *Against Culture: Development, Politics, and Religion in Indian Alaska*. Lincoln: University of Nebraska Press.

Dozier, Edward P. 1970. *The Pueblo Indians of North America*. Austin, Texas: Holt, Rinehart and Winston.

Drinnon, Richard. 1980. *Facing West: The Metaphysics of Indian Hating and Empire Building*. New York: New American Library.

Duggan, Lisa. 2004. *The Twilight of Equality? Neoliberalism, Cultural Politics, and the Attack on Democracy*. Boston: Beacon Press.

Dumont, Clayton. 2003. "The Politics of Scientific Objections to Repatriation." *Wicazō Śa Review* 18, no. 1: 109–28.

————. 2008. *The Promise of Poststructuralist Sociology: Marginalized Peoples and the Problem of Knowledge*. Albany: State University of New York Press.

Dyer, Ruth Caroline. 1975. *The Indians' Land Title in California: A Case in Federal Equity, 1851–1942*. San Francisco: R and E Research.

Editorial, Aljazeera.net. 2004. "Schwarzenegger: Stop Gay Marriages!" Aljazeera.net, February 20. http://www.aljazeera.net.

Editorial, cnn.com. 2003. "Bush Wants Marriage Reserved for Heterosexual Couples." CNN News, October 28. http://www.cnn.com.

Editorial, *Delaware Indian News*. 2002. "Court Rules in Favor of Delaware Recognition." *Delaware Indian News*, October 1.

Editorial, *Indian Country Today*. 2001. "Beware Blumenthal and BIA Recognition Reformers." *Indian Country Today*, April 18. http://www.indiancountry.com.

————. 2002. "Norton Speaks: Interior Secretary on Tribal Recognition, Gaming

Regulation, and the Trust Fund." *Indian Country Today*, September 17. http://www.indiancountry.com.

———. 2008. "An Olympic Opportunity for Declaration." *Indian Country Today*, April 19. http://www.indiancountry.com.

Editorial, Indianz.com. 2000. "Clinton Signs a Final Indian Bill." Indianz.com, December 29. http://www.indianz.com.

———. 2004a. "Schwarzenegger Seeks Revenues from Gaming Tribes." Indianz.com, January 7. http://www.indianz.com.

———. 2004b. "California Tribes Confront 'Dangers' Facing Gaming." Indianz.com, January 15. http://www.indianz.com.

———. 2004c. "California Tribe Proposes Own Gaming Initiative." Indianz.com, January 22. http://www.indianz.com.

———. 2004d. "Schwarzenegger Says Deal with Tribes Almost Ready." Indianz.com, March 31. http://www.indianz.com.

———. 2004e. "California Tribes Endorse Gaming Initiative." Indianz.com, July 19. http://www.indianz.com.

———. 2004f. "Schwarzenegger Says Tribes Ripped Off State." Indianz.com, October 14. http://www.indianz.com.

———. 2004g. "Schwarzenegger Wants Gaming Tribes to Open Books." Indianz.com, October 20. http://www.indianz.com.

———. 2004h. "States Not Willing to Credit Tribes for Sharing." Indianz.com, December 17. http://www.indianz.com.

———. 2005. "Override of Navajo Same-Sex Marriage Bill Sought." Indianz.com, May 16. http://www.indianz.com.

Editorial, *Maine Today*. 2002. "Anti-Gambling Forces Are Wise to Organize in Saco." *Maine Today*, August 21. http://www.mainetoday.com.

Editorial, NBC10. 2004. "N.J. Senate Approves Domestic Partnership Bill: Governor Expected to Sign Bill." NBC10 News, January 8. http://www.nbcphiladelphia.com.

Editorial, *New York Times*, National Desk. 2004. "Gay Marriage Licenses Coming to Oregon." *New York Times*, March 3.

Editorial, 365gay.com. 2004. "Gay Marriage Throws Indian Tribe into Turmoil." 365gay.com, May 18. http://www.365gay.com.

———. 2005. "New Move to Clock Gay Cherokee Marriage." 365gay.com, August 9. http://www.365gay.com.

Editorial, *Tulsa World*. 2006. "Cherokee Court Rules for Lesbian Couple." *Tulsa World*, January 4. http://www.tulsaworld.com.

Eichenwald, Kurt. 2005. *Conspiracy of Fools: A True Story*. New York: Broadway.

Ellis, Florence Hawley. 1951. "Pueblo Social Organization and Southwestern Archaeology." *American Antiquity* 17, 148–51.

———. 1967. "Where Did the Pueblo People Come From?" *El Palacio* (autumn).

Ellis, John. 2004. "Governor Fights Initiatives in Clovis: He Warns of Gaming

Threat If Two Measures Pass." *The Fresno Bee*, October 13. http://www.fresnobee
.com.

Ewen, Alexander, ed. 1994. *Voice of Indigenous Peoples: Native People Address the
United Nations*. Santa Fe, N. Mex.: Clear Light.

Ferguson, Christina D. 1993. "Martinez v. Santa Clara Pueblo: A Modern Day Les-
son on Tribal Sovereignty." *Arkansas Law Review* 46, no. 1: 275–301.

Field, Les W. 2003. "Unacknowledged Tribes, Dangerous Knowledge: The
Muwekma Ohlone and How Indian Identities Are 'Known.'" *Wicazō Ša Review* 18,
no. 2: 79–94.

Fixico, Donald L. 1986. *Termination and Relocation: Federal Indian Policy, 1945–1960*.
Albuquerque: University of New Mexico Press.

Fletcher, Matthew L. M. 2006. "Same-Sex Marriage, Indian Tribes, and the Constitution." *University of Miami Law Review* 61, 53–84.

———. 2007. "Bringing Balance to Indian Gaming." *Harvard Journal on Legislation*
44, no. 1: 39–95.

Forbes, Jack D. 1982. *Native Americans of California and Nevada*. Revised edn. Happy
Camp, Calif.: Naturegraph.

———. 1997. *Proposition 209: Radical Equalizer or Racist Trick? An Independent
Analysis*. Davis, Calif.: J. D. Forbes.

———. 2000. "Blood Quantum: A Relic of Racism and Termination." *Native Intelligence* (blog). http://nas.ucdavis.edu/jack-d-forbes/.

———. 2001. "Self-Termination Policy Proposed." *Windspeaker* 1, no. 1, http://www
.ammsa.com/.

Foreman, Grant. 1974. *Indian Removal: The Emigration of the Five Civilized Tribes of
Indians*. Norman: University of Oklahoma Press.

Foucault, Michel. 1972. *Power/Knowledge: Selected Interviews and Other Writings*.
New York: Pantheon.

———, ed. 1975. *I, Pierre Rivière, Having Slaughtered My Mother, My Sister, and
My Brother . . . : A Case of Parricide in the 19th Century*. Lincoln: University of
Nebraska Press.

———. 1977. "Nietzsche, Genealogy, History." *Language, Counter-Memory, Practice*,
139–64. Ithaca: Cornell University Press.

———. 1978. *History of Sexuality: An Introduction*. Vol. 1. New York: Vintage.

———. 1979. *Discipline and Punish: The Birth of the Prison*. New York: Vintage.

———. 1983. "The Subject and Power." *Michel Foucault: Beyond Structuralism and
Hermeneutics*, Hubert L. Dreyfus and Paul Rabinow, 208–28. Chicago: University
of Chicago Press.

Foust, Michael. 2004. "Paper Criticizes Kerry's Marriage Stance." *Baptist Press: Marriage Digest*, March 5. http://www.bpnews.com.

Frankenberg, Ruth. 1993. *White Race, Women Matters (Gender, Race, Ethnicity)*. New
York: Routledge.

Gardner, Jule. 2004. "The Great Gay Marriage Debate," http://www.pbs.com.

Garner, Van H. 1982. *The Broken Ring: The Destruction of the California Indians.* Tucson: Westernlore Press.

Garroutte, Eva Marie. 2003. *Real Indians: Identity and Survival of Native America.* Berkeley: University of California Press.

General Accounting Office (GAO). 2001a. "Indian Issues: Improvements Needed in Tribal Recognition Process." Washington: GAO.

———. 2001b. "Treaty of Guadalupe Hidalgo: Definition and List of Community Land Grants in New México: Exposure Draft." Washington: GAO.

Gilley, Brian Joseph. 2006. *Becoming Two-Spirit: Gay Identity and Social Acceptance in Indian Country.* Lincoln: University of Nebraska Press.

Gilroy, Paul. 1995. "Roots and Routes: Black Identity as an Outernational Project." *Racial and Ethnic Identity: Psychological Development and Creative Expression,* ed. Herbert W. Harris, Howard C. Blue, and Ezra E. H. Griffith, 15–30. London: Routledge.

Goldberg, Carole, and Duane Champagne. 2002. "Ramona Redeemed? The Right of Tribal Political Power in California." *Wicazō Śa Review* 17, no. 1: 43–63.

Goldberg, Michelle. 2007. *Kingdom Coming: The Rise of Christian Nationalism.* New York: W. W. Norton.

Goldberg-Ambrose, Carole. 1997. *Planting Tail Feathers: Tribal Survival and Public Law 280.* With the assistance of Timothy Carr Seward. Los Angeles: American Indian Studies Center, University of California, Los Angeles.

———. 2002a. "Descent into Race." *UCLA Law Review* 49: 1373–94.

———. 2002b. "Members Only? Designing Citizenship Requirements for Indian Nations." *University of Kansas Law Review* 50, no. 3: 437–71.

Goldtooth, Tom. 2008. "Protecting the Web of Life: Indigenous Knowledge and Biojustice." *Original Instructions: Indigenous Teachings for a Sustainable Future,* ed. Melissa Nelson, 220–28. Rochester, N.Y.: Bear and Company.

Gone, Joseph P. 2006. "Mental Health, Wellness, and the Quest for an Authentic American Indian Identity." *Mental Health Care for Urban Indians: Clinical Insights from Native Practitioners,* ed. Tawa M. Witko, 55–80. Washington: American Psychological Association.

Gonzales, Angela A. 2003. "Gaming and Displacement: Winners and Losers in American Indian Casino Development." *International Social Science Journal* 55, no. 175: 124–33.

Goodwin, Christine M. 2002. "Human Rights, Women's Rights, Aboriginal Rights: Indivisible and Guaranteed?" *Centrepiece: Newsletter of the Alberta Civil Liberties Research Centre* 8, no. 2. http://www.aclrc.com.

Green, Elizabeth. 1923. *The Indians of Southern California and Land Allotment.* Long Beach, Calif.

Green, Rayna. 1980. "Native American Women." *Signs* 6, no. 3: 497–513.

———. 1988. "The Tribe Called Wannabee: Playing Indian in America and Europe." *Folklore* 99, no. 1: 30–55.

————. 1990. "The Pocahontas Perplex: The Image of Indian Women in American Culture." *Unequal Sisters: A Multicultural Reader in U.S. Women's History*, ed. Ellen Carol DuBois and Vicki L. Ruiz, 15–21. New York: Routledge.

Grossberg, Lawrence. 1996. "On Postmodernism and Articulation: An Interview with Stuart Hall." *Stuart Hall: Critical Dialogues in Cultural Studies*, ed. David Morley and Kuan-Hsing Chen, 131–50. New York: Routledge.

Grossman, Joanna. 2004. "The New Jersey Domestic Partnership Law." *FindLaw: Legal News and Commentary*, January 13. http://writ.news.findlaw.com.

Guerrero, Marie Anna Jaimes. 1997. "Civil Rights versus Sovereignty: Native American Women in Life and Land Struggles." *Feminist Genealogies, Colonial Legacies, Democratic Futures*, ed. M. Jacqui Alexander and Chandra Talpade Mohanty, 101–21. New York: Routledge.

Haake, Claudia. 2002. "Identity, Sovereignty, Power: The Cherokee-Delaware Agreement of 1867, Past and Present." *American Indian Quarterly* 26, no. 3: 418–35.

Hales, Donna. 2006. "Top Court Scraps Tribe's Attempt to Block Gay Marriage." *Muscogee Phoenix*, January 5. http://www.muscogeephoenix.com.

Hamilton, Arnold. 2005. "Marriage Fight Taken to Cherokees." *Denton Record-Chronicle/The Daily Morning News*, August 16. http://www.dentonrc.com.

Haraway, Donna. 1989. *Primate Visions: Gender, Race, and Nature in the World of Modern Science*. New York: Routledge.

Harjo, Joy, Tiya Miles, and Sharon Holland, eds. 2006. *Crossing Waters, Crossing Worlds: The African Diaspora in Indian Country*. Durham: Duke University Press.

Harring, Sidney L. 1994. *Crow Dog's Case: American Indian Sovereignty, Tribal Law, and United States Law in the Nineteenth Century*. Cambridge: Cambridge University Press.

Harrington, John Peabody. 1916. "The Ethnogeography of the Tewa Indians." *Annual Report of the Bureau of American Ethnology* 29, no. 618. Washington: Government Printing Office.

Harris, Cheryl I. 1993. "Whiteness as Property." *Harvard Law Review* 106, no. 8: 1710–91.

Hedges, Chris. 2007. *American Fascists: The Christian Right and the War on America*. New York: Free Press.

Heizer, Robert F. 1972. *The Eighteen Unratified Treaties of 1851–1852 between the California Indians and the United States Government*. Department of Anthropology, University of California, Berkeley.

————. 1978. *The California Indians vs. the United States of America: Evidence Offered in Support of Occupancy, Possession and Use of Land in California by the Ancestors of Enrolled Indians of California*. Socorro, N. Mex.: Ballena.

————. 1979. *Federal Concern about Conditions of California Indians 1853 to 1913: Eight Documents*. Socorro, N. Mex.: Ballena.

————. 1993. *The Destruction of California Indians: A Collection of Documents from* the Period 1847 to 1865 in Which Are Described Some of the Things That Happened to Some of the Indians of California. Lincoln: University of Nebraska Press.

Heizer, Robert F., and Alan J. Almquist. 1977. The Other Californians: Prejudice and Discrimination under Spain, Mexico, and the United States to 1920. Berkeley: University of California Press.

Hermann, David, and Jim Miller. 2004. "Governor Targets Inland Ballot Measure." Riverside Press Enterprise, October 27. http://www.pe.com.

Hibbitts, Bernard. 2004. "More Gay Marriage Developments . . ." Jurist: Legal News and Research, March 5. http://www.jurist.com.

Hobsbawm, Eric, and Terence Ranger, eds. 1983. The Invention of Tradition. Cambridge: Cambridge University Press.

Hogan, Lawrence J. 1998. The Osage Indian Murders: The True Story of a Multiple Murder Plot to Acquire the Estates of Wealthy Osage Tribe Members. Frederick, Md.: Amlex.

Hogan, Linda. 1990. Mean Spirit. New York: Random House.

Hoge, William. 2007. "Indigenous Rights Declaration Approved." New York Times, September 14. http://www.nytimes.com.

Holly, Marilyn. 1990. "Handsome Lake's Teachings: The Shift from Female to Male Agriculture in Iroquois Culture. An Essay on Ethnophilosophy." Agriculture and Human Values VII, nos. 3 and 4: 80–94.

Hudson, Tim. 2006. "Some Delaware Members Concerned over Proposed Agreement with Cherokee." Bartlesville Examiner-Enterprise, August 29. http://www.examiner-enterprise.com.

Hunt, Alan, and Gary Wickam. 1994. Foucault and Law: Towards a Sociology of Law as Governance. London: Pluto Press.

Hurtado, Albert L. 1988. Indian Survival on the California Frontier. New Haven: Yale University Press.

Infoplease: Encyclopedia. n.d. "The American Gay Rights Movement: A Timeline," accessed April 2007, http://www.infoplease.com.

International Indian Treaty Council and Project Underground. 2003. Gold, Greed, and Genocide: The Untold Tragedy of the California Gold Rush. Berkeley, Calif.: Project Underground.

Ivison, Duncan, Paul Patton, and Will Sanders, eds. 2000. Political Theory and the Rights of Indigenous Peoples. Cambridge: Cambridge University Press.

Jackson, John L., Jr. 2005. Real Black: Adventures in Racial Sincerity. Chicago: University of Chicago Press.

Jacobi, Jeffrey S. 2006. "Two Spirits, Two Eras, Same Sex: For a Traditionalist Perspective on Native American Tribal Same-Sex Marriage Policy." University of Michigan Journal of Law Reform 39 (summer): 823–50.

Jacobs, Sue-Ellen. 1995. "Continuity and Change in Gender Roles at San Juan Pueblo." Women and Power in Native North America, ed. Laura F. Klein and Lillian A. Ackerman, 177–213. Norman: University of Oklahoma Press.

Jacobs, Sue-Ellen, Wesley Thomas, and Sabine Long, eds. 1997. *Two Spirit People: Native American Gender Identity, Sexuality, and Spirituality*. Urbana: University of Illinois Press.

Jaimes, M. Annette. 1992. "Federal Indian Identification Policy." *The State of Native America: Genocide, Colonization, and Resistance*, ed. M. Annette Jaimes, 123–38. Boston: South End Press.

Jenkins, Myra Ellen. 1974. *History of Laguna Pueblo Land Claims*. New York: Garland.

Johnson, George. 1997. "Alfonso Ortiz, 57, Anthropologist of the Pueblo, Dies." *New York Times*, January 31. http://www.nytimes.com.

Kabbany, Jennifer. 2006a. "Pechanga Denies Disenrolled Family's Appeal." *North County Times*, August 18. http://www.nctimes.com.

———. 2006b. "Expert Contradicts Pechanga Disenrollment." *North County Times*, September 23. http://www.nctimes.com.

Kannady, Christopher L. 2004/2005. "The State, Cherokee Nation, and Same-Sex Unions: In Re: Marriage License of McKinley and Reynolds." *American Indian Law Review* 29, no. 2: 363–81.

Kaplan, Amy. 2005. *The Anarchy of Empire in the Making of U.S. Culture*. Cambridge: Harvard University Press.

Kaplan, Esther. 2004. *With God on Their Side: George W. Bush and the Christian Right*. New York: New Press.

Kappler, Charles J., ed. 1975. *Indian Affairs, Laws, and Treaties: 1903–1929*. Vol. 4. Washington: Government Printing Office.

Karshmer, Barbara E. n.d. *Before the Assistant Secretary for Indian Affairs: In the Matter of the Recognition of the Pechanga Band of Mission Indians: Murphy vs. Pechanga: Response of the Pechanga Band*. Fresno, Calif.

Kauanui, J. Kēhaulani. 1999. "'For Get' Hawaiian Entitlement: Configurations of Land, 'Blood,' and Americanization in the Hawaiian Homes Commission Act of 1920." *Social Text* 17, no. 2: 123–44.

———. 2002. "The Politics of Blood and Sovereignty in Rice v. Cayetano." *Political and Legal Anthropology Review* 25, no. 1: 110–28.

———. 2005. "Precarious Positions: Native Hawaiians and U.S. Federal Recognition." *The Contemporary Pacific* 17, no. 1: 1–27.

———. 2008. *Hawaiian Blood: Colonialism and the Politics of Sovereignty and Indigeneity*. Durham: Duke University Press.

Kennedy, James, and Jerry Newcombe. 2004. *What's Wrong with Same-Sex Marriage?* Wheaton, Ill.: Crossway.

Kershaw, Sarah. 2005. "Oregon Supreme Court Invalidates Same-Sex Marriages." *New York Times*, April 15.

Ketchum, Dee. 2001. "Chief Ketchum Disputes Chief Smith's Letter: Letter to the Editor." *Cherokee Phoenix and Indian Advocate* XXV, no. 2.

Kickingbird, Kirke, Lynn Kickingbird, Charles J. Chibitty, and Curtis Berkey. 1977. *Indian Sovereignty*. Washington: Institute for the Development of Indian Law.

Klein, Christine A. 1996. "Treaties of Conquest: Property Rights, Indian Treaties, and the Treaty of Guadalupe Hidalgo." *New Mexico Law Review* 26, no. 205.

KOTV. 2004. "Gay Marriage Issue before the Cherokee Nation Supreme Court." The News on 6, May 18. http://www.kotv.com.

Kroft, Steve. 1994. "Wampum Wonderland." 60 Minutes: CBS News, September 18.

Lacan, Jacques. 1977. *Écrits: A Selection*. New York: W. W. Norton.

Laclau, Ernesto, and Chantal Mouffe. 1985. *Hegemony and Socialist Strategy: Towards a Radical Democratic Politics*. London: Verso.

LaDuke, Winona. 1999. *All My Relations: Native Struggles for Land and Life*. New York: South End Press and Honor the Earth.

Larson, Elizabeth. 2008. "Robinson Rancheria Moves Forward with Disenrollments." *Lake County News*, December 17. http://www.lakeconews.com.

Latour, Bruno. 1987. *Science in Action: How to Follow Scientists and Engineers through Society*. Cambridge: Harvard University Press.

Laurence, Robert. 1992. "A Quincentennial Essay on *Martinez v. Santa Clara Pueblo*." *Idaho Law Review* 28, no. 2: 307–47.

Laverty, Philip. 2003. "The Ohlone/Costanoan-Esselen Nation of Monterey, California: Dispossession, Federal Neglect, and the Bitter Irony of the Federal Acknowledgment Process." *Wicazō Śa Review* 18, no. 2: 41–77.

Leacock, Eleanor, and Jacqueline Goodman. 1976. "Montagnais Marriage and the Jesuits in the Seventeenth Century: Incidents from the Relations of Paul Le Jeune." *Western Canadian Journal of Anthropology* VI, no. 3: 77–91.

Leduff, Charlie. 2003. "The California Recall." *New York Times*, October 2.

Leong, Russell, and Amy Sueyoshi, eds. 2006. "Sister Subjects: In the Marriage Equality Debate." Special issue, *Amerasia Journal* 32, no. 1.

Light, Steven Andrew, and Kathryn R. L. Rand. 2005. *Indian Gaming and Tribal Sovereignty: The Casino Compromise*. Lawrence: University of Kansas Press.

Lipsitz, George. 1998. *The Possessive Investment in Whiteness: How White People Profit from Identity Politics*. Philadelphia: Temple University Press.

Locke, John. 2005. *The Selected Political Writings of John Locke*. New York: W. W. Norton.

Loew, Patricia. 2007. *Way of the Warrior*. Madison: Wisconsin Public Television.

Log Cabin Republicans. 2006. "About Log Cabin." http://online.logcabin.org.

Lomawaima, K. Tsianina. 1994. *They Called It Prairie Light: The Story of Chilocco Indian School*. Lincoln: University of Nebraska Press.

Lombardi, Michael. n.d. "Long Road Traveled I: From the Treaty of Temecula to the Pala Compact; Long Road Traveled II: Tribal Self-Sufficiency and the Battle for Proposition 1A; Long Road Traveled III: California Indian Self-Reliance and the Battle for 1A." *History of Tribal Gaming in California*. California Nations Indian Gaming Association. http://www.cniga.com.

López, Ian F. Haney. 1996. *White by Law: The Legal Construction of Race*. New York: New York University Press.

Lorenzo, June. 2005. "Summary of Land Rights in the United States." First Peoples Worldwide. http://www.firstpeoples.org.

Lowe, Lisa. 1996. *Immigrant Acts: On Asian American Cultural Politics.* Durham: Duke University Press.

Lyons, Oren. 2008. "A Democracy Based on Peace." *Original Instructions: Indigenous Teachings for a Sustainable Future,* ed. Melissa Nelson, 59–65. Rochester, N.Y.: Bear and Company.

Lyons, Oren, et al., eds. 1992. *Exiled in the Land of the Free: Democracy, Indian Nations, and the United States Constitution.* Santa Fe, N. Mex.: Clear Light.

MacKinnon, Catharine A. 1987. "Whose Culture? A Case Note on Martinez v. Santa Clara Pueblo." *Feminism Unmodified: Discourses on Life and Law,* 63–69. Cambridge: Harvard University Press.

Maniaci, Jim. 2005. "Council Overrides Veto: Vote Makes Same-Sex, Plural Marriages Illegal in Navajoland." *Gallup Independent,* June 4. http://www.gallup independent.com.

Mann, Barbara Alice. 2000. *Iroquoian Women: The Gantowisas.* New York: Land Press.

Markell, Patchen. 2003. *Bound by Recognition.* Princeton: Princeton University Press.

Marks, Mindy, and Kate Spilde Contreras. 2007. "Lands of Opportunity: Social and Economic Effects of Tribal Gaming on Localities." *Policy Matters: A Quarterly Publication of the University of California, Riverside* 1, no. 4: 1–11.

Martin, Allie. 2005. "Attorney: Tribal Same-Sex 'Marriage' Case Could Be End-Run around Oklahoma Law." *Agape Press,* August 2.

Mason, W. Dale. 2000. *Indian Gaming: Tribal Sovereignty and American Politics.* Norman: University of Oklahoma Press.

Matier, Phillip. 2003. "Recall Rumble Gets Going in Earnest as Clock Ticks Down, Tribes at the Center of Campaign Money Barbs, Accusations." *San Francisco Chronicle,* September 24. http://www.sfgate.com.

May, James. 2000. "California: To Be Indian, or Not to Be." *Indian Country Today,* August 9. http://www.indiancountry.com.

———. 2002. "The Fight against the State: Propositions 5 and 1A: California Indian Gaming." *Indian Country Today,* March 19. http://www.indiancountry.com.

McCulloch, Anne Merline, and David E. Wilkins. 1995. "'Constructing' Nations within States: The Quest for Federal Recognition by the Catawba and Lumbee Tribes." *American Indian Quarterly* 19, no. 3: 361–90.

McDonnell, Janet A. 1991. *The Dispossession of the American Indian, 1887–1934.* Bloomington: Indiana University Press.

McLean, Bethany, and Peter Elkind. 2003. *Smartest Guys in the Room: The Amazing Rise and Scandalous Fall of Enron.* New York: Portfolio Hardcover.

McLeod, Christopher, and Malinda Maynor, directors. 2001. *In the Light of Reverence.* Oley, Penn.: Bullfrog Films.

McLish, Thomas P. 1988. "Tribal Sovereign Immunity: Searching for Sensible Limits." *Columbia Law Review* 88, no. 1: 173–93.

Meranto, Oneida J. 2001. "From Buckskin to Calico and Back Again: An Historical Interpretation of American Indian Feminism." *New Political Science* 23, no. 3: 333–49.

Mihesuah, Devon A., ed. 2000. *The Repatriation Reader: Who Owns American Indian Remains?* Lincoln: University of Nebraska Press.

———. 2003. *Indigenous American Women: Decolonization, Empowerment, Activism.* Lincoln: University of Nebraska Press.

Miller, Bruce Granville. 2003. *Invisible Indigenes: The Politics of Nonrecognition.* Lincoln: University of Nebraska Press.

Miller, Jim. 2004a. "Tribal Agreement Said Close." *Riverside Press Enterprise,* March 31. http://www.pe.com.

———. 2004b. "Tribes Want Governor's Apology." *Riverside Press Enterprise,* October 19. http://www.pe.com.

Miller, Mark Edwin. 2004. *Forgotten Tribes: Unrecognized Indians and the Federal Acknowledgment Process.* Lincoln: University of Nebraska Press.

Miller, Robert J. 2005. "American Indian Treaty Glossary." *Oregon Historical Quarterly* 106, no. 3.

———. 2006. *Native America: Discovered and Conquered: Thomas Jefferson, Lewis and Clark, and Manifest Destiny.* Westport, Conn.: Praeger.

Monture, Patricia A. 2004. "The Right of Inclusion: Aboriginal Rights and/or Aboriginal Women." *Advancing Aboriginal Claims: Visions/Strategies/Directions,* ed. Kerry Wilkins, 39–66. Alberta, Canada: Purich.

Moreton-Robinson, Aileen. 2005. "Patriarchal Whiteness, Self-Determination and Indigenous Women: The Invisibility of Structural Privilege and the Visibility of Oppression." *Unfinished Constitutional Business? Rethinking Indigenous Self-Determination,* ed. Barbara A. Hocking, 61–73. Canberra, Australia: Aboriginal Studies Press.

Morgan, Lewis Henry. 1877. *Ancient Society: or, Researches in the Line of Human Progress from Savagery through Barbarism to Civilization.* Chicago: C. H. Kerr.

Morley, David, and Kuan-Hsing Chen, eds. 1996. *Stuart Hall: Critical Dialogues in Cultural Studies,* 131–50. New York: Routledge.

Morris, Glenn T. 1992. "International Law and Politics: Toward a Right to Self-Determination for Indigenous Peoples." *The State of Native America: Genocide, Colonization, and Resistance,* ed. M. Annette Jaimes, 55–86. Boston: South End Press.

Napoleon, Val. 2005. "Aboriginal Self Determination: Individual Self and Collective Selves." *Atlantis* 29, no. 2: 31–46.

National Center for Lesbian Rights (NCLR) Press Release. 2005. "Cherokee Court Rejects Petition to Block Same-Sex Marriage," August 3, http://www.nclrights.org.

National Conference of State Legislatures. 2007. "Same-Sex Marriage Timeline," http://www.ncsl.org.

National Congress of American Indians. 2006. "Support of Federal Legislation to Reinstate Federal Recognition to the Delaware Tribe of Indians." Resolution #SAC-06-063. http://www.ncai.org.

Native American Rights Fund (NARF). 2000. "The Federal Acknowledgment Process." http://www.narf.org.

———. 2002. "Dispelling the Myths about Indian Gaming." http://www.narf.org.

Nelson, Melissa, ed. 2008. *Original Instructions: Indigenous Teachings for a Sustainable Future*. Rochester, N.Y.: Bear and Company.

Newcomb, Steven T. 2008. *Pagans in the Promised Land: Decoding the Doctrine of Christian Discovery*. Golden, Colo.: Fulcrum.

Newman, Deirdre. 2005a. "Disenrolled Pechanga Members Specify Minimum Dollar Amount They Are Seeking in Lawsuit." *North County Times*, August 3. http://www.nctimes.com.

———. 2005b. "Disenrolled Pechanga Members Thwarted by Appellate Court." *North County Times*, August 9. http://www.nctimes.com.

Nguyen, Chris T. 2004. "Riverside Judge Says Due Process Tops Tribal Law." Associated Press, April 19.

Nicholas, Andrea Bear. 1994. "Colonialism and the Struggle for Liberation: The Experience of Maliseet Women." *University of New Brunswick Law Journal* 43: 223–39.

Nichols-Ledermann, Deborah, and James A. Rementer. 2008. "Introduction: Historical Information about the Lenape." *Long Journey Home: Oral Histories of Contemporary Delaware Indians*, ed. James W. Brown and Rita T. Kohn, xxii–xxvii. Bloomington: Indiana University Press.

Nietzsche, Friedrich. 1887. *On the Genealogy of Morals: A Polemic*. Translated by Douglas Smith (1996; repr., Oxford: Oxford University Press).

Niezen, Ronald. 2000. *Spirit Wars: Native North American Religions in the Age of Nation Building*. Berkeley: University of California Press.

———. 2003. *The Origins of Indigenism: Human Rights and the Politics of Identity*. Berkeley: University of California Press.

Norell, Brenda. 2005a. "Navajo President Vetoes Gay Marriage Ban." *Indian Country Today*, May 3. http://www.indiancountry.com.

———. 2005b. "2005 Diné Marriage Act Denounced." *Indian Country Today*, May 16. http://www.indiancountry.com.

———. 2005c. "Navajo Marriage Act Veto Draws Swift Reaction." *Indian Country Today*, May 23. http://www.indiancountry.com.

O'Brien, Jean M. 1997. *Dispossession by Degrees: Indian Land and Identity in Natick, Massachusetts, 1650–1790*. Lincoln: University of Nebraska Press.

O'Brien, Sharon. 1989. *American Indian Tribal Governments*. Norman: University of Oklahoma Press.

O'Leary, Tim. 2004a. "Judge Halts Expulsion of 130 Tribe Members: He Blocks a Committee from Descendants of Manuala Miranda — Temporarily." *Riverside Press Enterprise*, February 5. http://www.pe.com.

―――. 2004b. "Pechanga Panel Ejects 130 Adults from Tribe." *Riverside Press Enterprise*, March 20. http://www.pe.com.

―――. 2004c. "Tribal Dispute on Hold: A Judge Will Study Whether Disenrolled Members' Rights Have Been Violated." *Riverside Press Enterprise*, April 20. http://www.pe.com.

―――. 2004d. "No Longer a Family Matter: Those Disenrolled from Pechanga Cite Monetary and Emotional Setbacks." *Riverside Press Enterprise*, July 2. http://www.pe.com.

―――. 2006. "Pechanga Gives Family Final Notice of Ejection." *Riverside Press Enterprise*, August 21. http://www.pe.com.

Omi, Michael, and Howard Winant. 1986. *Racial Formation in the United States: From the 1960s to the 1980s*. New York: Routledge.

Ong, Aihwa. 1995. "Making the Biopolitical Subject: Cambodian Immigrants, Refugee Medicine and Cultural Citizenship in California." *Social Science Medicine* 40, no. 9: 1243–57.

Onions, C. T., ed., with G. W. S. Friedrichsen and R. W. Burchfield. 1996. *Oxford Dictionary of English Etymology*. Oxford: Clarendon.

Ono, Kent, and John M. Sloop. 2002. *Shifting Borders: Rhetoric, Immigration, and California's Proposition 187 (Mapping Racisms)*. Philadelphia: Temple University Press.

Ortiz, Alfonso. 1969. *The Tewa World: Space, Time, Being, and Becoming in a Pueblo Society*. Chicago: University of Chicago Press.

Otis, D. S. 1973. *The Dawes Act and the Allotment of Indian Lands*. Norman: University of Oklahoma Press.

Owens, Louis. 1998. *Mixedblood Messages: Literature, Film, Family, Place*. Norman: University of Oklahoma Press.

Parsons, Elsie Clews. 1939. *Pueblo Indian Religions*. Vols. 1 and 2. Lincoln: University of Nebraska Press.

Pavlik, Steven Andrew. 1985. "Issues and Developments in Navajo Education during the Peter McDonald Administrations, 1970 to 1982." M.A. thesis, University of Arizona.

―――. 1997. "Navajo Christianity: Historical Origins and Modern Trends." *Wicazŏ Ša Review* 12, no. 2: 43–58.

Pechanga Band of Luiseño Indians. 1978. *The Constitution and By-Laws of the Temecula Band of Luiseño Indians*. Adopted by the Pechanga General Council, Pechanga Indian Reservation, Temecula, Calif., December 10.

―――. 1979. *Enrolled Members of the Temecula Band of Luiseño Indians (the "Enrollment Book")*. Pechanga Indian Reservation, Temecula, Calif.

―――. 1996a. *Special Meeting Minutes: Enrollment Concerns*. Pechanga Indian Reservation, Temecula, Calif., February 25.

————. 1996b. *Enrollment Committee Guidelines and Procedures*. Pechanga Indian Reservation, Temecula, Calif.

Peckham, Tom. 2006. "Sovereignty Now or Sovereignty Later: Federal Recognition Legislation Proposed." *Delaware Indian News* 29, no. 1: 1, 4–5.

Perdue, Theda. 1981. *Nations Remembered: An Oral History of the Five Civilized Tribes, 1865–1907*. Santa Barbara, Calif.: Greenwood.

————. 1999. *Cherokee Women: Gender and Culture Change, 1700–1835*. Lincoln: University of Nebraska Press.

Perdue, Theda, and Michael D. Green, eds. 2004. *The Cherokee Removal: A Brief History with Documents*. 2nd ed. Boston: Bedford/St. Martin's.

Peroff, Nicholas C. 1982. *Menominee Drums: Tribal Termination and Restoration, 1954–1974*. Norman: University of Oklahoma Press.

Peter, Jennifer. 2004. "Massachusetts Supreme Court Rules Civil Unions Aren't Enough, Same-Sex Couples Entitled to Marriage." *The Boston Globe*, February 4. http://www.boston.com/news/globe.

Phillips, George Harwood. 1981. *The Enduring Struggle: Indians in California History*. San Francisco: Boyd and Fraser.

Pierpoint, Mary. 2001. "Cherokee vs. Delaware Recognition." *Indian Country Today*, January 24. http://www.indiancountry.com.

Pincetl, Stephanie S. 1999. *Transforming California: A Political History of Land Use and Development*. Baltimore: Johns Hopkins University Press.

Pommersheim, Frank. 1995. *Braid of Feathers: American Indian Law and Contemporary Tribal Life*. Berkeley: University of California Press.

Porter, Robert B. 1999. "The Demise of Ongwehoweh and the Rise of Native Americans: Redressing the Genocidal Act of Forcing American Citizenship upon Indigenous Peoples." *Harvard BlackLetter Law Journal* 15 (spring): 107–83.

Porteus, Liza. 2004. "Gay Marriage Ruling Likely to Be Campaign Issue." Fox News, February 4. http://www.foxnews.com.

Povinelli, Elizabeth. 2002. *The Cunning of Recognition: Indigenous Alterities and the Making of Australian Multiculturalism*. Durham: Duke University Press.

Previch, Chad. 2004. "Cherokee Council Bans Gay Unions." *The Oklahoman*, June 15. http://www.newsok.com.

Prindeville, Diane-Michele. 2004. "Feminist Nations? A Study of Native American Women in Southwestern Tribal Politics." *Political Research Quarterly* 57, no. 1: 101–12.

Prucha, Francis Paul. 1994. *American Indian Treaties: The History of a Political Anomaly*. Berkeley: University of California Press.

Puar, Jasbir K. 2007. *Terrorist Assemblages: Homonationalism in Queer Times*. Durham: Duke University Press.

Raibmon, Paige. 2006. *Authentic Indians: Episodes of Encounter from the Late-Nineteenth Century Northwest Coast*. Durham: Duke University Press.

Raine, George. 2003. "Actor Denies Going Negative in His New Ad, But Critics Say

He's Gone Back on Pledge." *San Francisco Chronicle*, September 23. http://www
.sfgate.com.

Rawls, James J. 1984. *Indians of California: The Changing Image*. Norman: University
of Oklahoma Press.

Reitman, Eric. 2006. "An Argument for the Partial Abrogation of Federally Recognized Indian Tribes' Sovereign Power over Membership." *Virginia Law Review*
92:793–866.

Resnik, Judith. 1989. "Dependent Sovereigns: Indian Tribes, States, and Federal
Courts." *University of Chicago Law Review* 56, no. 671.

———. 1999. "Multiple Sovereignties: Indian Tribes, States, and the Federal Government." *Judicature: The Journal of the American Judicature Society* 79, no. 3.
http://www.tribal-institute.org.

Rich, Adrienne. 1980. "Compulsory Heterosexuality and Lesbian Existence." *Signs* 5,
no. 4: 631–60.

Richland, Justin B. 2008. *Arguing with Tradition: The Language of Law in Hopi Tribal
Court*. Chicago: University of Chicago Press.

Riffe, Jed, director. 2005. *California and the American Dream*, part 1, *California's "Lost"
Tribes*. PBS.

Riley, Angela R. 2007. "(Tribal) Sovereignty and Illiberalism." *California Law Review*
95, no. 799.

Robinson, Judy Gibbs. 2006. "Tribe Seeks Former Status Lost in Court." *The Oklahoman*, August 18. http://www.newsok.com.

Rock, Joyce. 2004. "Baptists Taught Cherokee Bigotry." *Southern Voice Online*, October 1. http://www.sovo.com.

Romano, Lois. 2004. "Battle over Gay Marriage Plays Out in Indian Country." *Washington Post*, August 1.

Rosaldo, Renato. 1989. "Imperialist Nostalgia." *Representations* 26 (Spring), 107–22.

Roscoe, Will, ed. 1989. *Living the Spirit: A Gay American Indian Anthology*. New York:
St. Martin's.

Rose, Wendy. 1992. "The Great Pretenders: Further Reflections on White Shamanism." *The State of Native America: Genocide, Colonization, and Resistance*, ed.
M. Annette Jaimes, 403–22. Boston: South End Press.

Ross, Luana. 1998. *Inventing the Savage: The Social Construction of Native American
Criminality*. Austin: University of Texas Press.

Ruckman, S. E. 2006. "Delawares Closer to Federal Recognition." *The Oklahoman*,
August 16.

Rusco, Elmer R. 1990. "Civil Liberties Guarantees under Tribal Law: A Survey of
Civil Rights Provisions in Tribal Constitutions." *American Indian Law Review* 14,
no. 269.

Russell, Steve. 2008. "When Does Ethnic Fraud Matter?" *Indian Country Today*,
April 3. http://www.indiancountry.com.

Sahagun, Louis. 2004a. "Fight over Tribal Status Moved; a Federal Judge Remands

Lawsuit to State Court. More Than 100 Indians Could Be Stripped of Pechanga Identity and Lose Casino Revenues." *Los Angeles Times*, February 3.

———. 2004b. "Pechanga Band Ousts Scores of Tribal Members; the Action Costs Each Member $10,000 a Month in Casino Funds. An Appeal Is Expected." *Los Angeles Times*, March 20.

Sandoval, Chela. 1991. "U.S. Third World Feminism: The Theory and Method of Oppositional Consciousness in the Postmodern World." *Genders* 10:1–22.

Saxton, Alexander. 1990. *Rise and Fall of the White Republic: Class Politics and Mass Culture in Nineteenth-Century America*. New York: Verso.

Sears, Alan, and Craig Osten. 2003. *The Homosexual Agenda: Exposing the Principal Threat to Religious Freedom Today*. Nashville, Tenn.: B&H Publishing.

Secrest, William B. 2003. *When the Great Spirit Died: The Destruction of the California Indians, 1850–1860*. Sanger, Calif.: Word Dancer Press.

Secretariat of the Permanent Forum on Indigenous Issues. 2004. "The Concept of Indigenous Peoples." Background paper, workshop on data collection and disaggregation for indigenous peoples, United Nations, Department of Economic and Social Affairs (January 19–21). http://www.un.org.

Shanley, Kathryn. 1984. "Thoughts on Indian Feminism." *A Gathering of Spirit: A Collection by North American Indian Women*, ed. Beth Brant, 213–15. Ithaca, N.Y.: Firebrand Books.

Shaw, Shannon. 2005. "Indian Country: Domestic Violence in Epidemic Proportions." Stop Family Violence, November 8. http://www.stopfamilyviolence.org.

Shichor, David, and Dale K. Sechrest, eds. 1996. *Three Strikes and You're Out: Vengeance as Public Policy*. Thousand Oaks, Calif.: Sage.

Siegal, Robert. 2004. "Portland Issues Gay Marriage Licenses." NPR, March 3. http://www.npr.org.

Sifuentes, Edward. 2004. "Local Tribes Part of $1 Billion Deal with State." *North County Times*, June 21. http://www.nctimes.com.

Silva, Noenoe K. 2004. *Aloha Betrayed: Native Hawaiian Resistance to American Colonialism*. Durham: Duke University Press.

Skenandore, Francine R. 2002. "Revisiting Santa Clara Pueblo v. Martinez: Feminist Critiques on Tribal Sovereignty." *Wisconsin Women's Law Journal* 17, no. 347.

Skrentny, John David. 2001. *Color Lines: Affirmative Action, Immigration, and Civil Rights Options for America*. Chicago: University of Chicago Press.

Smith, Andrea. 2005. *Conquest: Sexual Violence and American Indian Genocide*. Boston: South End Press.

———. 2008. *Native Americans and the Christian Right: The Gendered Politics of Unlikely Alliances*. Durham: Duke University Press.

Smith, Chad. 2001a. "Letter from the Chief: Letter to the Editor." *Cherokee Phoenix and Indian Advocate* XXV, no. 1. http://www.cherokeephoenix.org.

———. 2001b. "History Not Rhetoric: Letter to the Editor." *Cherokee Phoenix and Indian Advocate* XXV, no. 3. http://www.cherokeephoenix.org.

Smith, Linda Tuhiwai. 1999. *Decolonizing Methodologies: Research and Indigenous Peoples*. Dunedin, New Zealand: University of Otago Press.

Snell, Teddye. 2005a. "Cherokee Court Hears Gay Marriage Case." *Tahlequah Daily Press*, August 4. http://www.tahlequahdailypress.com.

———. 2005b. "Councilors Join Cherokee Marriage Controversy." *Tahlequah Daily Press*, August 10. http://www.tahlequahdailypress.com.

———. 2006. "Councilors Support Delaware Separation Bill." *Cherokee Phoenix and Indian Advocate*, September. http://www.cherokeephoenix.org.

Snipp, C. Matthew. 1989. *American Indians: The First of This Land*. New York: Russell Sage Foundation.

Somerville, Siobhan B. 2000. *Queering the Color Line: Race and the Invention of Homosexuality in American Culture*. Durham: Duke University Press.

Soto, Onell R. 2008. "Tribal Members Expulsion Rejected: San Pasquel Indians Can Appeal Decision." *San Diego Union-Tribune*, December 2. http://www.signonsandiego.com.

Spilde, Katherine A. 1999. "Rich Indian Racism Is a Direct Attack on Tribal Sovereignty." *Hocak Worak* 5. Newsletter of the Ho-Chunk Nation.

Staff Writer, Bartlesville Examiner-Enterprise. 2004. "Delaware Tribe Recognition Rejected." *Bartlesville Examiner-Enterprise*, November 17. http://www.examiner-enterprise.com.

Stanton, Glen T., and Bill Maier. 2004. *Marriage on Trial: The Case against Same-Sex Marriage and Parenting*. Downers Grove, Ill.: InterVarsity Press.

Staver, Matthew D. 2004. *Same-Sex Marriage: Putting Every Household at Risk*. Nashville, Tenn.: B&H Publishing.

Stetson, C. L. 1980. "Tribal Sovereignty: Santa Clara Pueblo v. Martinez." *American Indian Law Review* 8, no. 139.

Stockes, Brian. 2001. "Report Finds Flaws in Tribal Recognition Process." *Indian Country Today*, November 9. http://www.indiancountry.com.

Stoler, Ann Laura. 2002. *Carnal Knowledge and Imperial Power: Race and the Intimate in Colonial Rule*. Berkeley: University of California Press.

Stout, Davis. 2004. "Bush Backs Ban on Constitution on Gay Marriage." *New York Times*, February 24. http://www.nytimes.com.

Strickland, Rennard. 1975. *Fire and the Spirits: Cherokee Law from Clan to Court*. Norman: University of Oklahoma Press.

Sturm, Circe. 2002. *Blood Politics: Race, Culture, and Identity in the Cherokee Nation of Oklahoma*. Berkeley: University of California Press.

Sueyoshi, Amy. 2006. "Friday the Thirteenth: Love, Commitment, and Then Catastrophe: Personal Reflections on the Marriage Equality Movement." *Amerasia Journal* 32, no. 1: xi–xvii.

Sweeney, James P. 2004. "Tribe Offers Tax Deal to Ease Limits on Gaming." *Copley News*, January 22. http://www.copleynews.com.

———. 2005. "Proposal Would Enable Joint Casino Projects—Legislation to Add

Barriers to Gaming Off of Reservations." *San Diego Union*, November 11. http://www.signonsandiego.com.

Swentzell, Rina. 2004. "Testimony of a Santa Clara Woman." *Kansas Journal of Law and Public Policy* 14, no. 1: 97–98.

Swidey, Neil. 2000. "Tribal Gamble: The Lure and Peril of Indian Gambling: Trump Plays Both Sides in Casino Bids." *Boston Globe*, December 13. http://www.boston.com/globe.

Tadiar, Neferti. 2009. *Things Fall Away: Philippine Historical Experience and the Makings of Globalization*. Durham: Duke University Press.

Taliman, Valerie. 2000. "Disenrolled Paiutes Fight for Heritage." *Indian Country Today*, September 27. http://www.indiancountry.com.

———. 2002a. "Las Vegas Paiutes Oust Entire Council." *Indian Country Today*, July 26. http://www.indiancountry.com.

———. 2002b. "Termination by Bureaucracy: Membership Denials in This New Economic Era." "Identity in the Crucible," special issue, *Native Americas: Hemispheric Journal of Indigenous Issues* (spring/summer): 8–17.

———. 2007. "United Nations Moves to Adopt Indigenous Declaration." *Indian Country Today*, September 14. http://www.indiancountry.com.

Tallbear, Kimberly. 2003. "DNA, Blood, and Racializing the Tribe." *Wicazō Ša Review* 18, no. 1: 81–107.

Tanner, Adam. 2006. "Top US Indian Court Upholds First Gay Marriage." *Brocktown News*, January 4. http://www.localnewsleader.com.

Taussig, Michael. 1987. *Shamanism, Colonialism, and the Wild Man: A Study in Terror and Healing*. Chicago: University of Chicago Press.

Taylor, Drew Hayden. 1998. *Funny, You Don't Look Like One: Observations from a Blue-Eyed Ojibway*. Penticon, British Columbia: Theytus Books.

———. 2008. *Me Sexy*. Vancouver, B.C.: Douglas & McIntyre.

Tengan, Ty P. Kāwika. 2008. *Native Men Remade: Gender and Nation in Contemporary Hawai'i*. Durham: Duke University Press.

Thompson, Don. 2004. "Schwarzenegger Fund-Raiser: Maloofs Deny Buying Favor: Palms Owners Reportedly Raising Campaign Funds While Negotiating Deal to Run Casino." *Las Vegas Review Journal*, September 1. http://www.reviewjournal.com.

Thornton, Russell. 1990. *American Indian Holocaust and Survival: A Population History Since 1942*. Norman: University of Oklahoma Press.

Tinker, George. 1993. *Missionary Conquest: The Gospel and Native American Cultural Genocide*. Minneapolis: Fortress Press.

———. 2008. *American Indian Liberation: A Theology of Sovereignty*. Maryknoll, N.Y.: Orbis Books.

Trafzer, Clifford E., and Joel R. Hyer, eds. 1999. *"Exterminate Them": Written Accounts of the Murder, Rape, and Slavery of Native Americans during the California Gold Rush, 1848–1868*. East Lansing: Michigan State University Press.

Trask, Haunani-Kay. 1993. *From a Native Daughter: Colonialism and Sovereignty in Hawai'i*. Monroe, Maine: Common Courage Press.

Treat, James, ed. 1996. *Native and Christian: Indigenous Voices on Religious Identities in the U.S. and Canada*. New York: Routledge.

Tsosie, Rebecca. 1997. "Negotiating Economic Survival: The Consent Principle and Tribal-State Compacts Under the Indian Gaming Regulatory Act." *Arizona State Law Journal* 29, no. 26.

———. 2002a. "Introduction: Symposium on Cultural Sovereignty." *Arizona State Law Journal* 34, no. 1.

———. 2002b. "Reclaiming Native Stories: An Essay on Cultural Appropriation and Cultural Rights." *Arizona State Law Journal* 34, no. 1.

———. 2005. "The New Challenge to Native Identity: An Essay on 'Indigeneity' and 'Whiteness.'" *Journal of Law and Policy* 18: 55–98.

United States. 1904. *Allotment of Lands to Delaware Indians*. Washington: Government Printing Office.

———. 1909. *General Allotment Act and Amendments*. Washington: Government Printing Office.

———. 1991. *The Native Allotment Handbook*. [Anchorage, Alaska]: Bureau of Land Management, Alaska State Office, Division of Conveyance Management.

United States Congress. 1966. *California Indians Judgment Fund, 1966*. House Committee on Interior and Insular Affairs. Subcommittee on Indian Affairs. Hearings, Eighty-ninth Congress, 2d sess., May 2 and 3. Washington: U.S. Government Printing Office.

Valencia-Weber, Gloria. 2004. "Santa Clara Pueblo v. Martinez: Twenty-Five Years of Disparate Cultural Visions: An Essay Introducing the Case for Reargument before the American Indian Nations Supreme Court." *Kansas Journal of Law and Policy* 14, no. 1: 49–58.

Valencia-Weber, Gloria, and Christine Zuni. 1995. "Domestic Violence and Tribal Protection of Indigenous Women in the United States." *St. John's Law Review* 69: 69–135.

Van Kirk, Sylvia. 1983. *Many Tender Ties: Women in Fur-Trade Society, 1670–1870*. Norman: University of Oklahoma Press.

Vecsey, Christopher, ed. 1993. *Handbook of American Indian Religious Freedom*. New York: Crossroad.

Venne, Sharon Helen. 1998. *Our Elders Understand Our Rights: Evolving International Law Regarding Indigenous Rights*. Penticton, British Columbia: Theytus.

Vizenor, Gerald. 1994. *Manifest Manners: Postindian Warriors of Survivance*. Hanover, N.H.: University Press of New England.

Vollman, Tim. 2004. "Revisiting *Santa Clara Pueblo v. Martinez*: What Can We Learn Thirty Years Later?" Address at the 29th Federal Bar Association, Indian Law Conference, April 15–16.

Wagenlander and Heisterkamp, LLC. 2002. "What Is Tribal Sovereign Immunity?"

Presentation at the National American Indian Housing Council. Annual Convention, Washington, D.C.

Wanamaker, Tom. 2002a. "Who's Next for Class III Gaming." *Indian Country Today*, June 12. http://www.indiancountry.com.

———. 2002b. "Recognition, Unions and a Joint Venture." *Indian Country Today*, July 3. http://www.indiancountry.com.

———. 2002c. "Anti-Gamers Rail against Recognition: Threaten Tribal Economics." *Indian Country Today*, September 4. http://www.indiancountry.com.

———. 2002d. "No Casinos in My Backyard." *Indian Country Today*, September 26. http://www.indiancountry.com.

———. 2004. "Let the Games Begin: Victims of Success?" *Indian Country Today*, February 4. http://www.indiancountry.com.

Wardell, Morris. L. 1938. *A Political History of the Cherokee Nation*. Norman: University of Oklahoma Press.

Warrior, Robert Allen. 1994. *Tribal Secrets: Recovering American Indian Intellectual Traditions*. Minneapolis: University of Minnesota Press.

Washburn, Kevin K. 2001. "Recurring Problems in Indian Gaming." *Wyoming Law Review* 1, no. 427.

Washburn, Wilcomb E. 1975. *The Assault on Indian Tribalism: The General Allotment Law (Dawes Act) of 1887*. Philadelphia: Lippincott.

Weaver, Dariel. 2004. "Rhea County Mulls Gay Ban." *The Orbis*, March 24. http://www.vanderbiltorbis.com.

Werner, Erica. 2003. "Money from Casino-Owning Tribes Could Play Big Role in California Recall Campaign." Associated Press, August 24.

Weslager, C.A. 1978. *The Delaware Indian Westward Migration*. Wallingford, Penn.: Middle Atlantic Press.

Whitt, Laurelyn. 2009. *Science, Colonialism, and Indigenous Peoples: The Cultural Politics of Law and Knowledge*. New York: Cambridge University Press.

Wiegand, Steve. 2004. "Governor Spells Out His Ballot Views." *Sacramento Bee*, July 8. http://www.sacbee.com.

Wilkins, David E. 1997. *American Indian Sovereignty and the U.S. Supreme Court: The Masking of Justice*. Austin: University of Texas Press.

———. 2002. *American Indian Politics and the American Political System*. Lanham, Md.: Rowman and Littlefield.

———. 2004. "Exiling One's Kin: Banishment and Disenrollment in Indian Country." *Western Legal History* 17, no. 2: 235–62.

Wilkins, David E., and K. Tsianina Lomawaima. 2001. *Uneven Ground: American Indian Sovereignty and Federal Law*. Norman: University of Oklahoma Press.

Wilkinson, Charles F. 1987. *American Indians, Time, and the Law*. New Haven: Yale University Press.

———. 2005. *Blood Struggle: The Rise of Modern Indian Nations*. New York: W. W. Norton.

Williams, Colleen. 2007. "Special Report: Without a Tribe." NBC4 News, Los Angeles, California, February 20.

Williams, Robert A., Jr. 1990. *The American Indian in Western Legal Thought: The Discourses of Conquest.* New York: Oxford University Press.

———. 1997. *Linking Arms Together: American Indian Treaty Visions of Law and Peace.* New York: Oxford University Press.

———. 2005. *Like a Loaded Weapon: The Rehnquist Court, Indian Rights, and the Legal History of Racism in America.* Minneapolis: University of Minnesota Press.

Wilmer, Franke. 1993. *The Indigenous Voice in World Politics.* Newbury Park, Calif.: Sage.

Wilson, Angela Waziyatawin, and Michael Yellow Bird, eds. 2005. *For Indigenous Eyes Only: A Decolonization Handbook.* Santa Fe, N. Mex.: School of American Research Press.

Wing, Adrien Katherine, ed. 1997. *Critical Race Feminism: A Reader.* New York: New York University Press.

Woodward, Bob. 2003. *Bush at War.* New York: Simon and Schuster.

———. 2004. *Plan of Attack.* New York: Simon and Schuster.

———. 2007. *State of Denial.* New York: Simon and Schuster.

———. 2008. *The War Within: A Secret White House History, 2006–2008.* New York: Simon and Schuster.

Wunder, John R., ed. 1999. *Native American Sovereignty.* New York: Garland.

Yamamura, Kevin. 2004. "Governor's Remarks Draws Ire: Gaming-Tribe Group, NAACP Call Schwarzenegger's 'Ripping Us Off' Campaign Utterance Insensitive." *Sacramento Bee,* October 20. http://www.sacbee.com.

Yellow Bird, Michael. 2005. "Decolonizing Tribal Enrollment." *For Indigenous Eyes Only: A Decolonization Handbook,* ed. Angela Waziyatawin Wilson and Michael Yellow Bird, 179–88. Santa Fe, N. Mex.: School of American Research Press.

Young, Iris Marion. 1990. *Justice and the Politics of Difference.* Princeton: Princeton Paperbacks.

———. 2007. *Global Challenges: War, Self-Determination and Responsibility for Justice.* Cambridge: Polity Press.

Zimring, Franklin E., Gordon Hawkins, and Sam Kamin. 2001. *Punishment and Democracy: Three Strikes and You're Out in California.* New York: Oxford University Press.

Zion, James W. 2006. "Indian Tradition and Custom in Adjudication under Rules of Evidence." Tribal Court Clearinghouse. http://www.tribal-institute.org.

Zuni Cruz, Christine. 2000/2001. "Tribal Law as Indigenous Social Reality and Separate Consciousness: Incorporating Customs and Traditions into Tribal Law." *Tribal Law Journal* 1. http://tlj.unm.edu/.

Joanne Barker is an associate professor of American Indian Studies at San Francisco State University. She is the editor of *Sovereignty Matters: Locations of Contestation and Possibility in Indigenous Struggles for Self-Determination* (2005).

Library of Congress Cataloging-in-Publication Data

Barker, Joanne, 1962–
Native acts : law, recognition, and cultural authenticity / Joanne Barker.
p. cm.
Includes bibliographical references and index.
ISBN 978-0-8223-4838-2 (cloth : alk. paper)
ISBN 978-0-8223-4851-1 (pbk. : alk. paper)
1. Indians of North America — Ethnic identity.
2. Indians of North America — Government relations — History.
3. Ethnicity — United States. 4. United States — Race relations.
I. Title.
E98.E85B375 2011
323.1197 — dc22   2011006306